TEACHING NUMBER IN THE CLASSROOM

WITH 4-8 YEAR OLDS

Education at SAGE

SAGE is a leading international publisher of journals, books, and electronic media for academic, educational, and professional markets.

Our education publishing includes:

- accessible and comprehensive texts for aspiring education professionals and practitioners looking to further their careers through continuing professional development

- inspirational advice and guidance for the classroom

- authoritative state of the art reference from the leading authors in the field.

Find out more at: **www.sagepub.co.uk/education**

TEACHING NUMBER IN THE CLASSROOM
WITH 4-8 YEAR OLDS

2ND EDITION

ROBERT J. WRIGHT

GARRY STANGER

ANN K. STAFFORD

JIM MARTLAND

Los Angeles | London | New Delhi
Singapore | Washington DC

Los Angeles | London | New Delhi
Singapore | Washington DC

SAGE Publications Ltd
1 Oliver's Yard
55 City Road
London EC1Y 1SP

SAGE Publications Inc.
2455 Teller Road
Thousand Oaks, California 91320

SAGE Publications India Pvt Ltd
B 1/I 1 Mohan Cooperative Industrial Area
Mathura Road
New Delhi 110 044

SAGE Publications Asia-Pacific Pte Ltd
3 Church Street
#10-04 Samsung Hub
Singapore 049483

Editor: Marianne Lagrange
Editorial assistant: Rachael Plant
Production editor: Thea Watson
Copyeditor: Jane Fricker
Marketing manager: Dilhara Attygalle
Cover design: Wendy Scott
Typeset by: C&M Digitals (P) Ltd, Chennai, India
Printed and bound in Great Britain by Ashford
Colour Press

Library of Congress Control Number: 2013957015

British Library Cataloguing in Publication data

A catalogue record for this book is available from
the British Library

ISBN 978-1-4462-8268-7
ISBN 978-1-4462-8269-4 (pbk)

At SAGE we take sustainability seriously. Most of our products are printed in the UK using FSC papers and boards.
When we print overseas we ensure sustainable papers are used as measured by the Egmont grading system.
We undertake an annual audit to monitor our sustainability.

To Eli and Millie
Eliana, Samuel, Kirralee, Amy, Mitchell and Sarah
Dillon
James A. Wheldon, Georgina and Jac

Brief Contents

List of Tables   xvi
Website Content   xvii
Contributors   xx
Acknowledgments   xxiii

Introduction   1

PART I   5

1 Approaching, Designing and Organizing Instruction   5
2 General Introduction to Part II   23

PART II   33

3 Number Words and Numerals   33
4 Early Counting and Addition   53
5 Structuring Numbers 1 to 10   71
6 Advanced Counting, Addition and Subtraction   92
7 Structuring Numbers 1 to 20   111
8 Two-digit Addition and Subtraction: Jump Strategies   135
9 Two-digit Addition and Subtraction: Split Strategies   161
10 Early Multiplication and Division   178

Glossary   206
Appendix: Instructional Settings   212
Bibliography   214
Index   222

Contents

List of Tables   xvi
Website Content   xvii
Contributors   xx
Acknowledgments   xxiii

Introduction   1
    Purpose   1
    Structure   1
    Notes to the Reader   3

PART I   5
1 Approaching, Designing and Organizing Instruction   5
    Approaching Instruction   5
    Designing Instruction   10
    Organizing Instruction   18

2 General Introduction to Part II   23
    Structure of Chapters in Part II   23
    Teaching Number in the Early Years – Contrasting Traditional and
      Emerging Approaches   26
    Teaching Place Value – A New Approach   28

PART II   33
3 Number Words and Numerals   33
    Topic Overview   33
      Learning about Number Words   33
      Learning about Numerals   34
    Assessment Task Groups   36
      A3.1: Forward Number Word Sequences   37
      A3.2: Number Word After   37
      A3.3: Backward Number Word Sequences   38
      A3.4: Number Word Before   38
      A3.5: Numeral Identification   39
      A3.6: Numeral Recognition   39
      A3.7: Sequencing Numerals   40
      A3.8: Ordering Numerals   40
      A3.9: Locating Numbers in the Range 1 to 100   41

Instructional Activities   41
    IA3.1: Count Around   42
    IA3.2: Numbers on the Line   42
    IA3.3: Counting Choir   43
    IA3.4: What Comes Next?   43
    IA3.5: Stand in Line   45
    IA3.6: Secret Numbers   46
    IA3.7: Can You See Me?   46
    IA3.8: Take Your Place   47
    IA3.9: Where Do I Go?   48
    IA3.10: Teddy Bear Walk   49
    IA3.11: The Numeral Roll   50
Learning Trajectories   51

4   Early Counting and Addition   53
Topic Overview   53
    The Importance of Counting   53
    Levels of Sophistication in Counting   53
    Counting versus Saying a Number Word Sequence   54
    Perceptual Counting   54
    Beginning Addition through Counting   55
    Counting-from-one versus Counting-on   55
    Counting as Coordinating Words and Items   56
    Emergent, Perceptual and Figurative Counting   56
    Determining the Most Sophisticated Level   57
Assessment Task Groups   57
    A4.1: Comparing Small Collections   57
    A4.2: Increase and Decrease in the Range 1 to 6   58
    A4.3: Establishing the Numerosity of a Collection 58
    A4.4: Establishing a Collection of Specified Numerosity   59
    A4.5: Establishing the Numerosity of Two Collections   59
    A4.6: Additive Tasks Involving Two Screened Collections   60
    A4.7: Counting and Copying Temporal Sequences and Temporal Patterns   60
Instructional Activities   61
    IA4.1: Diffy Game   61
    IA4.2: Number Row Count   62
    IA4.3: Domino Addition   62
    IA4.4: Addition Spinners   63
    IA4.5: Counters in a Row   64
    IA4.6: On the Mat   65
    IA4.7: Toy Box   66
    IA4.8: Chains   66
    IA4.9: Give Me Five   67
    IA4.10: Pass It On   68

IA4.11: Hide and Add   69
IA4.12: Rhythmic Patterns   69
Learning Trajectory   70

5   Structuring Numbers 1 to 10   71
Topic Overview   71
Combining and Partitioning Small Numbers   71
Spatial Patterns   72
Finger Patterns   73
Five and Ten as Reference Points in the Range 1 to 10   74
Assessment Task Groups   75
A5.1: Making Finger Patterns for Numbers in the Range 1 to 5   76
A5.2: Making Finger Patterns for Numbers in the Range 6 to 10   76
A5.3: Naming and Visualizing Domino Patterns 1 to 6   77
A5.4: Naming and Visualizing Pair-Wise Patterns on a Ten-Frame   77
A5.5: Naming and Visualizing Five-Wise Patterns on a Ten-Frame   78
A5.6: Partitions of 5 and 10   79
A5.7: Addition and Subtraction in the Range 1 to 10   79
Instructional Activities   80
IA5.1: Bunny Ears   81
IA5.2: The Great Race   82
IA5.3: Quick Dots   83
IA5.4: Make Five Concentration   84
IA5.5 Five- and Ten-Frame Flashes   85
IA5.6: Memory Game   86
IA5.7: Domino Flashes   87
IA5.8: Domino Fish   88
IA5.9: Domino Snap   88
IA5.10: Make Ten Fish   89
IA5.11: Ten-Frame Bingo   89
IA5.12: Domino Five Up   89
IA5.13: Make Ten Ping Pong   90
Learning Trajectory   91

6   Advanced Counting, Addition and Subtraction   92
Topic Overview   92
Advanced Counting-by-ones Strategies   92
Screened Collections versus Word Problems   94
Choosing Numbers for Additive and Subtractive Tasks   95
Assessment Task Groups   96
A6.1: Additive Tasks Involving Two Screened Collections   97
A6.2: Missing Addend Tasks Involving Two Screened Collections   97
A6.3: Removed Items Tasks Involving a Screened Collection   98
A6.4: Missing Subtrahend Tasks Involving a Screened Collection   99

A6.5: Comparative Subtraction Involving Two Screened Collections   99
A6.6: Subtraction with Bare Numbers   100
Instructional Activities   100
IA6.1: Class Count-On and Count-Back   101
IA6.2: Hundred Chart Activities   101
IA6.3: Activities on a Bead Bar or Bead String   102
IA6.4: Bucket Count-On   103
IA6.5: Bucket Count-Back   103
IA6.6: Number Line Count-On   104
IA6.7: It's in the Bag   105
IA6.8: Team Mats   106
IA6.9: What's in the Box?   106
IA6.10: Under the Cloth   107
IA 6.11: Train Track   108
IA6.12: Frogs on the Lily Pads   108
IA6.13: Making Ice   109
Learning Trajectory   109

7   Structuring Numbers 1 to 20   111
Topic Overview   111
Using the Arithmetic Rack   111
Making and Reading Numbers 1 to 20   112
Adding Two Numbers with the Sum in the Range 1 to 20   113
Subtraction in the Range 1 to 20   116
From Using the Rack to Mental Strategies   117
Working Flexibly with Doubles and Near Doubles, and Five and Ten   117
Assessment Task Groups   118
A7.1: Naming and Visualizing Pair-Wise Patterns for 1 to 10   118
A7.2: Naming and Visualizing Five-Wise Patterns for 1 to 10   119
A7.3: Naming and Visualizing Pair-Wise Patterns for 11 to 20   120
A7.4: Naming and Visualizing Five-Wise and Ten-Wise Patterns for 11 to 14   120
A7.5: Naming and Visualizing Ten-Wise Patterns for 15 to 20   121
A7.6: Addition using Doubles, Fives and Tens – Addends Less than 11   121
A7.7: Subtraction using Doubles, Fives and Tens – Subtrahend and Difference
    Less than 11   122
A7.8: Addition using Doubles, Fives and Tens – One Addend Greater than 10   122
A7.9: Subtraction using Doubles, Fives and Tens – Subtrahend or Difference
    Greater than 10   123
Instructional Activities   123
IA7.1: Double Decker Bus Flashes   124
IA7.2: Getting On and Off the Bus   125
IA7.3: Dot Snap   126
IA7.4: Making Combinations to Twenty Fish   126
IA7.5: Using Ten-Plus Combinations   127
IA7.6: Five and Ten Game   129

	IA7.7: Chocolate Boxes	129
	IA7.8: Double Ten-Frame Facts	130
	IA7.9: Bead Board	131
	IA7.10: Clear the Board	132
	Learning Trajectories	133

8	Two-digit Addition and Subtraction: Jump Strategies	135
	Topic Overview	135
	Fostering the Development of Jump Strategies	136
	Learning to Add and Subtract through a Decuple	138
	Learning to Increment and Decrement 2-digit Numbers	139
	Fostering the Development of a Range of Strategies	140
	Assessment Task Groups	142
	A8.1: Forward and Backward Number Word Sequences by Tens, on and off the Decuple	142
	A8.2: Adding from a Decuple and Subtracting to a Decuple	142
	A8.3: Adding to a Decuple and Subtracting from a Decuple	143
	A8.4: Incrementing and Decrementing by Tens on and off the Decuple	144
	A8.5: Incrementing Flexibly by Tens and Ones	145
	A8.6: Adding Tens to a 2-Digit Number and Subtracting Tens from a 2-Digit Number	146
	A8.7: Adding Two 2-Digit Numbers without and with Regrouping	146
	A8.8: Subtraction Involving Two 2-Digit Numbers without and with Regrouping	147
	A8.9: Addition and Subtraction using Transforming, Compensating and Other Strategies	148
	Instructional Activities	148
	IA8.1: Walk-about Sequences	149
	IA8.2: Bead String with Ten Catcher	149
	IA8.3: Leap Frog	150
	IA8.4: Jump to 100	153
	IA8.5: Jump from 100	155
	IA8.6: Target Number	155
	IA8.7: Jump Addition and Subtraction Worksheets	156
	IA8.8: Jump Addition and Subtraction Cards	157
	IA8.9: Jump Addition and Subtraction Spinners	157
	IA8.10: What's the Question?	158
	IA8.11: Race to 50	158
	Learning Trajectory	159

9	Two-digit Addition and Subtraction: Split Strategies	161
	Topic Overview	161
	Higher Decade Addition and Subtraction	161
	Fostering the Development of Split Strategies	163
	Extending to 3-digit Addition, Subtraction and Place Value	164

Assessment Task Groups 165
  A9.1: Higher Decade Addition and Subtraction without and with
    Bridging the Decuple 166
  A9.2: Partitioning and Combining Involving 2-Digit Numbers 167
  A9.3: Combining and Partitioning Involving Non-Canonical
    (Non-Standard) Forms 167
  A9.4: Addition Involving Two 2-Digit Numbers without and with Regrouping 168
  A9.5: Subtraction Involving Two 2-Digit Numbers without and with Regrouping 169
Instructional Activities 169
  IA9.1: Follow the Pattern 170
  IA9.2: Counting by Tens 170
  IA9.3: Ten More or Ten Less 171
  IA9.4: Add or Subtract Tens 171
  IA9.5: Playing with Money 172
  IA9.6: Addition Tasks with Screened Materials 172
  IA9.7: Subtraction Tasks with Screened Materials 173
  IA9.8: Split the Subtrahend (Decuples) 173
  IA9.9: Making Bundles of Ten 174
  IA9.10: Make and Break Numbers 174
Learning Trajectory 176

10 Early Multiplication and Division 178
Topic Overview 178
  Repeated Equal Groups and Sharing 178
  Number Word Sequences of Multiples – Skip Counting 179
  Counting Repeated Equal Groups 180
  Division as Sharing or Measuring 180
  Abstract Composite Unit 181
  Using Arrays 182
  Commutativity and Inverse Operations 183
  Extending Multiplication and Division Knowledge 184
Assessment Task Groups 184
  A10.1: Counting by Twos, Fives, Tens and Threes 185
  A10.2: Multiplication – Items and Groups Visible 185
  A10.3: Multiplication – Items Screened and Groups Visible 186
  A10.4: Multiplication – Items and Groups Screened 187
  A10.5: Quotitive Division – Number in Each Group Given 187
  A10.6: Partitive Division – Number of Groups Given 188
  A10.7: Multiplication using Arrays 188
  A10.8: Division using Arrays 190
  A10.9: Multiplication Basic Facts Involving 2, 10 and 5 as Multipliers 190
  A10.10: Relational Thinking: Commutative and Distributive Principles 191
  A10.11: Relational Thinking: Multiplication and Division as Inverses 191

Instructional Activities   192
    IA10.1: Count Around – Multiples   192
    IA10.2: Trios for Multiples   193
    IA10.3: Quick Draw Multiples   194
    IA10.4: Rolling Groups   194
    IA10.5: Lemonade Stand   196
    IA10.6: Array Flip   197
    IA10.7: Dueling Arrays   198
    IA10.8: Mini Multo   199
    IA10.9: Four's a Winner   200
    IA10.10: I Have/Who Has   202
    IA10.11: Multiplication Match-up   202
    IA10.12: Introducing Division   203
    IA10.13: Division Array Cards   204
Learning Trajectory   205

Glossary   206
Appendix: Instructional Settings   212
Bibliography   214
Index   222

List of Tables

1.1 Classroom Instructional Framework for Early Number Learning   11

1.2 Design of display chart for four-group rotation model   21

1.3 Design of display chart for three-group rotation model   21

2.1 Outline of the structure of Chapters 3 to 10   24

2.2 Contrasting traditional and emerging approaches to number instruction in the first two years of school   27

2.3 Responses of a child with, and a child without, sound knowledge of the ten and ones structure of teen numbers   30

3.1 Learning Trajectory: Number Words   51

3.2 Learning Trajectory: Numerals   52

4.1 Learning Trajectory: Early Counting and Addition   70

5.1 Learning Trajectory: Structuring Numbers 1 to 10   91

6.1 Advanced counting-by-ones strategies, task types and solutions   93

6.2 Learning Trajectory: Advanced Counting, Addition and Subtraction   110

7.1 Learning Trajectory: Structuring Numbers 1 to 20 – Addition   133

7.2 Learning Trajectory: Structuring Numbers 1 to 20 – Subtraction   134

8.1 Learning Trajectory: 2-Digit Addition and Subtraction – Jump Strategies   159

9.1 Learning Trajectory: 2-Digit Addition and Subtraction – Split Strategies   176

10.1 Learning Trajectory: Early Multiplication and Division   205

Website Content

This book is supported by a brand new companion website (www.sagepub.co.uk/wrighttnc) which offers extra tips, videos and other resources for anyone using the text.

The website features a Facilitator's Guide, intended as a companion to the book, to be used either individually or in group study to help you get the most out of the material.

There is a section for all ten chapters from the book, and each chapter is supported by:

- Additional notes from the authors.
- An agenda to help you work through the chapter content.
- Suggestions for using and adapting Assessments and Instructional Activities from the book (Chapters 3–10).
- A planning matrix (Chapters 3–10).

There is also additional material to support the Instructional Activities in the book.

Look out for the following symbols in the text:

 Additional online resources that can be printed for use in the activity.

 An online video demonstration with tips for the most effective ways of working.

These resources can be used in one-on-one intervention teaching, small-group instruction, classroom learning station instruction, and as home activities instead of traditional homework sheets.

A full list of available resources is shown below.

Videos

- IA 4.12 Rhythmic Patterns
- IA 5.1   Bunny Ears
- IA 5.12 Domino Five Up
- IA 6.1   Count On, Count Back
- IA 6.4   Bucket Count-on
- IA 6.7   It's in the Bag
- IA 6.9   What's in the Box
- IA 7.10 Clear the Board
- IA 8.4   Jump to 100
- IA 8.5   Jump from 100

Printable resources

Chapter 3

Arrow spinner
Blank number grid
Blank numeral ladder
Digit cards
Find the missing numbers on the hundred
    square
Teddy Bear Walk
Large numerals 1–32
Pairs game
What Comes Before? worksheet
Number grid – 771–870
Number grid – 941–1040
Numeral cards – 1–118
Numeral rolls 1–120, 101–220
Screened hundred square
What Comes Next? worksheet

Chapter 4

Domino Addition cards
Addition Spinners

Chapter 5

Birds in Trees
Dice/numeral cards
Traditional Dominos game
Dot spinner
Five dot cards
Five-frame 1–4
Five-frames – blank
Five-frame combinations
Five-frames – numeral cards
Five-frames – small cards
Five-wise Fish
Five-wise cards
Five-wise ten-frames
Fives combinations record sheet
The Great Race game board

Quick Dots
Dice/numeral cards
Make a Number Fish
Making 6 numeral cards
Spinners
Five-frame minibus
Using ten-frame and ten-frame minibus
Ten-frame five-wise flash cards
Ten-frames – numeral cards
Ten-frames – blank
Ten-frames – tens
Ten-frames – pair-wise
Ten-frames – mini
Ten-frames – red and green
Ten-frames – 0 to 10
Ten-frames – parts of ten
Domino Pattern Cards

Chapter 6

Hundred chart
9 Plus game
19 Plus game
20 Minus game
Addition facts grid
Decuple minus
Expression cards
Jumping to 50 game
Make 10 activity
Near ten addition activity sheet

Chapter 7

Double Decker Bus
Double Decker Bus work sheet
Double and near double cards
Double ten-frame worksheet
Ten-wise cards (11–20)
Five and Ten game sheet
Clear the Board sheet
Double ten-frame blank cards

Chapter 8

20 Plus game
32 Minus game
51 Minus game
48 Plus game
67 Plus game
70 Plus game
Add or subtract 12
How many more to make 100?
How many more to make 60?
Leap Frog 1
Leap Frog 2
Leap Frog 3
Leap Frog 4
Leap Frog 5
Jump to 100
Jump addition and subtraction
    worksheet
Jump addition and subtraction
    spinners
What's the Question? record sheet
Race to 50

Chapter 9

Arrow cards
How Many Dots?
Ten-frame worksheet

Chapter 10

10 x 10 dot array
Array Bingo cards
Dot tiles in geometric arrangements
    (3s, 4s, 5s)
How Many in Each Box?
Rolling Groups worksheet
Lemonade Stand
Dueling Array cards
Four's a Winner
Multiplication Match-up worksheet
Multiplication Match-up cards
Multiples of 2
Multiples of 3
Multiples of 4
Multiples of 5

Contributors

Authors

Dr Robert J. (Bob) Wright holds Bachelor's and Master's degrees in mathematics from the University of Queensland (Australia) and a doctoral degree in mathematics education from the University of Georgia. He is an adjunct professor in mathematics education at Southern Cross University in New South Wales. Bob is an internationally recognized leader in assessment and instruction relating to children's early arithmetical **knowledge** and strategies, publishing four books and many articles and papers in this field. His work over the last 20 years has included the development of the Mathematics Recovery program which focuses on providing specialist training for teachers to advance the numeracy levels of young children assessed as low-attainers. In Australia and New Zealand, Ireland, the UK, the USA, Canada, Mexico and elsewhere, this program has been implemented widely and applied extensively to classroom teaching and to average and able learners as well as low-attainers. He has conducted several research projects funded by the Australian Research Council including the most recent project focusing on assessment and intervention in the early arithmetical learning of low-attaining 8–10-year-olds.

Garry Stanger has had a wide-ranging involvement in primary, secondary and tertiary education in Australia. He has held positions of head teacher, deputy principal and principal, and has been a Mathematics consultant with the New South Wales Department of Education. He has also taught in schools in the USA. He has worked with Robert Wright on the Mathematics Recovery project since its inception in 1992 and has been involved in the development of the Count Me In Too early numeracy project. His last project before finally retiring was working with Jenny Bednall, Head of Junior School, Trinity South and the 30 teachers at the Trinity College schools in South Australia.

Ann K. Stafford's academic background includes graduate study at Southern Cross University, Australia, the University of Chicago and Clemson University. She received a Master's degree from Duke University and an undergraduate degree from the University of North Carolina at Greensboro. Her professional experience includes teaching and administrative roles in K-5 classrooms and supervision in the areas of mathematics, gifted, early childhood and remedial as well as teaching and research positions at Clemson University. She has led in the writing and development of Early Childhood and Mathematics Curricula for the School District of Oconee County, South Carolina. Ann has received numerous professional awards and grants for outstanding contributions to the region and state for mathematics and leadership. She was the leader in the implementation and classroom applications of Mathematics Recovery in the USA and currently is an academic consultant.

Jim Martland is a member of the International Board of Mathematics Recovery and Founder of the Mathematics Recovery Council (UK and Ireland). He was a Senior Fellow in the

Department of Education at the University of Liverpool. In his long career in education he has held headships in primary and middle schools and was Director of Primary Initial Teacher Training. In all the posts he continued to teach and pursue research in primary mathematics. His current work is with local education authorities in the UK and Canada, delivering professional development courses on assessing children's difficulties in numeracy and designing and evaluating teaching interventions.

Contributors

Amy Shiloh Ernst is a mathematics specialist in Harford County, Maryland. She has been a Mathematics Recovery teacher and leader since 1999. She has been involved in several mathematics projects in her district, including Mathematics Recovery training and implementation, curriculum revision, assessment production, staff development and program evaluation. She completed her Master's in Education at Loyola College in Maryland.

Kurt Kinsey is co-owner and consultant for Mountain States Mathematics, working together with schools and school systems to improve the mathematics educational experience for students. With a BS and MEd in mathematics education, his teaching background includes secondary mathematics, mathematics intervention at the early and middle levels, and teacher in-service and graduate-level coursework. Kurt was a founding member of US Math Recovery Council (USMRC), served on the USMRC Board of Directors, and worked as a member of the USMRC Instructional Strategy Group and as faculty for the USMRC Summer Institute. He is co-author of the Add+VantageMR professional development program and a contributing author for the Math Recovery Intervention Specialist (MRIS) and MRIS Leadership courses. Current projects include on-going development of the Strength in Number professional development programs and providing leadership and program development for the First People's Center for Education, a non-profit organization supporting schools serving indigenous children.

Lucinda 'Petey' MacCarty, MEd, of Sheridan, Wyoming is co-owner of Mountain States Mathematics, an educational consulting organization. Petey has a passion for mathematics teaching and learning. Her career began as a secondary mathematics teacher and expanded to intervention specialist and K-12 mathematics coordinator. This district leadership role included curriculum development, assessment design and alignment, interventions and professional development for mathematics content and pedagogy. Beginning in 1999 Petey helped to design the professional development programs for Math Recovery Intervention Specialists and Math Recovery Leaders. In 2003 Petey along with the original developers of Mathematics Recovery helped to establish the non-profit US Math Recovery Council (USMRC). Petey continued to help the USMRC expand and evolve by co-authoring the Add+VantageMR professional development programs and taking leadership roles within the USMRC. Petey co-designed the Strength in Number professional development programs used by the non-profit First People's Center for Education. Petey is currently a lead developer for the organization and works directly with schools serving Native American, Alaska Natives and Native Hawaiian children across the US. Her goal is to help students and adults realize they can be successful with mathematics, giving them greater access to the world before them.

Charlotte Madine is an independent education consultant with over 15 years' experience in school improvement; she has worked with individuals, schools and local authorities to improve teaching and learning. Charlotte was a Senior Adviser with the National Strategies (UK) where she led programs of work implementing national policy and strategy to secure improved standards in literacy and numeracy. Prior to this she has been a teacher, an advisory teacher and a numeracy consultant for Knowsley MBC in the North West of England. She has extensive experience of teaching children from ages 5 to 11 years. Charlotte has a Certificate in the Advanced Study of Education (Mathematics Recovery) from the University of Liverpool, England and has extensive national and international experience in providing professional development for teachers in early intervention in mathematics. She has an active role in the Mathematics Recovery Council UK and Ireland.

Joan McCarthy is a numeracy consultant formerly from Wigan Education Authority UK, where she worked in an advisory and training capacity for the Learning Support Services. She has been involved with the Mathematics Recovery program since its introduction to the UK in 1996, becoming a trainer in 1998 and a numeracy consultant in 2002. She is an experienced primary school practitioner having taught pupils aged 5–11 during her teaching career. Joan now provides professional development in mathematics for classroom teachers in the UK and Ireland. She holds a Certificate and Diploma in the Advanced Study of Education (Mathematics Recovery) from the University of Liverpool, England.

Chris Porter is a Mathematics Recovery consultant training teachers and trainers across the UK and Ireland. She has been involved with Mathematics Recovery from its early days. More recently she has been part of a small team of consultants training across Ireland supporting the development of the Mathematics Recovery program. Chris has extensive experience of teaching primary age children. Studying for a further degree in Mathematics Education in the 1990s kindled her interest in children's mathematical development. Taking up the post of numeracy consultant for Salford Local Authority in 2000 involved supporting schools and teachers to develop and strengthen their teaching which led to standards being raised.

Julia Sheridan has extensive experience of classroom teaching of children from age 5 to 11 years. She trained as a Mathematics Recovery researcher in 1997 under the tutorship of Jim Martland and with Jim as her mentor went on to become a Mathematics Recovery trainer. After working as an advisory teacher for her local education authority and a numeracy consultant for the National Numeracy Strategy in England, she now works as an independent consultant providing Mathematics Recovery training for teachers on behalf of the Mathematics Recovery Council, UK and Ireland. Whilst providing Mathematics Recovery training extensively throughout the Republic of Ireland she has supported the development of 'Mata sa Rang', a classroom program based upon Mathematics Recovery, and mentors new Mathematics Recovery trainers. She has a Master's Degree (Education) and a Certificate in the Advanced Study of Education (Mathematics Recovery) from the University of Liverpool, England.

Pam Tabor is an independent researcher located in Havre de Grace, Maryland. Her previous experience includes functioning as a school-based mathematics specialist for nearly 20 years. During that time she served as a US Math Recovery Council board member. Her current research interests are in early childhood mathematics, implementation of the Common Core, gifted and talented education and meeting the needs of students with autism. She has presented at numerous conferences nationally and internationally.

Acknowledgments

This book is a culmination of several interrelated research projects conducted over the last 20 years, many of which come under the collective label of Mathematics Recovery. All these projects have involved one or more of the authors or contributors undertaking research, development and implementation in collaboration with teachers, schools and school systems. These projects have received significant support from the participating schools, school systems and jurisdictions.

The authors wish to express their sincere gratitude and appreciation to all the teachers, students and project colleagues who have participated in, and contributed to, these projects. We also wish to thank the following organizations for funding and supporting one or more projects which have provided a basis for writing this book: the government and Catholic school systems of the north coast region of New South Wales, Australia; the Australian Research Council; the New South Wales Department of Education and Training; the School District of Oconee County and the South Carolina Department of Education; many other school districts across the United States; the University of Liverpool and Wigan, Sefton, Salford, Stockport, Knowsley and Cumbria Education Authorities in England; Flintshire County Council in Wales; the Ministry of Education in the Bahamas; the Catholic Education Office, Melbourne (Australia); the First Peoples Center for Education (USA); the Department of Education and Science, Ireland; the Kentucky Center for Mathematics; the Frontier School Division, Manitoba, Canada; the University of Strathclyde; and Glasgow, Edinburgh and Stirling Education Authorities in Scotland; Fundación Educación, voces y vuelos, IAP in Mexico; and Trinity College, South Australia.

The authors, SAGE Publications and the International Mathematics Recovery Council wish to express their grateful appreciation to the principal, staff, parents and children of Wallyford Primary School and the officers of East Lothian Council for permission to produce the instructional activities for the website.

We also wish to thank the children and staff in schools in Edinburgh, Flintshire, Wigan, Mexico and the USA for agreeing to appear in the photographs.

Dr Penny Munn – a Tribute

The Mathematics Recovery program has lost a distinguished and highly respected colleague. Penny died of cancer in June 2011. She was a developmental psychologist and undertook research at Cambridge and Strathclyde Universities. She was joint editor of the *Journal of Early Years Education* and Chair of the Mathematics Recovery Council of the United Kingdom and Ireland from its inception. Penny was instrumental in the development and spread of Mathematics Recovery in Scotland. She put young children at the center of her research and teaching and her work will continue to influence educationalists and academics for some considerable time to come.

Series Page

The four books in this series provide practical help to enable schools and teachers to give equal status to early numeracy intervention and classroom instruction. The authors are internationally recognized as leaders in the field of numeracy intervention and **early number** instruction, and draw on considerable practical experience of delivering training courses and materials.

The books are:

- *Early Numeracy: Assessment for Teaching & Intervention* (2nd edn), Robert J. Wright, Jim Martland and Ann K. Stafford, 2006.

  Early Numeracy demonstrates how to assess students' mathematical knowledge, skills and strategies in addition, subtraction, multiplication and division.

-  *Teaching Number: Advancing Children's Skills & Strategies* (2nd edn), Robert J. Wright, Jim Martland, Ann K. Stafford and Garry Stanger, 2006.

  This book sets out in detail nine principles which guide the teaching together with 180 practical, exemplar teaching procedures to advance children to more sophisticated strategies for solving arithmetic problems.

- *Developing Number Knowledge: Assessment, Teaching & Intervention with 7–11-year-olds*, Robert J. Wright, David Ellemor-Collins and Pamela Tabor, 2012.

  Developing Number Knowledge provides more advanced knowledge and resources for teachers working with older students.

- *Teaching Number in the Classroom with 4–8-year-olds* (2nd edn), Robert J. Wright, Garry Stanger, Ann K. Stafford and Jim Martland, 2014.

  This book shows how to extend the work of assessment and intervention with individual and small groups to working with whole classes.

The series provides a comprehensive package on:

1   How to identify, analyse and report children's arithmetic knowledge, skills and strategies.
2   How to design, implement and evaluate a course of intervention.
3   How to include both assessment and teaching in the daily numeracy program in differing class organizations and contexts.

The series draws on a substantial body of recent theoretical research supported by international, practical application. Because all the assessment and teaching activities have been empirically tested, the books are able to show the teacher the possible ranges of students' responses and patterns of their behavior.

The books are a package for professional development and a comprehensive resource for experienced teachers concerned with early numeracy intervention and for the primary teacher responsible for teaching numeracy from kindergarten to upper primary levels.

Introduction

The authors of this book have worked extensively on research and development projects in early numeracy for at least the last 20 years. Much of our research in the early 1990s focused on the development of the **Mathematics Recovery** program – a program of intensive instruction for children encountering significant difficulties in early **number** learning. From the mid-1990s onward, this program has been used extensively in the United States, the United Kingdom, Ireland, Australia, Canada, Mexico and elsewhere. In many of the school districts where Mathematics Recovery has been implemented, the program has provided the basis for major transformations in approaches to teaching early numeracy to all children.

We have spent countless hours on the provision of school-based and system-based professional development and support, focusing on early numeracy assessment and instruction.

The theory and approaches presented in this book have their origins in constructivist-based research into early number learning. This includes Leslie Steffe's constructivist teaching experiment research and Paul Cobb's classroom teaching experiment research, as well as research into early number learning by Bob Wright. This book also draws significantly on approaches to teaching number developed by researchers in the Freudenthal Institute.

Purpose

This book is a detailed and comprehensive guide to the classroom teaching of early numeracy. Our two earlier books – *Early Numeracy: Assessment for Teaching & Intervention* and *Teaching Number: Advancing Children's Skills & Strategies* – focus mainly on the provision of specialist, intervention teaching of low-attaining children. This book also complements our more recent book – *Developing Number Knowledge: Assessment, Teaching & Intervention with 7–11-year-olds* which focuses on the classroom teaching of number to an older range of students.

Structure

The book is organized into two parts. Part I focuses on our general approach to teaching early numeracy and Part II focuses on the teaching of specific topics of early numeracy.

Part I General Approach to Teaching Early Numeracy

Part I consists of two chapters: Chapter 1 focuses on approaching, designing and organizing instruction and Chapter 2 provides a general introduction to Part II.

Chapter 1 consists of three sections.

- The first presents nine principles of classroom teaching which have been used extensively by the authors and others as a guide to classroom teaching. This section also includes a discussion of **progressive mathematization**, that is, advancement in mathematical sophistication. Finally, this section includes the Classroom Instructional Framework for Early Number (CIFEN) which provides guidance for the development of instructional sequences, that is, sequences of interrelated instructional topics that progressively build an important aspect of children's early number knowledge.
- The second section provides a description and illustration of the use of the Teaching and Learning Cycle for designing instruction.
- The third section presents models which demonstrate different approaches to classroom organization for instruction. Block scheduling is also discussed.

Chapter 2 provides a detailed overview of Part II.

- The first section sets out the common structure that applies to Chapters 3 to 10.
- Section 2 focuses on aspects of the teaching of number typical of the earlier years in this range, say 4–6-year-olds.
- Section 3 focuses on aspects of the teaching of number typical of the later years in this range, say 6–8-year-olds.

Part II Teaching Specific Early Numeracy Topics

Part II of the book is organized into eight chapters, each of which presents an important topic of early numeracy. Each chapter consists of four sections.

- Topic Overview – A comprehensive overview of the topic of early number learning that is the focus of the chapter.
- Assessment Task Groups – sets out in detail up to 11 assessment task groups relevant to the topic of the chapter, which can be used by the teacher to assess comprehensively the extent of children's knowledge of the topic. Assessment in this form provides a crucial basis for instruction. An assessment task group is a group of assessment tasks in which all the tasks are very similar to each other. The tasks in each assessment task group focus on a particular aspect of the number topic in the chapter. Each task group includes details of how to present the assessment tasks and notes on the purpose of the task, children's responses, and so on.
- Instructional Activities – sets out in detail up to 13 instructional activities relevant to the topic of the chapter. Each instructional activity has the following five-part format: title, intended learning, description, notes and materials. These activities are designed so that they are easily incorporated into lessons.
- Learning Trajectories – each learning trajectory provides a progression of learning topics that draw on the overview, assessment tasks and instructional activities presented in the first three sections.

Notes to the Reader

Assessment Tasks and Instructional Activities

The chapters in Part II of this book contain many assessment task groups and instructional activities. Many of the assessment task groups can be easily adapted for use as instructional activities and many of the instructional activities can be easily adapted for use as assessment tasks.

Mapping topics to other books in the series

Some of the topics covered in this book directly link with chapters or sections in the other books in this series. Relevant key topics from *Teaching Number* (the 'green book') and chapters from *Developing Number Knowledge with 7–11 year-olds* (the 'red book') are indicated at the beginning of each chapter, so for example for Chapter 7:

  Key topics: 8.5   Chapter: 4

Glossary, Appendices, and Bibliography

This book includes an extensive Glossary of technical terms used in the book. There is also an Appendix at the back of the book which contains descriptions of the key instructional settings used in the book. Additionally, there is a comprehensive bibliography of relevant works.

Conventions for Reading and Writing Numbers

The readers of our books are from a range of countries and we are aware that, internationally, there are differing conventions for reading and writing numbers and so on. Examples are saying 'one hundred and four' or 'one hundred four'; and writing '3 104' or '3,104'. Because our books are published in London, as a general rule we follow the conventions used in the United Kingdom. We trust that, when readers encounter a convention different from the one to which they are accustomed, they will adjust the text accordingly.

PART I

1

Approaching, Designing and Organizing Instruction

Summary

This chapter consists of three sections. The first presents nine principles of classroom teaching which have been used extensively by the authors and others as a guide to classroom teaching. Also included in this section is the Classroom Instructional Framework for Early Number (CIFEN) which provides guidance for the development of learning trajectories, that is, sequences of interrelated instructional topics that progressively build an important aspect of children's early number knowledge. The second section provides a description and illustration of the use of the Teaching and Learning Cycle for designing instruction. In the third section, models are presented which demonstrate different approaches to classroom organization for instruction. Block scheduling is also discussed.

Approaching Instruction

The purpose of this section is to set out key ideas in the general approach to teaching number in the classroom that is advocated in this book. These key ideas are presented in the following two topics: (a) Guiding Principles for Classroom Teaching (GPCT); and (b) the Classroom Instructional Framework for Early Number (CIFEN). This section draws on some of the ideas in our two earlier books: *Early Numeracy: Assessment for Teaching & Intervention* (2nd edn) (Wright et al., 2006a) and *Teaching Number: Advancing Children's Skills & Strategies* (2nd edn) (Wright et al., 2006b).

Guiding Principles for Classroom Teaching

In the 1990s, we conducted several research and development projects in which we worked in collaboration with teachers and school systems. In these projects, we developed the following set of nine guiding principles of teaching. In more recent years, we have conducted additional research and development projects in which these principles have been applied extensively to guide the teaching of number in the early years of school:

1   The teaching approach is inquiry based, that is, problem based. Children routinely are engaged in thinking hard to solve numerical problems which for them are quite challenging.
2   Teaching is informed by an initial, comprehensive assessment and ongoing assessment through teaching. The latter refers to the teacher's informed understanding of children's current knowledge and problem-solving strategies, and continual revision of this understanding.
3   Teaching is focused just beyond the 'cutting-edge' of the child's current knowledge.
4   Teachers exercise their professional judgement in selecting from a bank of teaching procedures each of which involves particular instructional settings and tasks, and varying this selection on the basis of ongoing observations.
5   The teacher understands children's numerical strategies and deliberately engenders the development of more sophisticated strategies.
6   Teaching involves intensive, ongoing observation by the teacher and continual **micro-adjusting** or fine-tuning of teaching on the basis of her or his observation.
7   Teaching supports and builds on children's intuitive, verbally based strategies and these are used as a basis for the development of written forms of arithmetic which accord with the child's verbally based strategies.
8   The teacher provides the child with sufficient time to solve a given problem. Consequently the child is frequently engaged in episodes which involve sustained thinking, reflection on her or his thinking and reflecting on the results of her or his thinking.
9   Children gain intrinsic satisfaction from their problem-solving, their realization that they are making progress, and from the verification methods they develop.

Each of these principles is now discussed in more detail.

Principle 1

The teaching approach is inquiry based, that is, problem based. Children routinely are engaged in thinking hard to solve numerical problems which for them are quite challenging.

The inquiry-based approach to teaching number is sometimes referred to as learning through problem-solving or problem-based learning. In this approach, the central learning activity for children is to solve tasks that constitute genuine problems, that is, problems for which the children do not have a ready-made solution. What follows is that the issue of whether a particular task is appropriate as a genuine problem largely depends on the extent of the children's current knowledge.

Principle 2

Teaching is informed by an initial, comprehensive assessment and ongoing assessment through teaching. The latter refers to the teacher's informed understanding of children's current knowledge and problem-solving strategies, and continual revision of this understanding.

Assessment for providing specific and detailed information to inform instruction is the critical ingredient in our approach to teaching early number. It is essential to conduct a detailed assessment of children's current number knowledge, and to use the results of assessment in designing instruction. In each of Chapters 3 to 10, the second section of the chapter contains detailed descriptions of assessment tasks and notes on their use. These have the explicit purpose of informing the design of instruction. The second aspect of this principle, ongoing assessment through observation and reflection, is equally as important as initial assessment.

Principle 3

Teaching is focused just beyond the 'cutting-edge' of the child's current knowledge.

This principle accords with Vygotsky's notion of zone of proximal development, that is, instruction should be focused just beyond the child's current levels of knowledge in the areas where the child is likely to learn successfully through sound teaching. This principle is very important in our focus on the teaching of early number. The principle highlights the importance of assessment to inform teaching. Assessment provides the teacher with a profile of children's knowledge and the teacher focuses instruction so that children will be moved beyond their current levels of knowledge.

Principle 4

Teachers exercise their professional judgement in selecting from a bank of teaching procedures each of which involves particular instructional settings and tasks, and varying this selection on the basis of ongoing observations.

This principle highlights the need to develop a bank of instructional procedures and to understand the role of each procedure, in terms of its potential to bring about advancements in children's current knowledge. In each of Chapters 3 to 10, the third section of the chapter includes up to 13 examples of learning activities which can be used to develop an appropriate bank of teaching procedures. Also, the second section of each chapter contains an extensive set of assessment tasks. These tasks constitute an additional source of instructional procedures because the tasks are easily adapted for instruction.

Principle 5

The teacher understands children's numerical strategies and deliberately engenders the development of more sophisticated strategies.

This principle highlights the need for teachers to have a working model of children's knowledge of early number and the ways in which children's knowledge typically progresses. In each of Chapters 3 to 10, the first section of the chapter provides a detailed overview of the development of an aspect of early number knowledge. Our belief is that teachers can develop an appropriate working model through reading, reflecting and observing, in conjunction with their teaching practice.

Principle 6

Teaching involves intensive, ongoing observation by the teacher and continual micro-adjusting or fine-tuning of teaching on the basis of her or his observation.

This principle highlights the importance of observational assessment in determining children's specific learning needs, and the need for this assessment to be ongoing and to lead to action, that is, the fine-tuning of instruction on the basis of ongoing assessment.

Principle 7

Teaching supports and builds on the child's intuitive, verbally based strategies and these are used as a basis for the development of written forms of arithmetic which accord with the child's verbally based strategies.

This principle highlights that children's initial number knowledge is by and large verbally based rather than involving written forms. Thus we suppose that children's initial counting and calculating strategies mainly involve mentally computing with sound images of number words and number word sequences. The further development of number knowledge involves a gradual process of incorporating written symbols, including but not limited to numerals, and linking these symbols to already acquired verbally based number knowledge.

Principle 8

The teacher provides the child with sufficient time to solve a given problem. Consequently the child is frequently engaged in episodes which involve sustained thinking, reflection on her or his thinking and reflecting on the results of her or his thinking.

In our research and development work in early number learning over the last 20 years and longer, we have always emphasized the importance of sustained thinking and reflection for the learning of mathematics. The topic of early number learning is well suited to significant problem-solving by children. This problem-solving and the mental processes of thinking hard and reflecting during problem-solving are, we believe, a fundamental aspect of early number learning.

Principle 9

Children gain intrinsic satisfaction from their problem-solving, from their realization that they are making progress, and from the verification methods they develop.

This principle relates to Principle 8. Our experience in working closely with teachers and children for many years on the topic of early number learning is that when young children work hard at problem-solving and their problem-solving is successful, this is typically a very positive experience for the learner. To go further, we argue that this kind of learning constitutes a kind of cognitive therapy, having intrinsic rewards beyond such processes as teacher affirmation and peer recognition.

Progressive Mathematization

This section draws on the recent book: *Developing Number Knowledge: Assessment, Teaching & Intervention with 7–11-year-olds* (Wright et al., 2012), and also draws on ideas in our two earlier books: *Early Numeracy: Assessment for Teaching & Intervention* (2nd edn) (Wright et al., 2006a) and *Teaching Number: Advancing Children's Skills & Strategies* (2nd edn) (Wright et al., 2006b). The term 'progressive mathematization' is used to describe the progression of children's learning and thinking in terms of advancement in mathematical sophistication. Recently we have described ten themes or dimensions of progressive mathematization (Wright et al., 2012; Ellemor-Collins and Wright, 2011b). By and large, these dimensions transcend specific topics in early number instruction. Thus the dimensions typically provide guidance for advancing children's early number knowledge and are applicable to a range of topics. Below we overview four dimensions which are particularly important in early number learning.

Extending the range of numbers

One way to progress children's learning is to extend the range of numbers that is currently the focus of their work. For example, on the topic of learning to say a **backward number word sequence** (BNWS) (Chapter 3) the sequence from 1 to 10 can be extended to 20. Learning to add and subtract in the range 1 to 10 (Chapter 5) can be extended to the range 1 to 20 (Chapter 7). We strongly advocate that teachers should continually seek opportunities to progress children's learning in this way. The instructional strategy of extending the range of numbers is incorporated into the learning trajectories that appear in Chapters 3 to 10 (Part II).

Distancing the setting

We use the term **setting** to refer to a situation used by the teacher when posing arithmetical tasks. Settings can be: (a) materials (e.g. **numeral track**, ten-frame, counters), (b) informal written, (c) formal written, or (d) verbal. The term setting refers not only to the material, writing or verbal statements but also encompasses the ways in which these are used in instruction and feature in students' reasoning. As in the case of extending the range of numbers (see above), we advocate an explicit instructional agenda to progress from (a) the student seeing the materials, to (b) the teacher **flashing** the materials, to (c) the student seeing the materials only after they have responded to a task, perhaps to check their response, to (d) posing tasks in a verbal or written form where no materials are available. The instructional strategy of distancing the setting is incorporated into the learning trajectories that appear in Chapters 3 to 10.

Complexifying

Complexifying refers to making the current mathematics more complex. For example, progressing from (a) adding to finding a missing addend, (b) adding a 10 to adding a 10 and two ones, and (c) doubling a number to doubling a number and adding one. Again, we advocate an instructional agenda of complexifying at every opportunity and this dimension of mathematizing is also incorporated into the learning trajectories.

Notating

Notating refers to children making their own written record that accords with a **strategy** they have used to solve an arithmetical task. Notating can be used in conjunction with distancing the setting (see above). In this way children can progress from solving arithmetical tasks presented using a material setting to solving tasks presented in verbal or written from. Notating is highlighted in Guiding Principle 7 (see above).

The Classroom Instructional Framework for Early Number

One of the key ideas underlying the approach to teaching early number presented here is that it is important for the teacher to be aware of the longer-term goals of instruction. Thus a year or half-year program in early number should not be regarded as a list of topics with little or no connections among the topics. By way of contrast, the program should be seen as one or more sequences of closely related topics where children's success on each topic depends very much on the extent to which they have developed sound knowledge of foregoing topics. Thus the Classroom Instructional Framework for Early Number (CIFEN) provides detailed guidance for teachers in the development of learning trajectories, where a learning trajectory is a sequence of interrelated, instructional topics that progressively build an important aspect of children's early number knowledge.

Table 1.1 describes the CIFEN. The CIFEN sets out a progression of early number topics that typically would span the first three or four years of school. The listing of the topics in separate columns indicates that the topics are somewhat distinct from each other. Nevertheless, this does not indicate that the topics should necessarily be taught separately from each other. By way of contrast, instructional activities can serve to integrate learning across these distinct topics. Topics are arranged in columns in the table to indicate their order in the progression of teaching. Our intention is that the organization of topics in CIFEN will be interpreted and adapted by teachers in a range of ways according to issues such as the specific curriculum being followed and the availability of resources. Finally, as indicated in Table 1.1, Chapters 3 to 10 (Part II) of this book provide detailed information on the teaching of each of the topics listed in the table. In particular, in each of Chapters 3 to 10 the fourth and final section consists of one or two learning trajectories. Each of these learning trajectories provides a detailed progression of instructional topics. These are complemented by the CIFEN which provides a sense of broader, less finely grained learning trajectories.

Designing Instruction

In designing instruction, many teachers have found it useful to use the Teaching and Learning Cycle (Figure 1.1) in conjunction with the Guiding Principles for Classroom Teaching (GPCT) set out earlier in this chapter. The Teaching and Learning Cycle has four key elements for teachers to consider in planning instruction for children.

Table 1.1 Classroom Instructional Framework for Early Number Learning

Number Words	Numerals	Counting	Structuring Numbers	Addition & Subtraction	Multiplication & Division
Chapter 3	**Chapter 3**	**Chapter 4** **Early Counting**	**Chapter 5** **Structuring Numbers 1–10**	**Chapter 8** **Jump Strategies**	**Chapter 10**
Number word sequences 1–10	Numerals 1 to 5	Counting small collections • emergent counting • perceptual counting	Finger patterns 1 to 10	Number word sequences by 10s on and off the decuple	Repeated equal groups – items and groups visible
Number word sequences 1–30	Numerals 1 to 10	Counting two visible collections	Dice patterns	Adding and subtracting to and from a decuple	Repeated equal groups – items screened
Number word sequences 1–100	Numerals 1 to 20	Temporal sequences	Pair-wise patterns to 10	Incrementing by tens, on and off the decuple	Repeated equal groups – items and groups screened
	Numerals 1 to 100	Early addition • figurative counting • counting-on	Partitioning 5 and 10	Jump strategy to add and subtract without re-grouping	Introduction to division
	Numerals to 100 and beyond		Five-wise patterns 6 to 10	Jump strategy to add and subtract involving re-grouping	Multiplication and division using arrays
			Addition and subtraction in range 1 to 10	Mental strategies to add and subtract 2-digit numbers	Linking multiplication and division
		Chapter 6 **Advanced Counting**	**Chapter 7** **Structuring Numbers 1–20**	**Chapter 9** **Split Strategies**	
		Counting-on	Pair-wise patterns to 20	Addition and subtraction in higher decades without bridging a decuple	
		Counting-back	Five-wise patterns to 20	Partitioning and combining involving 2-digit numbers	
		Addition and subtraction with screened collections	Ten-wise patterns to 20	Split strategy to add and subtract with re-grouping	
			Addition and subtraction using pairs, fives and tens	Split strategy to add and subtract involving re-grouping	

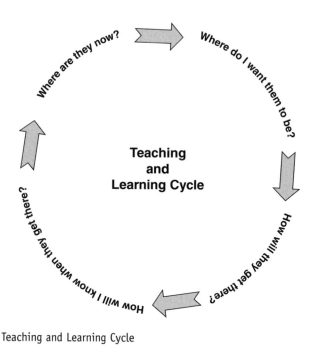

Figure 1.1 The Teaching and Learning Cycle

The Teaching and Learning Cycle

Where Are They Now?

Part II of this book (Chapters 3 to 10) contains assessment tasks that enable teachers to establish a clear picture of children's number knowledge. This is an essential phase of the Teaching and Learning Cycle and relates to Principles 2 and 3 in the GPCT.

Where Do I Want Them to Be?

Part II of this book (Chapters 3 to 10) contains what we regard as the essential number topics in teaching young children. This phase of the Teaching and Learning Cycle relates to Principle 5 in the GPCT.

How Will They Get There?

In the third section of this chapter we outline suggestions for organizing classrooms and for using the activities described in Part II (Chapters 3 to 10) in lessons to support the development of children's number knowledge. This phase of the Teaching and Learning Cycle relates to Principles 4, 6, 7 and 8 in the GPCT.

Characteristics of problem-centered lessons   Consider the following characteristics when selecting number lesson activities:

- Activities should require children to use strategic thinking rather than automatic or procedural responses. There are times when you might design activities to enhance factual knowledge but activities should largely involve problematic rather than routine tasks.

- Activities should allow children to use their current number knowledge. If the activities are too advanced, there is a risk that children will become frustrated in attempting to undertake the activities.
- Children should acquire some mathematical knowledge from engaging in an activity. If the tasks are too simple, children will not have an opportunity to advance their number knowledge.

How Will I Know When They Get There?

This also refers to the importance of assessment in the Teaching and Learning Cycle, and again we refer you to the assessment tasks and ideas on how they can be used that are outlined in Chapters 3 to 10. This phase of the Teaching and Learning Cycle relates to Principle 9 in the GPCT.

The following three lesson plans use instructional activities drawn from Chapters 3 to 10.

Lesson 1

Comment

The main activity in this lesson is the Numbers on the Line instructional activity (IA3.2). This might appear to be an activity that requires only routine thinking. However, for many young children, the placement of numerals might require a strategy, for example, counting-up or counting-back from one or from a visible numeral.

Introductory Activity (Warm-ups)

Forward number word sequences: 1 to 20; 8 to 15.
Backward number word sequences: 10 to 1; 12 to 5; 20 to 10.

Whole-class Activity

See Instructional Activity IA3.2: Numbers on the Line.
Smallest number is 3 and largest is 17.

- Individuals are invited to select a number card and peg it on the line in the correct position.
- After each card is pegged, ask the class if it is in the correct position.
- When all cards are pegged, say the forward and backward sequences together, pointing to each card.
- Have the children close their eyes while the teacher turns a card over. What number has been turned over? How did you know?
- Observe those children who look at the number before and those who count from the beginning of the sequence.
- Repeat this, turning two cards over, then several.
- Turn all the cards over except one (for example, 11). Point to other cards before and after the 11 and ask how they found the numbers.
- Leave the cards pegged to the line for later in the lesson.

Explain the pairs activity: see Instructional Activity IA3.9: Where Do I Go? Demonstrate this activity on the floor with the class in a circle.

Pairs – IA3.9: Where Do I Go?

The intention of this activity is to build facility with number word sequences and identifying numerals. Choose pairs with children of similar levels. Alter the packs of cards according to the level of the pair. Some pairs could have cards from 1 to 10 and others might have cards from 8 to 17 or 15 to 30.

Whole-class Discussion

Use the number line to review children's progress. Pose some number after and number before tasks.

Lesson 2

Comment

The activities used in this lesson (Memory Game, Make Ten Fish and Ten-frame Snap) might also appear to be quite routine. Nevertheless, it is how the teacher customizes the activity and when it is given that are critical to whether or not it is problematic for children. One child might require some strategic thinking to solve a task, whereas for a more advanced child the answer might be straight forward.

Whole-class Activity

See Instructional Activity IA5.1: Bunny Ears.
The intention of this activity is to develop finger patterns for six to ten.
The teacher asks the class to: *Make an eight! Make a six!*

Children are selected to show the pattern they made. Some might have a double pattern and others might have a five-plus pattern or some other arrangement of the fingers.
The teacher might also ask the class to try to make a double pattern or a five-plus pattern.

Small-group Activities

The class has been divided into three groups that will rotate through three activities – one per day for the next three days. The groups have been organized by the teacher according to the children's tens combination levels.

Activity A – Instructional Activity IA5.6: Memory Game.
Activity B – Instructional Activity IA5.10: Make Ten Fish.
Activity C – Ten-frame Snap, a variation of Instructional Activity IA5.9: Domino Snap.

Each activity uses ten-frame cards. Each group has a helper to explain the activity and guide the children. The teacher is one of the helpers and the others are paraprofessionals, parents or volunteers.

Whole-class Discussion

The class comes together and the teacher flashes some ten-frame combinations on an image projector, asking: *What did you see? How many dots?*

Lesson 3

Comment
This whole-class lesson is based on addition and **missing addend tasks**. After the introductory tasks, one missing addend task is given. Typically this task will elicit a range of solution strategies.

Whole-class Introduction
The class has been using the **empty number line** to record their solutions of addition tasks involving two 2-digit addends. The teacher tells a story like: *There are 37 girls in the group and 25 boys. How many children are there altogether?* She asks the class to think about how they would work this out and uses an empty number line to illustrate their thinking. Child A starts at 37 and makes two ten jumps (57) and then counts five ones to get to 62 (Figure 1.2).

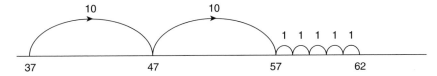

Figure 1.2 The empty number line: child A

Child B starts at 37 and also makes two ten jumps (57) and then uses three of the five to make 60 then adds the remaining two to make 62 (Figure 1.3).

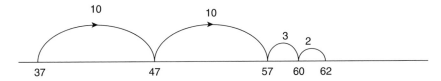

Figure 1.3 The empty number line: child B

Child C adds three to make 40, then two to make 42 and then makes two ten jumps: 52 then 62 (Figure 1.4).

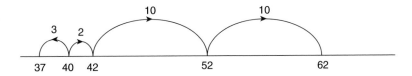

Figure 1.4 The empty number line: child C

Small Group/Individual Activities

The teacher gives the class this problem: there are 28 people on a bus. How many more people can fit on the bus if it can carry a total of 55 passengers? Children are given ten minutes to solve this task and then they will reassemble and discuss how they solved the problem. They are not directed into groups but are allowed to work in pairs or individually. The teacher walks around the room observing children's solutions and answering questions. After children complete this problem, they are asked to write a similar problem and solve it.

Whole-class Discussion

When the class comes together, the teacher asks several children to explain their strategies and asks the class to comment or question these children. Child D jumps 2 to 30, then 5 to 35 and then tens to 55 (Figure 1.5).

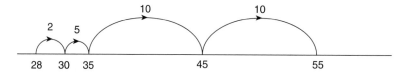

Figure 1.5   The empty number line: child D

Child E makes two ten jumps to 48, then 2 to 50 and 5 to 55 (Figure 1.6).

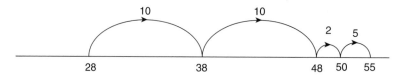

Figure 1.6   The empty number line: child E

Child F counts by ones from 28 to 55 and keeps track with fingers and also uses recording to keep track of the tens. The teacher asks several questions in order to check whether or not children have understood the various strategies. The teacher noticed several children who completed the task faster than most of the other children. The teacher directed them to invent a number problem of their own and to show how they solved it.

Discussion of Lessons 1, 2 and 3

To what extent do these lessons reflect the characteristics of problem-centered lessons as described in this section? Lesson 3 is the most problem-centered of the three lessons. However, in Lessons 1 and 2 the teacher aims to target the activities so that they require inquiry-based thinking rather than using routine procedures. The teacher does this first by gauging children's levels of knowledge in each of the areas being targeted and then by planning activities that will extend each child. Even in the case of an activity such as Ten-frame Snap (Lesson 2), which might not be regarded as a problem-centered activity, the teacher can select the cards to be used that will extend but not be too difficult for the participants. This can be done as follows:

For children that have not learned the combinations to ten, the teacher could use the cards shown in Figure 1.7.

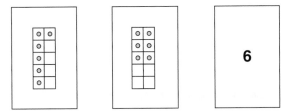

Figure 1.7   Five-wise and pair-wise settings for 6

For children who are learning the ten-plus and doubles combinations to 20, the cards shown Figure 1.8 in could be used.

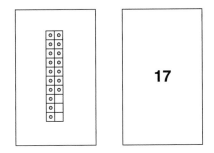

Figure 1.8   Ten-plus cards

For those children who are **facile** with the ten-plus combinations, the teacher might decide to use cards with other combinations (near ten combinations for example) as illustrated in Figure 1.9.

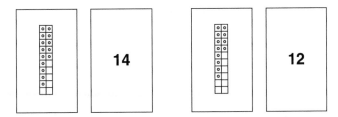

Figure 1.9   Near ten-plus cards

In the activities above, children can be engaged in problem-based learning, if their current levels of knowledge are determined, and activities are designed that will foster advancement of their knowledge.

The instructional activities are not intended to be prescriptive. Some can be used without modification. Other activities might need modification to be suitable for the children with whom you are working. Our intention is that these activities will serve as models to assist teachers in designing new activities for a range of situations.

Organizing Instruction

In our work with classroom teachers we have observed a range of successful approaches to classroom organization for instruction. We have also observed teachers who use several approaches to achieve a range of goals. In this section we describe three commonly used approaches that, we believe, provide models which can be informative for teachers.

1 Collaborative Learning Model

Ms Smith has a class of 25 children. In Ms Smith's class, mathematics is timetabled daily for 70 minutes during the morning session. Ms Smith particularly values whole-class teaching and collaborative learning in her mathematics lessons. Ms Smith uses a range of similar formats for her lessons. Below are two examples of these formats:

Format 1

10 minutes of warm-ups

30 minutes of whole-class teaching

20 minutes of seat work

10 minutes of teacher-led discussion.

The initial 10 minutes in Ms Smith's lesson is a fast-paced session focusing on activities to strengthen and consolidate children's knowledge of particular topics. One activity that Ms Smith has been using in the last couple of weeks involves flashing ten-frames. The children's task is to state quickly the number of dots on the upper row, the number of dots on the lower row, the number of dots altogether, and the number of dots needed to make 10. The second part of this lesson focuses on whole-class teaching. As an example, Ms Smith was working on the topics of strengthening children's facility with number word sequences in the range 1 to 100, and reading 2-digit numerals. Ms Smith worked with each of these interrelated topics in turn, posing tasks to her children and calling on children to respond and to comment on the responses of others. Ms Smith also led the class in whole-class activities such as counting-on from a given number, reading numerals and arranging a group of **numeral cards** in numerical order. The third part of this lesson involves children working at their desks on independent learning activities. Some children are working in pairs and others are working individually. This work relates closely to the topics that were taught in the second part of the lesson. In addition, Ms Smith has used independent learning activities at different levels in terms of children's knowledge of the topics of focus. In this way, she is able to differentiate her instruction according to her knowledge of children's current levels of knowledge and learning needs. In the final part of this lesson, Ms Smith leads a whole-class discussion of some of the tasks from the independent learning activities. Several children are called on to explain their solutions and Ms Smith takes every opportunity to explain key ideas and consolidate children's knowledge.

Format 2

10 minutes of warm-ups

5 minutes of whole-class explanation of activities

40 minutes of group activities involving rotation

15 minutes of teacher-led discussion and consolidation.

In this format, the initial part of Ms Smith's lesson is the same as it is in the first format. The main focus of this lesson is for children to work in groups of four to six children and to rotate through six different workstations. When available, helpers are used at some of the work stations. A helper might be a paraprofessional, a parent helper or a child helper from a higher grade. The activity at each workstation can be varied according to children's particular learning needs. Before the children move to their workstations, Ms Smith spends five minutes explaining any new activities and addressing difficulties with activities that arose in a previous session. In the last part of the lesson, Ms Smith poses questions to the whole class, focusing on the activities of each workstation in turn, and concludes this part with general questions on the topics currently being learned. Typically, Ms Smith uses this format on Thursdays or Fridays, when parent and child helpers are more readily available.

2 Learning Pairs and Discussion Model

In Mr Jorjez's classroom the following format is used:

10 minutes of whole-class teaching

5 minutes of introducing problems for the day

30 minutes of children working individually or in pairs on inquiry-based learning

25 minutes of whole-class, teacher-orchestrated discussion.

Mr Jorjez has a class of 20 children. He particularly values inquiry-based learning, that is, learning through problem-solving, and thinks it is important for children to be given opportunities to discuss with each other the tasks they are trying to solve. Such discussion he believes can enhance sense-making and the development of more sophisticated mathematical knowledge. The first part of Mr Jorjez's lesson involves teacher-led whole-class activities. These activities are very much like the warm-up activities used by Ms Smith (Collaborative Learning Model) and consolidate specific aspects of number knowledge or develop children's **automaticity** with number facts for example.

The main focus of Mr Jorjez's lesson is for the children to work on developing solutions to tasks which are intended to be genuine problems in the sense that the children do not have a ready-made response. For example, they do not have a procedural or algorithmic method to solve these problems. Before this part of the lesson begins, Mr Jorjez works with the whole class to read the tasks and to briefly discuss them. In this way children begin to think about the tasks and to formulate initial solution methods that might be attempted. During this part, Mr Jorjez gets an initial sense of the ways children might construe the tasks, and the kinds of solution methods they might attempt. In the third part of the lesson, children work to solve the tasks that have been discussed by the teacher and the whole class. Children can choose to work in pairs or individually, and there is opportunity to seek assistance from other children or from the teacher. The lesson involves children working on a relatively small number of tasks, typically no more than four.

The final part of the lesson involves a whole-class, teacher-led discussion of the tasks. This part begins with the teacher reading the first task, and calling on volunteers to go to the whiteboard and explain their solutions. Each child is obliged to listen and to attempt to understand the particular solution method being explained. In this way, the teacher carefully orchestrates discussion of each task in turn. A range of solution methods is developed, and Mr Jorjez takes every opportunity to highlight and emphasize methods that he regards as having potential to lead to more sophisticated number thinking. In this part of the lesson, methods of recording solutions are developed. These methods accord with children's strategies and have an important communicative function.

3 Rotational Groups Model

Ms Thompson has a class of 20 children. She particularly values whole-class teaching that is closely aligned to children's current levels of knowledge and that is complemented by seat work activities that are especially chosen to support her whole-class teaching. She also values independent and collaborative learning activities. The children are organized into four groups of approximately equal numbers of children. In Ms Thompson's class, mathematics is timetabled for one hour per day, in the morning. Children are organized in the groups according to their current progress in learning mathematics. She does not expect that children will remain in the group to which she originally allocated them. Ms Thompson is aware that children progress in mathematics at different rates. She has observed that sometimes children appear to plateau in their learning and at other times they make surprising progress in a relatively short period of time. For these reasons Ms Thompson is continually monitoring children's learning and progress, and reallocating children to their groups accordingly.

Ms Thompson uses a four-group rotation model to organize her mathematics lessons. The mathematics hour is partitioned into four periods of 15 minutes. Ms Thompson uses a display chart like the one shown in Table 1.2 to facilitate her classroom organization and management. A three-group rotation model could also be used (Table 1.3). At weekly intervals she will reallocate the groups to each line in the model. This ensures that, for each group, there is variety from week to week, in the order in which children rotate through the four kinds of activities. For example, in Table 1.2, for the red group the rotation is teacher, seat work, learning station, learning station. In the following week, the groups are rotated upwards in the left-hand column – blue to the first row, yellow to the second row, green to the third row and red to the fourth row. Over a period of four weeks, each group has experienced each of the four rotations in the table.

In the learning station activities, children can work individually or in small groups on independent instructional activities such as number games or computer-based activities. During the periods of learning station activities, children have opportunities to work with children from a different group and, over the course of four weeks, each group has opportunities to work with any other group.

Ms Thompson's main role is to have a highly interactive teaching session with each group in turn. This involves tailoring the content of each group-teaching session as closely as possible to

Table 1.2   Design of display chart for four-group rotation model

Period/ Group	1	2	3	4	Children
Red	Teacher	Seat work	Learning station	Learning station	Niara, Phyllis, Tynasia, Tre, Bill
Blue	Learning station	Teacher	Seat work	Learning station	Pam, Dominick, Harry, Addis, Heather
Yellow	Learning station	Learning station	Teacher	Seat work	Shanea, Devin, Ty-Keisha, Cole, Joline
Green	Seat work	Learning station	Learning station	Teacher	Jill, Jade, Marissa, Mark, Kim

Table 1.3   Design of display chart for three-group rotation model

Period/ Group	1	2	3	Children
Red	Teacher	Seat work	Learning station	Michael, Jalisa, Avery, Thomas, Summer, Bonnie, Amy
Blue	Learning station	Teacher	Seat work	Ansley, Tanner, Makayla, Horace, Leslie, Janette, Michael
Yellow	Seat work	Learning station	Teacher	Rick, Jedda, Kalindi, Aaliyah, Sharon, Matthew, Simone

the learning needs of that group. Also, the seat work involves independent learning activities focused on the work currently taught in the group-teaching session. In this way, the seat work period focuses on practice and consolidation that is specific to that group and closely tuned to the content currently being learned by that group. The learning station periods provide opportunities for instructional games and novel learning that differs from and complements the teaching and seat work sessions.

Block Scheduling

We have seen a diverse range of approaches for organizing mathematics instruction. As well as the approaches exemplified above, we have seen several approaches based on block scheduling and reorganization of classes. Green Hills School, for example, has one third grade, one fourth grade and one fifth grade, with about 30 children in each grade. There is a block schedule of 70 minutes for mathematics, across these grades during the middle session of each day. During this mathematics period, the children are allocated to one of five classes so that each class contains children who have been assessed as being close together in terms of their learning needs in mathematics. This involves scheduling two additional teachers (five teachers in all) during the mathematics period. Additionally, rather than allocate equal numbers of children to each of the five classes, the class of children with the most significant learning needs is allocated a smaller number of children, say 12 to 14; whereas the class of high-attaining children is allocated a larger number of children, say 24 children.

2
General Introduction to Part II

Summary

This chapter consists of three sections and provides a detailed overview of Part II of the book. The first section sets out the common structure that applies to Chapters 3 to 10. The second and third sections provide a broad overview of the approaches to teaching number to 4–8-year-olds that are the focus of Chapters 3 to 10. Section two focuses on aspects of the teaching of number typical of the earlier years in this range, say 4–6-year-olds, and section three focuses on aspects of the teaching of number typical of the later years in this range, say 6–8-year-olds.

In Part II (Chapters 3 to 10) we set out a coherent and detailed approach to the teaching of specific number topics to 4–8-year-olds. Chapter 3 focuses on children's initial learning about number words and numerals. Chapter 4 focuses on the development of counting and children's early notions of addition involving the use of counting strategies. Chapter 5 focuses on developing early number knowledge that de-emphasizes the use of counting-by-ones and instead emphasizes ways of **combining** and **partitioning** numbers without counting, in the range 1 to 10. Chapter 6 builds on Chapter 4, focusing on the advanced counting-by-ones strategies that children use for solving addition and subtraction problems. Chapter 7 builds on Chapter 5 and focuses on combining and partitioning numbers without counting in the range 1 to 20. Chapters 8 and 9 focus on children's beginning knowledge of place value and addition and subtraction involving two 2-digit numbers. Finally, Chapter 10 focuses on children's early multiplication and division learning.

Structure of Chapters in Part II

Each of the chapters in Part II (Chapters 3 to 10) has a common structure consisting of four sections: a topic overview, assessment task groups, instructional activities and one or two learning trajectories. In each chapter, the first section – topic overview – includes detailed descriptions of the chapter topic and, when relevant, describes its relation to the topics of earlier or later chapters. Table 2.1 provides an outline of the structure of each chapter and includes the numbers of assessment task groups, instructional activities and learning trajectories.

Table 2.1 Outline of the structure of Chapters 3 to 10

Chapter	Overview	# ATs	# IAs	# LTs
3 Number words and numerals	√	9	11	2
4 Early counting and addition	√	7	12	1
5 Structuring numbers 1 to 10	√	7	13	1
6 Advanced counting addition and subtraction	√	6	13	1
7 Structuring numbers 1 to 20	√	9	10	2
8 Jump strategies	√	9	11	1
9 Split strategies	√	5	10	1
10 Early multiplication and division	√	11	13	1
Totals		63	93	10

ATs = Assessment Task Groups IAs = Instructional Activities LTs = Learning Trajectories

Assessment Task Groups

In each chapter, the second section (assessment tasks) contains up to 11 assessment task groups. Across these eight chapters there is a total of 63 task groups. An assessment task group is a group of assessment tasks in which all of the tasks are very similar to each other. Thus each task group focuses on a particular aspect of early number knowledge related to the topic of the chapter. Collectively, the task groups in a given chapter constitute a comprehensive approach to assessing and documenting a child's knowledge related to the chapter topic. For example, the task groups in Chapter 3 provide a comprehensive set of assessment tasks related to the particular aspects of children's early number knowledge that relate to number words and numerals.

The Rationale for the Assessment Task Groups

One of the basic assumptions underlying this book is that, prior to commencing the teaching of any topic in the early number curriculum, it is critically important to have a very sound understanding of children's current knowledge of that topic. For this reason the assessment task groups appear before the instructional activities rather than after them. The task groups are not intended as prescriptive procedures to be strictly adhered to. Rather, they are intended as examples of assessment tasks that, we believe, can provide a detailed picture of the children's knowledge of the early number topic in question.

Format of the Assessment Tasks

Throughout the chapters in Part II, the assessment tasks have the following three-part format: materials, what to do and say, and notes. This format is ideally suited for use in a one-to-one interview with a child. Nevertheless, we find this format useful for providing a simple and straightforward explanation of each assessment task that can be easily adapted by teachers to a range of applications. The notes section at the end of each task might refer to any of the following: the purpose of the task; why the task is important; possible variations to the task and possible limits to the variations; descriptions of the responses typical of children; features of children's solutions which should be particularly noted; and possible links to other task groups.

Ways to Use the Assessment Tasks

There are five important ways that the reader might use or adapt the assessment tasks: (a) observational assessment; (b) large group or whole-class written assessments; (c) individualized assessment; (d) videotaped assessment interview; and (e) as a source of instructional activities. Each of these is described in more detail.

Observational Assessment
The tasks are intended to provide a context where teachers can advance their knowledge of children's thinking and learning in early number. This might involve using the tasks in informal, opportunistic ways that involve little or no change to the regular classroom routine. This approach constitutes what is often called observational assessment, that is, assessment that involves questioning and observing children at their desks, as opportunities might arise throughout the day. Finally, this approach might include the use of a class or group list to profile children's current levels of knowledge.

Written Assessment
Although the tasks are written in a ready form for individualized assessment, they can be adapted for administration to groups rather than individuals, for example, many of the tasks could be adapted to a written format for large-group (whole-class) administration.

Individualized Assessment
The tasks can, of course, be used in individualized assessments conducted by the class teacher or support personnel, with all children in the class or a particular subgroup, for example, those children who seem to have persistent difficulties with a particular topic.

Videotaped Assessment Interviews
This approach involves using a simple videotaping process (e.g. camera on tripod) to record an individualized assessment interview. Incorporating videotaping in this way has several advantages, one of which is that the videotaped assessment interview can be a very rich source of professional learning for teachers. Also, the process of videotaping for later analysis frees the interviewer from the need, during the interview, to describe or categorize the children's responses. This significantly increases the potential for productive observation, interaction and reflection, on the part of the teacher, during the course of the interview.

Assessment Tasks as a Source of Instructional Activities

Virtually all the assessment tasks are ideally suited for adaptation to instructional activities. Further, because the assessment tasks are organized into task groups, the tasks within a task group or across several groups typically constitute a form of learning trajectory. Again, although the tasks are presented in a format for one-to-one interaction, they are easily adapted to situations involving small- or large-group instruction. To emphasize this point, in each chapter, the assessment sections are intended to provide the reader with not only a significant source of instructional activities, but also one or more learning trajectories. In this way, the assessment tasks complement the set of instructional activities that appear in the third section of each chapter (see below).

Assessment Tasks as a Source of Teachers' Learning

A final point about the assessment tasks is that we believe the most effective use teachers can make of these, at least initially, is with the deliberate purpose of advancing their professional knowledge and learning. This might involve, for example, a school-based, team-based approach to professional learning. Ideally, this is undertaken with an instructional leader who is expert in the approach to early number learning that is presented in this book.

The Instructional Activities

In each of Chapters 3 to 10, the third section contains up to 13 instructional activities related to the early number topic addressed in that chapter. Across these eight chapters, there is a total of 93 instructional activities. Each instructional activity has the following five-part format: title, intended learning, description, notes and materials.

Learning Trajectories

In each of Chapters 3 to 10, the fourth and final section contains one or two learning trajectories. In each learning trajectory, the first column provides a progression of learning topics that constitute a trajectory or path of learning. The second column links sections of the topic overview (i.e. the first part of the chapter) to specific topics in the learning trajectory. The third and fourth columns list respectively, assessment task groups and instructional activities relevant to specific topics in the learning trajectory.

Teaching Number in The Early Years – Contrasting Traditional and Emerging Approaches

The traditional approaches to teaching number in the early years were typically organized as follows: (a) an initial focus on a range of topics which are typically referred to as 'pre-number'; (b) learning about numbers and operations (addition, subtraction, and so on) in the range 1 to 10; and (c) extending this learning to numbers and operations in the range 11 to 20. The topic of pre-number involves activities with everyday materials and simple learning materials (for example, small plastic objects). One such activity focuses on children sorting or classifying objects according to a common attribute, color, shape, and so on. Another example, matching, involves materials such as cups and saucers. Given, say, six cups and six saucers, the child's task is to match each cup to a saucer. This activity is often referred to as putting items into one-to-one correspondence. Learning about numbers and operations in the range 1 to 10 would typically involve a focus on each number in the range 1 to 10 in turn. So learning about

Table 2.2 Contrasting traditional and emerging approaches to number instruction in the first two years of school

Traditional approaches	Emerging approaches
Study of the 'pre-number' topics provides a basis for learning about numbers and should occur before learning about numbers.	Pre-number topics can enhance development of logical and number knowledge but are not necessarily an essential prerequisite for early number knowledge.
Children should study numbers in the range 1 to 10 for an extended period before focusing on numbers beyond 10. Similarly, then study numbers in the range 11 to 20.	Teachers should develop children's verbal (in the sense of spoken and heard rather than written) knowledge of number words and their knowledge of numerals, extending beyond 20 and beyond 100 as soon as possible.
Children should study each number in turn to learn about its cardinality, its numeral, and number combinations involving the number.	Teachers should take a flexible and open-ended approach to learning about number words and numerals.
It is important for children to work with spatial patterns and count the dots in spatial patterns to learn about cardinality in the range 1 to10.	Instructional activities involving flashing spatial patterns can help children learn to combine and partition numbers in the range 1 to 10 without counting by ones.
Teaching cardinality and ordinality of numbers in the range 1 to 10 is important.	Teachers should de-emphasize the teaching of cardinality and ordinality.
Children should be encouraged to use materials to solve early number problems for as long as they seem to need or rely on the materials.	Teachers should use instructional strategies as soon as possible that help to advance children to levels where they do not rely on seeing materials.
When children first learn about numbers in the range 11 to 20 it is important to teach the associated ideas of place value. Similarly for numbers in the range 20 to 100.	Children should learn about the number words and numerals beyond ten, long before they learn about place value involving 2-digit numbers.
Children should learn about place value before they learn about addition and subtraction involving numbers beyond 10.	Children can learn about addition and subtraction involving numbers beyond 10 before they learn about place value.
Place value should be formally taught using base-ten materials, before children learn addition and subtraction involving multi-digit numbers.	Place value knowledge should arise from children's developing strategies for addition and subtraction involving 2- and 3-digit numbers.

'six' would include learning to associate the numeral '6', the spoken and written word 'six' and a simple representation of the quantity of six, for example, a die pattern consisting of two rows of three dots. The study of six would also include learning about addition combinations involving six, and perhaps also subtraction and multiplication involving six. Similar approaches would be taken with numbers in the range 11 to 20.

The three topics just described are in large part the focus of children's number work in the first two years of school (4–6-year-olds). The origins of this approach are the reforms in curricula and teaching of mathematics in the early years of school, which occurred in several countries including the United Kingdom, the United States and Australia, in the late 1950s and early 1960s. Piaget's theory of young children's number development was one of the major influences on these earlier reforms.

The pre-number activities (sorting, matching, classifying, and so on) are still regarded as appropriate learning activities for young children because the activities are likely to contribute to the development of logical and numerical thinking. What is no longer accepted is the view that for every child in the first year of school, an extended period focusing on these activities is essential as a basis for the subsequent development of number knowledge.

In summary, traditional approaches to early number instruction:

- began with a topic called pre-number focusing on subjects such as sorting, matching, classifying, and putting objects into one-to-one correspondence
- then focused on the study of numbers in the range 1 to 10 in turn
- included addition, subtraction, and perhaps multiplication involving each number in turn
- then extended study of numbers to numbers in the range 11 to 20 in turn
- were introduced in several countries around 1960 and
- were strongly influenced by Piaget's theory of young children's number development.

Table 2.2 sets out some of the key features of traditional approaches to the teaching of number in the early years of school and contrasts these with emerging approaches. The emerging approaches summarized in Table 2.2 are described in detail in Part II (Chapters 3 to 10).

Teaching Place Value – A New Approach

To the extent that it is an important topic in early number learning, place value refers to understanding the tens and ones structure of 2-digit numbers and the hundreds, tens and ones structure of 3-digit numbers. In the middle and upper elementary years, place value knowledge involving 2- and 3-digit numbers is extended to numbers in the thousands, millions, and so on, and to decimals.

Difficulties with Place Value

As stated above, children's initial important ideas about place value relate to 2- and 3-digit numbers, and there are many indications that, in certain contexts in which they do simple arithmetic, older children either have very little knowledge of initial place value, or at least are unable to access their place value knowledge when performing operations (addition, subtraction, etc.) on 2- and 3-digit numbers.

Place Value: A Traditional View

In the last 40 or so years, the prevailing view about place value knowledge has been that it is a necessary foundation for addition and subtraction involving multi-digit numbers (the numbers from 10 onward). Thus children would be taught the place value of teen numbers prior to adding and subtracting in the range 11 to 20 and, similarly, children would be taught place value in the range 20 to 100 prior to addition and subtraction in this range. This view of the teaching of place value arose around the mid-1970s, as part of a broader development involving the use of base-ten materials for the teaching of place value and for the teaching of the standard column algorithms for addition, subtraction, and so on. This development in the mid-1970s was part of a broader back-to-basics movement in the teaching of number which, by and large, was a reaction to the overly formal 'new mathematics' of the 1960s and early 1970s. Thus this 'traditional view' of the central role of the teaching of place value, and the use of base-ten materials to teach place value, is a relatively recent phenomenon.

Conceptual Place Value: An Alternative Approach

In this book we present an alternative approach to the teaching of place value and when it should be taught. We refer to this approach as conceptual place value (see Wright et al., 2012). According to this approach, children can develop important initial place value knowledge through the operations of addition and subtraction with multi-digit numbers. Therefore, learning addition and subtraction in the range 1 to 20 can lead to a sound knowledge of what we call the 'ten and ones structure of teen numbers' (knowing 14 is 10 and 4. and so on) and similarly, learning addition and subtraction involving two 2-digit numbers can result in a sound knowledge of the tens and ones structure of numbers in the range 20 to 100 (knowing 36 is 30 and 6, and so on). We are not arguing here that base-ten materials have no useful role to play in number learning. Rather, we advocate the use of base-ten materials in ways that differ from the way these materials are used in the traditional approach. This alternative approach to using base-ten materials is the focus of Chapter 9.

Teaching Place Value through Addition and Subtraction

The Ten and Ones Structure of Teen Numbers

The notion of sound knowledge of the ten and ones structure of teen numbers is explained in Table 2.3. The table shows three kinds of tasks relating to this topic, and the contrasting responses of two children to these tasks. A child who has little or no knowledge of the ten and ones structure of teen numbers is likely to respond to the three tasks in ways the same as or

Table 2.3   Responses of a child with, and a child without, sound knowledge of the ten and ones structure of teen numbers

Tasks	With sound knowledge of ten and ones structure	Without sound knowledge of tens and ones structure
1. Here is a bundle of ten sticks. Here are six more sticks. How many sticks in all?	Spontaneously answers 'sixteen'.	Counts on from ten to sixteen while looking at each of the six sticks in turn or attempts to count all of the sticks from one.
2. Here are four sticks (cover with a screen), and here are 10 more sticks (place out a pile of 10 sticks), how many sticks in all?	Spontaneously answers 'fourteen'.	Counts on from four to fourteen while looking at each stick in the pile of 10 or counts from one to four, while looking at the screen, and then continues to count each of the ten sticks in the pile.
3. Place out a numeral card for '18'. Point to the numeral '1' in '18' and ask the child 'what does this stand for?'	Answers 'ten'.	Answers '1'.

similar to those described in the third column. The child who has sound knowledge of the ten and ones structure of teen numbers is likely to respond in ways like those shown in the second column. This assumes that the children have not been trained to give the correct response to these tasks. Children who respond in the mature way (as in the second column) on the first and second task only or the first task only, have partially developed knowledge of this topic.

An Additive Sense of Place Value

In the discussion above we explain what it means for a child to know the ten and ones structure of the teen numbers and the tens and ones structure of numbers in the range 20 to 100. Our view is that this knowledge constitutes the important initial learning about place value. We refer to this as an additive sense of place value. In the case of 3-digit numbers, for example, an elaborated understanding of place value would include knowing that, for 546: (a) 546 is equal to 500 plus 40 plus 6; (b) 500 is equal to 5 times 100, 40 is equal to 4 times 10, 6 is equal to 6 times one; (c) the place value in the hundreds is 10 times the place value in the tens, and the place value in the tens is 10 times the place value in the ones. The child who has an additive sense of place value knows (a) above, but might have little or no sense of (b) and (c).

Addition, Subtraction and Place Value in the Range 1 to 100

As a general rule, children's knowledge of place value within a range of numbers (for example, 11 to 20, 20 to 100), will develop in association with their development of mental strategies for adding and subtracting within that range of numbers. In particular, the development of knowledge of the ten and ones structure of teen numbers is likely to occur when children develop the strategies described in Chapter 7. In other words, the development of flexible strategies for addition and subtraction in the range 1 to 20 – including the use of adding through 5, adding through 10, using doubles and partitioning numbers – will incorporate development of the ten and ones structure of teen numbers. In similar vein, developing flexible strategies for addition and subtraction involving two 2-digit numbers will incorporate development of the tens and ones structure of 2-digit numbers. The development of these strategies is the focus of Chapter 8 and Chapter 9.

Learning to Add and Subtract with Two 2-digit Numbers

Formal Algorithms for Adding and Subtracting

Adding and subtracting multi-digit numbers has been and continues to be an important topic in primary mathematics. Approaches in the past emphasized teaching children the **formal algorithms** for addition and subtraction. The term 'formal algorithms' refers to the standard, written algorithms for addition and subtraction, that is, the procedures in which the numbers are written in columns and one works from right to left adding (or subtracting) in each column. In the approach to teaching number presented in this book, the formal algorithms are still regarded as important, but they are taught after children have developed facile, informal, mental strategies.

Informal Strategies versus Formal Algorithms

An important reason for delaying the teaching of the formal algorithms is that children's informal strategies typically are significantly different from formal algorithms. In the case of informal strategies children typically work from left to right, and often work with the whole number, rather than one column at a time. When children who have not developed facile informal strategies are taught the formal algorithms, they tend not to develop informal strategies because their learning of the formal algorithms tends to interfere with their development of informal strategies. Because of this, the approaches to this topic presented in this book focus on delaying the teaching of the formal algorithms until children learn facile informal strategies.

Children who can increment and decrement by tens on and off the **decuple**, and who have facile strategies for addition and subtraction in the range 1 to 20, are ready to extend their knowledge to the development of informal strategies for addition and subtraction involving two 2-digit numbers. Children who have not been taught the formal written algorithms will use a range of strategies to add and subtract with two 2-digit numbers. Many of these strategies fall into two classes of strategies: (a) jump strategies, and (b) split strategies. The strategies are demonstrated in Figures 2.1, 2.2, 2.3 and 2.4.

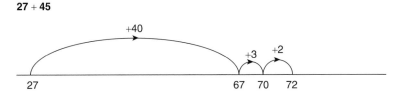

Figure 2.1 2-digit addition using a jump strategy

82 – 28

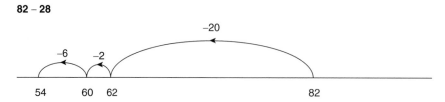

Figure 2.2 2-digit subtraction using a jump strategy

27 + 45: 20 + 40 ———→ 60

7 + 5 ———→ 12

60 + 12 ———→ 72

Figure 2.3 2-digit addition using a split strategy

82 – 28: 80 – 20 ———→ 60

12 – 8 ———→ 4

60 – 10 ———→ 50

50 + 4 ———→ 54

Figure 2.4 2-digit subtraction using a split strategy

In Chapter 8, the focus is on instructional approaches that are particularly suited to developing jump strategies and related kinds of strategies. In Chapter 9, the focus is on instructional approaches that are particularly suited to developing split strategies. We take the view that instruction can focus on one or both of these approaches, and that the focus on jump strategies can precede the focus on split strategies or vice versa.

PART II

3

Number Words and Numerals

Summary

This chapter focuses on children's early learning about number words and numerals. Developing facility with number word sequences and learning to name numerals constitute important aspects of early numeracy, and the view taken in this book is that these topics are deserving of a renewed emphasis. This chapter presents new information about how children learn these topics and approaches to instruction that take account of children's learning.

 Key topics: 5.1, 5.2, 6.1, 6.2, 7.1, 7.2, 8.2   Chapter: 3

Topic Overview

Learning about the names of numbers (number words) and the symbols for numbers (numerals) is a very important part of early number learning.

Numbers. Numbers are ideas or concepts. The number six for example, is the idea of 'six-ness'.

Number words. Number words are the names for numbers. We can distinguish between names that are spoken or heard and names that are written or read. In this chapter the term 'number words' will usually refer to spoken or heard number words.

Digits. The **digits** are the ten basic symbols in the numeration system (the system of **symbolizing** numbers). Thus the digits are the symbols 0, 1, 2, 3, 4, 5, 6, 7, 8, 9.

Numerals. Numerals are the written symbols for numbers, for example, 27, 346, 8. The ten digits from 0 to 9 can also be referred to as numerals.

Learning about Number Words

Young children encounter number words very frequently. For many infants, as soon as they start to make sense of spoken language, number words are commonly used. The infant or young child is likely to encounter number words in senses such as their age or that of a sibling or friend, and the house number on a street. Number words will also be encountered in conversations referring to simple quantities, such as *Bill has two sisters* or *There are three birds*.

Number Word Sequences

As well as encountering particular number words, children will also encounter number words in the context of a sequence of words, for example, *one, two, three, … ten*. This is referred to as a **forward number word sequence** (FNWS) or the FNWS from one to ten. Children might also encounter these words spoken in the reverse order, that is the **backward number word sequence** (BNWS) from ten to one.

Facility with FNWSs and BNWSs

The extent to which a child has knowledge of FNWSs is referred as the child's facility with FNWSs. In similar vein, one can refer to the child's facility with BNWSs. Some school entrants, for example, have good facility with the FNWS from one to thirty and beyond, while others may know only the first few words of the sequence (one, two, three). Typically, children will have less facility with BNWSs than with FNWSs, for example, a child might be able to say the FNWS from one to twenty-nine but not be able to say the BNWS from eight to one.

Number Word After and Number Word Before

Being able to say FNWSs and BNWSs is one important aspect of the young child's emerging facility with number words. A second important facility is being able to say one or two words after or before a given word. For example, when asked to 'say the number after eight', one child might answer immediately, 'nine'. Another child might say the words forward from one and then answer 'nine' – referred to as 'dropping back to one'. A third child might not be able to answer 'nine'.

Learning about number words and number word sequences is a very prominent aspect of early number knowledge, and one of the earliest aspects to emerge. Instruction to develop children's facility with number words is regarded as very important. This is because facility with number words provides an important basis for the development of what are called 'early arithmetical strategies' – the first strategies that children use in additive and subtractive situations.

Learning about Numerals

As well as learning about number words, another important aspect of early number involves learning about numerals. This includes learning to: (a) identify numerals; (b) write numerals; and (c) recognize numerals, and to learn about **numeral sequences**. Identifying numerals is also referred to as naming numerals or reading numerals, for example, where a teacher displays 10 and the child's task is to say 'ten'. An example of recognizing numerals is that a teacher puts a collection of numeral cards from 11 to 20 on a desk, not in numerical order, and asks the child, 'Which number is twelve?'. Numeral sequences refers to presenting the numerals in a sequence, for example, the numeral sequence from 11 to 20.

The Numerals from 1 to 10

Children will typically learn the names of the numerals from 1 to 10 through frequent association of the numeral and its name. This can occur through activities with the numerals individually or with the numeral sequence from 1 to 10. Thus children's early learning of numerals occurs in much the same way as children learn the names of letters. Indeed, in the early stages of learning about numerals, some children might not distinguish between numerals and letters.

The Numerals from 11 to 20

Children can and should learn the names of the numerals from 11 to 20 in much the same way as they learn the names of the numerals to 10, that is by frequent association of the numeral and its name, again through activities with the numerals individually, and with numeral sequences. For several reasons learning the numerals in the teens can be difficult for children. For one thing, their more established knowledge of the number words and numerals from 1 to 10 interacts with their emerging knowledge of teen number words and numerals. Also, the names of the teen numbers are such that they cause difficulties for children learning to associate these names with numerals. This is discussed in more detail below. A final point is that children can and should become skilful at associating number words with numerals in the teens, that is, naming numerals in the teens, long before they understand that the left hand digit (1) in each of the numerals from 11 to 19 indicates or stands for the number ten. In the same way that children develop a sight vocabulary of very common words – 'home, 'dog', and so on – they can develop a sight vocabulary of numerals. In this way children initially associate the name 'fifteen' with the numeral 15 without necessarily understanding why the digits 1 and 5 are used to write the numeral for fifteen.

The Numerals from 20 to 99

When children start to encounter the numerals from 20 onward, they begin to learn a naming system which is very close to a regular or transparent system. Children can come to know for example, that a 2-digit numeral of the form '6…', has the name 'sixty-', and that the second part of the name of '6…' is the name of the digit in the right-hand place. For most children, learning implicit rules or principles of this kind is not difficult. As in the case of numerals in the teens, children can and should learn the names of numerals from 20 to 99 long before they necessarily know that the left-hand digit in a numeral such as 46 indicates four 10s. Learning the place value features of the digits in multi-digit numerals is complex. This can and should be learned much later than when children first learn to name these numerals.

Three-digit Numerals

An important point about the naming system for 3-digit numerals is that there is a very regular system to the way one deals with the left-hand digit in a 3-digit numeral. In all cases, for example, 461, 207, 117, the numeral is read by simply first saying 'four hundred', 'two hundred', 'one hundred', and so on. Learning this implicit rule or principle is relatively easy for children. Thus, children who have a sound knowledge of numerals and number words in the range 1 to 100 can be taught the names of 3-digit numerals with relative ease, and, as in the case of 2-digit numerals, children can and should learn the names of 3-digit numerals long before they know in detail about the place value features of 3-digit numerals.

Difficulties with Names of 2-digit Numbers

Many researchers and writers on early number have highlighted difficulties associated with the particular number names. This problem arises in the English language, other European languages, and some other languages but does not arise in certain East Asian languages (for example, Chinese, Japanese, Korean). The problem mainly concerns the number names: 'eleven', 'twelve' … 'nineteen', but also names such as 'twenty', 'thirty' and 'fifty'. In the East Asian languages, the numeral 11, for example, is literally read as 'one ten one', that is, 'one ten one' is the spoken number word for 11. Similarly, the number word for 15 is 'one ten five', for 20 is 'two ten', and for 58 is 'five ten eight'. The system of number words in the East Asian languages is described as transparent. In virtually all languages and cultures, children typically learn the number word system before they learn the numeral system, that is, they learn the spoken sequence of number words before they learn the sequence of numerals.

The important point is that, in English and other languages with the difficulty just described, when children come to learn the numeral system, the non-transparent number naming system can result in significant and persistent difficulties for many children. This arises when children are learning to read numerals, that is, learning to make links from the numeral system to the number word system, which they already know to some extent at least. Consider the case of a child who has been learning the names of numerals in the teens. For example, this child has learned to read 18 by first saying 'eight'. Confronted with the task of reading 27, a typical response for this child is to look at the digit on the right-hand side and say 'seven …', and after a moment's reflection to say 'seventy-two'. In similar vein, children who are learning to read numerals in the range 20 to 100 will often have difficulty writing numbers in the teens. The child has the sound 'sixteen' in their mind, so they first write the digit 6, and after some reflection, they might correctly write 1 to the left of the 6. A final example is that some children seem to have extreme difficulty with associating the numeral 12 and the spoken number word 'twelve'. In this regard 12 typically is much more difficult than 11. In the case of 11, reversing the order of the digits is not an issue. Children will often read 12 as 'twenty' or 'twenty-one'. If a child is asked to select the larger of two numbers (presented on cards as the numerals 12 and 18), a child might select 12 because they read 12 as 'twenty-one'.

ASSESSMENT TASK GROUPS

List of Assessment Task Groups

A3.1: Forward Number Word Sequences
A3.2: Number Word After
A3.3: Backward Number Word Sequences
A3.4: Number Word Before
A3.5: Numeral Identification
A3.6: Numeral Recognition
A3.7: Sequencing Numerals
A3.8: Ordering Numerals
A3.9: Locating Numbers in the Range 1 to 100

TASK GROUP A3.1: Forward Number Word Sequences

Materials: None.

What to do and say: *Start counting from one. I will tell you when to stop.* Stop the child at 32. *Start counting from forty-seven.* Stop the child at 55. And so on.

Notes:

- Children might have particular difficulties progressing to the next decade, for example, after 29.
- Listen carefully for omissions. Children might omit decuples or double-digit numbers such as 66.
- Children who can say the sequence through 99, 100, 101, etc. might say 200 after 109.
- Listen carefully to pronunciation. Children might confuse the pronunciation of teens and decuples, for example *fifty* instead of *fifteen*.

TASK GROUP A3.2: Number Word After

Materials: None.

What to do and say: *I am going to say a number and I would like you to say the number that comes after the number I say. What comes after six? After eleven?* And so on.

Photo 3.1   Using the numeral roll for FNWS and NWA (1)

Photo 3.2   Using the numeral roll for FNWS and NWA (2)

Notes:

- Children who can say the sequence from one to beyond ten will not necessarily be successful on these tasks.
- Children might need to drop back, to solve these tasks, for example, for *after seven?* the child says *one, two, three, four, five, six, seven, … eight!*
- Children might confuse decuples and teens, for example, for *after sixteen?* they might say *seventy!*

TASK GROUP A3.3: Backward Number Word Sequences

Materials: None.

What to do and say: *Count back from ten. Count backwards from twenty-three. I will tell you when to stop.* Stop the child at 8. *Count back from forty-three.* Stop the child at 36. And so on.

Notes:

- Children are typically more facile with forward sequences than with backward sequences.
- Children who can say the forward sequence beyond 30 might have difficulty with backward sequences involving the teens.
- Children might have difficulties progressing to the next lowest decade, for example, *42, 41, …?*; or *42, 41, 40, …?*.
- Children might confuse teens and decuples, *23, 22, 21, 20, 90, 80,* and so on.
- Children might say the next lowest decuple, *52, 51, 40, 49, 48,* and so on, or omit a decuple, *52, 51, 49, 48,* and so on.
- Children might omit a word in the backward sequence which they do not omit in the forward sequence, for example, *sixteen, fifteen, fourteen, twelve, eleven,* and so on. This error can be persistent and can result in errors when using the backward sequence for subtraction, for example, 17 – 4 as *sixteen, fifteen, fourteen, twelve!*

TASK GROUP A3.4: Number Word Before

Materials: None.

What to do and say: *I am going to say a number and I would like you to say the number that comes before the one I say. What comes before three? Before eight?* And so on.

Notes:

- Children who can say the sequence from ten or more, back to one, will not necessarily be successful on these tasks.

- Children might use a dropping back strategy. This involves saying a forward number word sequence to figure out the number word before (for example, for *before six?* the child responds *one, two, three, four, five, six, … five!*).
- Children might confuse number word after with number word before.

TASK GROUP A3.5: Numeral Identification

Materials: Set of numeral cards from 1 to 10, not in numerical order. Similarly, a set of numeral cards from 11 to 20, and a set of cards for selected numerals in the range 21 to 100 (about 12 to 15 of these).

What to do and say: Display the cards in turn. *Tell me the number on the card.*

Notes:

- Children might say a forward number word sequence. For example, when identifying the numeral 5, the child says *one, two, three, four, five!*
- Depending on your sense of the children's level, you can start with the set of cards from 11 to 20.
- Children who can easily identify the numerals from 11 to 20 will very likely be able to identify the numerals from 1 to 10. A common error is to identify 12 as 20 or 21. Numerals from 13 to 19 might be read as decuples. For example, 13 is read as *thirty*.
- Children might identify 2-digit numerals incorrectly, for example, saying *seventy-two* for

Photo 3.3 Numeral identification

27. Most likely this arises from applying inappropriately a method of reading teen numerals (for example, 17 is read from right to left *seven* then *teen*) to 2-digit numerals.

TASK GROUP A3.6: Numeral Recognition

Materials: Set of five or more numeral cards, for example, the cards from 1 to 10 or 11 to 20.

What to do and say: Arrange the cards randomly on the desk. *Which number is six? Three?* And so on.

Note:

- Children might be able to recognize numerals that they cannot identify. For example, the child cannot identify the numeral 12 when an individual card with the numeral 12 is displayed, but can successfully respond to a task such as *Which number is the 12?* – for example, using a set of cards for the numbers from 11 to 20. These children seem to have difficulty in generating a sound image of the word 'twelve'.

TASK GROUP A3.7: Sequencing Numerals

Photo 3.4   Sequencing numerals

Materials: Sets of numeral cards as follows: 1 to 10; 10, 20, 30, … 100; 46, 47, … 55.

What to do and say: Arrange the ten cards from 46 to 55 randomly on the desk. *Put these numbers in order, starting from the smallest.* Similarly, use the set of cards from 1 to 5, 1 to 10 or the decuple cards.

Notes:

- We use the term **sequencing** when the numerals in question are a segment of a regular sequence such as the numerals from one onward, a sequence of decuples (60, 70, 80, 90 etc.) or a sequence of multiples of three (15, 18, 21 etc.). We use the term 'ordering' when this is not the case.
- If the child is not fluent at **numeral identification** (for example, for the numerals from 46 to 55) then they will probably have difficulty in sequencing the numerals.
- A common response is to take account of the 'ones' only: 50, 51, 52, 53, 54, 55, 46, 47, 48, 49.
- An alternative phrasing is to use the term 'least' rather than 'smallest'.

TASK GROUP A3.8: Ordering Numerals

Materials: Sets of four numeral cards such as the following: 8, 12, 18, 31.

What to do and say: Arrange the four cards randomly on the desk. *Put these numbers in order starting from the smallest.*

Notes:

- We use the term sequencing when the numerals in question are a segment of the numeral sequence from one onward. We use the term 'ordering' when this is not the case.
- Typically these tasks are much easier for children who are facile at identifying numerals.
- For some children the relative difficulty of these tasks depends on the number of numerals to be ordered, for example, ordering three numerals is much easier than ordering six numerals.
- Errors of **ordering numerals** can sometimes result from incorrectly reading (identifying) numerals, for example, the child reads 12 as 'twenty-one' and therefore orders the numerals as follows: 8, 18, 12, 31.

TASK GROUP A3.9: Locating Numbers in the Range 1 to 100

Materials: A strip of cardboard about 20 inches (50 cm) long with a number line showing the decuples, 0, 10, 20, 30 ... 100, evenly spaced. Numeral cards for numbers in the range 1 to 100 (for example, 6, 13, 22, 25, and so on).

What to do and say: Arrange the number line on the desk. *Read the numbers on the line*. Select one of the numeral cards (22). *Read this number. Show me where this number would be on the number line*. Similarly with the other numeral cards.

Notes:

- The number line can include evenly spaced marks for each number. Alternatively these can be omitted.
- Children who cannot identify numerals are likely to find this task quite difficult.

INSTRUCTIONAL ACTIVITIES

List of Instructional Activities

IA3.1: Count Around
IA3.2: Numbers on the Line
IA3.3: Counting Choir
IA3.4: What Comes Next?
IA3.5: Stand in Line
IA3.6: Secret Numbers
IA3.7: Can You See Me?
IA3.8: Take Your Place

IA3.9: Where Do I Go?
IA3.10: Teddy Bear Walk
IA3.11: The Numeral Roll

ACTIVITY IA3.1: Count Around

Intended learning: To extend knowledge of forward number word sequences.

Materials: None.

Description: Children stand in a circle and count around, each child saying the next number in the sequence. Start the count at one. The child who says the number 12 sits down. The next child begins the count again at one. The activity continues until only one child is left standing.

- Extend to crossing decuples.
- Use shorter or longer sequences.
- Vary the range of numbers (for example, start at 45 and sit down on 53).
- Extend to backward number word sequences.

Notes:

- Children might omit numbers, say them in the incorrect order or not be able to give the next number, particularly when crossing a decuple.
- Ask questions such as: *Who will sit down next? Who will say five? Who will be left standing?*
- Suitable for whole class or groups.

ACTIVITY IA3.2: Numbers on the Line

Intended learning: To sequence numerals.

Materials: A length of rope or string, pegs, numeral cards.

Description: Place a set of numeral cards from 16 to 25 face down on the floor, in a pile, in pseudorandom order. Ask a child to take a card and peg it on the line. Ask a second child to take the next card from the pile and place it appropriately on the line. Continue until all the numbers have been pegged on the line in the correct sequence. Ask children to read the numbers aloud to check. If any numbers are in the wrong place, discuss and ask a child to re-position.

- Use shorter or longer sequences.
- Vary the range of numbers, for example from 126 to 135.

- Read the sequences backwards as well as forwards.
- Extend to non-consecutive numbers, for example 46, 48, 51 54, 60.

Notes:

- When children are about to place their card, ask questions such as: *Is it more or less than …? Will you place it to the left or right of …? Which two numbers should it go between?*
- Vocabulary includes: more, less, higher, lower, before, after.
- Suitable for whole class or groups.

ACTIVITY IA3.3: Counting Choir

Intended learning: To count in ones, tens and hundreds.

Materials: Baton, a set of cards (labeled *ONES*, *TENS*, *HUNDREDS*).

Description: Divide the class into three groups. The teacher takes the role of conductor holding a baton (pointer). The teacher begins the count, for example 21, 22, 23, 24, and then points the baton at one of the groups who continue the count in unison, for example 25, 26, 27 … until the teacher points the baton at another group. This group, in turn, continues the count. The teacher moves the baton from group to group pseudorandomly bringing in sections of the choir. Similarly with other starting numbers. Give one group a card labeled *ONES*, the second group a card labeled *TENS*, and the third a card labeled *HUNDREDS*. The teacher begins the count again, for example 7, 8, 9 and then points to the *ONES* group. The *ONES* group continues the count in ones, for example 10, 11, 12, 13. The teacher moves the baton to the *TENS* group. The *TENS* group continues the count in tens, for example 23, 33, 43, 53. The teacher then moves the baton to the *HUNDREDS* group. The *HUNDREDS* group continues the count in hundreds, for example 153, 253, 353, 453. Similarly with other start numbers. Vary the activity by counting in ones only, in ones and tens, extending to counting in thousands, or counting backwards by ones, tens or hundreds.

Notes:

- Suitable for whole class or large group.
- Children can be grouped according to their facility in counting by ones, tens and hundreds.
- Children might experience difficulties when crossing decuples or going beyond 999.

ACTIVITY IA3.4: What Comes Next?

Intended learning: To be able to say the number after any given number.

Materials: Numeral track.

Description: Tell the children that you are going to count and that when you stop counting, you want them to say the next number. Say: *One, two, three, four, five*. Children shout, whisper or sing: *Six!*

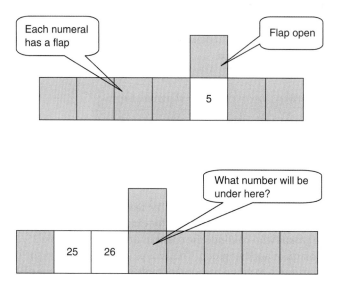

Figure 3.1   Numeral track

Photo 3.5   Numeral track activities

Continue with other number word sequences, for example *seventeen, eighteen, nineteen, twenty*.... Use shorter sequences for example *twenty-five, twenty-six* .... Display the numeral track from 25 to 34. Lift the flaps to show 25 and 26. Say the numbers with the children and ask: *What number will be under here (27)? What comes next?* Take several responses and then choose a child to lift the flap and reveal the number. Continue, starting with other sequences. Progress to lifting one flap only (29) and challenging the children to give the next number (30).

- Vary the activity by using longer sequences on the numeral track for example 1 to 30 or 26 to 55.
- Change the activity to saying the number before a given number.
- This activity can also be used to develop backward number word sequences.

Notes:

- Children might need to count from one, to give the next number.
- Some children might have difficulty when shorter sequences are used, for example, two numbers only.
- Suitable for whole class or groups. Vocabulary includes: next number, number after, number before.

Photo 3.6 Numeral track: crossing a decuple

ACTIVITY IA3.5: Stand in Line

Intended learning: To extend knowledge of backward number word sequences and numerals.

Materials: Set of numeral cards from 1 to 30.

Description: Assuming there are 18 children, use the sequence of numerals from 1 to 18. Give each child one numeral card. Ask a child to come to the front and hold up their card, for example 16. Children must look at their own card and decide who has the number before 16 (15). The child holding number 15 stands to the left of the first child (holding number 16). Continue the line until it has six children in it and shows the sequence from 16 to 11. The teacher can decide to continue the numbers until they reach one or some other number. Each child in turn displays and says their number. All of the children read the number sequence backwards in unison and then repeat with their eyes closed.

- Use a range of starting numbers.
- Vary the range of numbers, for example from 74 to 57.
- Build sequences forward as well as backward.
- Focus on crossing decuples forwards and backwards.
- When the children are standing in line choose several to turn their cards over. Can the children still say the BNWS correctly?

Notes:

- Children might omit numbers, say them in the incorrect order or not be able to give the next number, particularly when crossing a decuple.
- Suitable for whole class or groups.
- Vocabulary includes: more, less, higher, lower, before, after, larger, smaller, in between.

ACTIVITY IA3.6: Secret Numbers

Intended learning: To order non-sequential numerals.

Materials: Large numeral cards, sets of smaller cards (for working in pairs).

Description: Provide six non-sequential numerals on cards, for example 17, 23, 28, 31, 36, 42. Select two children. Give the largest number (42) to one child and the smallest (17) to another. Place the two children with their cards about three metres apart. Select a third child to choose one of the remaining numbers. They must keep their number secret and decide where to stand in between 17 and 42. Ask: *What could the number be?*

Establish that it must be more than 17 and less than 42. Ask the child to reveal their secret number. Continue with a second secret number, then a third and fourth until all the cards are in the correct order.

- Vary by using other sets of cards.
- Vary the range of numbers used.

Notes:

- Suitable for whole class or small groups.
- Adapt for pairs by providing sets of cards for children to order and record.

ACTIVITY IA3.7: Can You See Me?

Intended learning: To identify and recognize digits from 1 to 9.

Materials: Large numeral cards (1 to 5 or 1 to 10), screen, small numeral cards

Description: The teacher:

- displays a collection of large numeral cards – each card has one of the numerals from 1 to 5, this can be extended to 10 as needed
- after the children have had a chance to look at the cards, places them face down in a pile
- selects one of the cards and screens the numeral (in Figure 3.2 the numeral 3 has been selected and screened)
- gradually reveals part of the numeral asking: *What number could this be?*
- after several responses, displays a little more of the numeral until eventually the entire numeral is revealed
- this procedure is followed with other numerals.

Notes:

- As an additional activity, ask the children to draw the numeral in the air, trace it on their partner's hand or back, or write it on a whiteboard.
- Have the children find the numeral from a larger collection of numeral cards. Each child or pair could be provided with a set of small numeral cards.
- The technique of gradually moving the screen to reveal the numeral can involve moving the screen in one of several ways, for example, moving the screen down or moving the screen to the left.

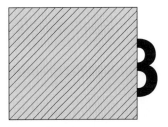

Figure 3.2   What number could this be?

ACTIVITY IA3.8: Take Your Place

Intended learning: To sequence and order numerals.

Materials: Two dice (or spinners) numbered 1 to 6, or 1 to 9, sets of digit cards 1 to 9.

Description: Ask a child to roll two dice to generate a 2-digit number. The child holds up the **digit cards** to represent that number, for example 26. A second child rolls the dice, takes the digit cards and makes a second 2-digit number, for example 34. Ask: *Which is more, 26 or 34? Where should 34 go?* A third child rolls the dice, selects the cards and makes a third 2-digit number, for example 21. Ask: *Is it higher or lower than 26? Where should it go?* Roll again to generate a fourth number and ask similar questions. Check that the numbers are in the correct order. Ask the child with number 26: *Why are you standing in between 21 and 34?* (Encourage explanations such as *I am more than 21 and less than 34*.) Repeat the activity several times.

- Vary the activity by using one die or spinner numbered 1–9 and order 1-digit numbers.
- Extend by using two 1–9 dice or spinners.
- Use a 0–9 spinner to generate the ones digit thus allowing for decuples.
- Extend by using three dice to generate 3-digit numbers.

Notes:

- Suitable for whole class, groups or pairs.
- Children might read 2-digit numerals incorrectly from right to left, for example, 72 is read as 'twenty-seven'.
- When doing this activity in pairs, children could be asked to record their numbers.
- It is important to ask appropriate questions and encourage explanations from children.
- Extend children's vocabulary to include: higher, lower, more, less, larger, smaller.

ACTIVITY IA3.9: Where Do I Go?

Photo 3.7 Where Do I Go?

Intended learning: To identify numerals 1 to 10 and to order numerals correctly.

Materials: 40 cards (numbers 1 to 10 in four different colors), four colored circle cards.

Description: The teacher decides which numbers to use for the activity. This will depend on the children's ability to identify numerals and also their forward number word sequence range. For example, a child might be able to say the FNWS to 20 but be unable to identify some of the numerals from 1 to 20 and to count collections of up to 20 items. The teacher can decide to work in a range such as: 1 to 5, 1 to 10, 1 to 15 or 1 to 20. If working in the 1 to 10 range, the numerals 1 to 10 are written four times on cards, each time in a different color (e.g. red, yellow, green and blue). Four other cards displaying a circle of each of the four colors are also needed. The teacher places the four colored circles in a column, shuffles all the other cards (40 if working in the 1 to 10 range), and then places ten cards face down at the side of each circle. The teacher asks a child to turn over any card. If, as above, the child was to turn a red 8 (see Figure 3.3), the teacher then explains that this card is presently in the yellow row and must be placed in the red row in the eighth position. The child might need to start at one and count each card to determine the eighth position. The child then picks up the card in the eighth position in the red row and replaces it with the red 8. This new card must then be placed in its correct position. The game ends when each card is in its correct position as shown in Figure 3.3.

Notes:

- This activity is appropriate for children having difficulty coordinating number words and items or having difficulty with numeral identification.
- Children might observe that the numbers in a given column are the same.
- If they make a mistake in their counting the numbers in a given column are not the same and the error is apparent.
- This activity is useful for children who have difficulty with the identification and ordering of teen numbers.
- If the child turns over a card that is already in its correct position, any other card is turned over.
- Initially, two rows (two colors) rather than four could be used in order to reduce the complexity of the activity.

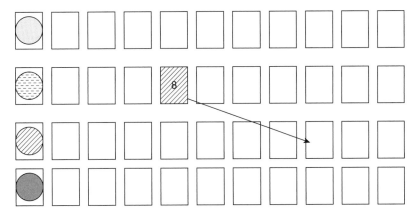

Figure 3.3   Where Do I Go?

- Children who count from one, often find more efficient ways to determine a card's placement. This is especially the case if cards in the range 1 to 20 are used. For example, it's more efficient to realize that 19 is one less than 20 rather than to count up to 19 from 1.
- This activity is suitable for individuals, pairs or small groups where children take turns in placing cards.

ACTIVITY IA3.10: Teddy Bear Walk

Intended learning: To use counting-on and counting-back or more advanced strategies in addition and subtraction.

Materials: Teddy Bear Walk board, a teddy bear or counter for each player.

Description: Players take turns to: (a) roll a die; (b) predict which square their teddy bear will walk to by taking the number of steps indicated on the die; (c) move their teddy bear the number of steps and check whether or not their calculation was correct. The game ends when one teddy bear reaches the end of the walk.

Notes:

- Typically the die (or spinner) has the numerals 1, 2 and 3. When appropriate, a die with 1 and 2 only could be used.
- To include subtraction activities, when a teddy bear lands on a shaded square the next roll will be a subtraction task and the teddy bear will need to retrace steps.
- Observe the strategies used to solve the addition and subtraction tasks.
- The board can be altered according to children's levels of knowledge.
- This activity will support students' learning of the numeral sequence.

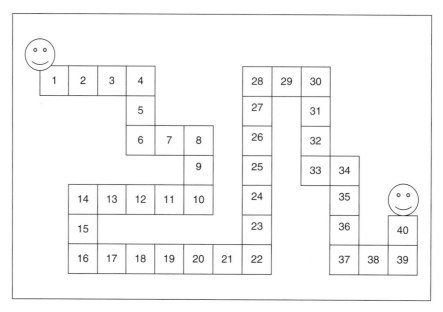

Figure 3.4   Teddy Bear Walk

ACTIVITY IA3.11: The Numeral Roll

Photo 3.8   Numeral roll activities

Intended learning: To extend knowledge of numerals to 100, forward number word sequences and backward number word sequences to 100, and facility in counting-on or counting-back from given numbers in that range.

Materials: Numeral roll.

Description: The **numeral roll** has a long sequence of numerals (e.g. 1 to 120) and is used in conjunction with a ten-lid screen so that one or more numerals can be displayed in turn going forwards or backwards. Activities using the numeral roll should be given before activities with a hundred chart. This is because the numeral roll consists of a single line of numerals whereas on the hundred chart the numerals are arranged in ten rows (1 to 10, 11 to 20, 21 to 30, etc.).

Activities include:

- Displaying the roll and having children say each number in a sequence as the teacher points to it, either forwards or backwards.
- **Screening** the sequence of numerals and displaying them one at a time.
- Displaying a numeral in a window and asking questions like – *What number is next? What is this number (two or three more)? What number comes before this number (two or three back)?* Then unscreening the numeral so that the child can check.
- Proceeding along the sequence forwards or backwards, unscreening one numeral at a time: (a) first seeing then saying (*See then say*), and (b) first saying then seeing (*Say then see*).

Notes:

- The decades (1 to 10, 11 to 20, etc.) can appear in alternating colors (e.g. 1 to 10 on white card, 11 to 20 on pink card, 21 to 30 on white card, etc.), highlighted to provide convenient reference points.
- The teacher can cut up a hundred chart into rows of ten and place them in order to constitute a numeral roll.
- A large numeral roll for the group can be used but small rolls should be available for individual children.
- An interactive white board can be used.
- The numeral roll can be extended or shortened according to children's levels of knowledge.

Learning Trajectories

Note:

- The two learning trajectories – number words and numerals – should be followed in parallel rather than in sequence.

Table 3.1 Learning Trajectory: Number Words

Topics	Page Ref.	Assessment Task Groups	Instructional Activities
FNWSs to 10 Forward number word sequences and number word after in the range 1 to 10	33–34	A3.1 A3.2	IA3.1 IA3.4 IA3.6 IA3.11
BNWSs to 10 Backward number word sequences and number word before in the range 1 to 10	33–34	A3.3 A3.4	IA3.1 IA3.4 IA3.6 IA3.11

(Continued)

Table 3.1   (Continued)

Topics	Page Ref.	Assessment Task Groups	Instructional Activities
FNWSs and BNWSs to 20 Forward number word sequences and number word after in the range 1 to 20 Backward number word sequences and number word before in the range 1 to 20	33–34	A3.1 A3.2 A3.3 A3.4	IA3.3 IA3.4 IA3.6 IA3.11
FNWSs and BNWSs to 100 Forward number word sequences and number word after in the range 1 to 100 Backward number word sequences and number word before in the range 1 to 100	33–34	A3.1 A3.2 A3.3 A3.4	IA3.3 IA3.4 IA3.6 IA3.11

Table 3.2   Learning Trajectory: Numerals

Topics	Page Ref.	Assessment Task Groups	Instructional Activities
Numeral identification and recognition Range 1 to 10 Range 1 to 20 Range 1 to 100	34–36	A3.5 A3.6	IA3.2 IA3.5 IA3.6 IA3.7 IA3.8
Sequencing numerals Range 1 to 10 Range 1 to 20 Range 1 to 100	34–36	A3.7	IA3.2 IA3.5 IA3.9 IA3.10 IA3.11
Ordering numerals Range 1 to 10 Range 1 to 20 Range 1 to 100	34–36	A3.8	IA3.2 IA3.6 IA3.8

4

Early Counting and Addition

Summary

This chapter focuses on the early development of counting, where counting is regarded as an activity oriented to solving an arithmetical task such as figuring out how many items in a collection or how many items in all when two small collections are put together. The chapter provides a detailed description of a progression of counting types of increasing sophistication – emergent, perceptual and figurative counting – and how these types of counting provide the basis for children's early addition strategies.

 Key topics: 5.3, 5.6, 6.3

Topic Overview

The Importance of Counting

Counting is regarded as an extremely important aspect of early number instruction. Counting is very prominent in young children's early mathematical activity and seems to be virtually a natural and spontaneous activity for children in the first two or three years of school, and also for many preschoolers. Further, it is well known by teachers and others that many children in the middle and upper primary years make extensive use of counting when solving arithmetical problems, that is, problems that involve any of the four operations – addition, subtraction, multiplication and division. To make this point another way, counting is a prominent aspect of much of the so-called 'mental arithmetic' or mental computation done by children in the primary years and beyond.

Levels of Sophistication in Counting

There are various levels of mathematical sophistication in the ways children use counting and it is important for teachers to have some understanding of these. Teachers who have a good knowledge of these are better able to develop instructional approaches focused on developing more sophisticated arithmetical strategies in their children. The levels of sophistication in counting will be described in detail in this chapter.

Counting versus Saying a Number Word Sequence

Chapter 3 focused on children learning about number words including learning to say forward number word sequences and backward number word sequences. In that section we did not use the term 'counting' as a label for a child's activity of saying a FNWS. This is because we find it useful to distinguish between, on the one hand, the activity of merely reciting the sequence of number words and, on the other hand, the activity of saying the words in a context where the child is purposefully keeping track of items. The latter activity is referred to as counting, and the distinction just described has been highlighted by several researchers and writers (for example, Steffe and Cobb, 1988). This distinction relates to a qualitative difference between the mental activity associated with merely saying a FNWS, and the mental activity associated with counting, where each number word is associated with an item.

Perceptual Counting

Perceptual counting refers to situations in which the items to be counted are available for the child to see. Counting that is not perceptual counting refers to situations in which the child knows how many counters are in a small collection (for example, four) but those counters are screened and not available for the child to see.

Using Perceptual Counting to Establish the Numerosity of a Collection
Collections have the property of **numerosity**. The numerosity of a collection is its how-manyness. An example of perceptual counting is when a teacher puts a collection of 15 counters on the desk (the child does not know how many counters there are) and asks the child how many counters there are. Typically, the child would move the counters in turn, or at least point at them one by one, and coordinate each movement or point with a number word. Thus one would say the child uses counting to establish the numerosity of a collection of counters.

Using Perceptual Counting to Establish a Collection of Specified Numerosity
Another example is when a teacher puts a large pile of counters (say 50) on the desk, and asks the child to get eight counters. Again, the child typically would move the counters one by one in coordination with saying the number words from one to eight. In this case one would say the child uses counting to establish a collection of specified numerosity.

Using Perceptual Counting to Establish the Numerosity of Two Collections
Another example of perceptual counting is when a teacher places out seven red counters and five blue counters and asks the child how many counters in all. Typically, the child would begin by counting the counters in one of the collections and continue to count the items in the second collection. For some children, tasks involving counting the items in two visible collections (for example, seven red and five blue) seem to be more difficult than tasks involving counting the items in one collection (for example, twelve red counters).

Beginning Addition through Counting

The activity of perceptual counting is described above. In the case of perceptual counting, the items to be counted are available for the child to see. More advanced levels of counting occur when children count to solve problems involving items which are not available to be seen. Consider a task involving eight counters under one screen and five under a second screen. The two collections are briefly displayed for the child and the child is told how many in each. Also, for ease of demarcation, the first collection comprises red counters and the second comprises blue counters. The child's task is to figure out how many counters in all. From an adult perspective this is a trivial arithmetic problem involving addition of two numbers in the range 1 to 10. But from the perspective of the child for whom the task is problematic, this is a task about counters and numbers. The arithmetical idea of addition is currently somewhat remote for the child. The task just described is referred to as an **additive task** involving two screened collections of counters. The counters used in this way constitute a setting in which the child can begin to develop notions of adding numbers.

Counting-from-one versus Counting-on

Consider a child who is known in advance to be capable of perceptual counting (see above). The child is presented with the additive task involving two screened collections (8 + 5). Typically, young children will respond to this kind of task in one of four ways: the perceptual counter, the figurative counter, the counting-on child and the **non-count-by-ones** child. Each of these four types of responses is now explained.

The Perceptual Counter
The perceptual counter is unable to use counting to solve the task and is the least advanced in terms of arithmetic sophistication. Currently, perceptual counting is this child's most advanced kind of counting.

The Figurative Counter
The figurative counter looks at the first screen while counting from one to eight, and then looks at the second screen while counting from nine to thirteen. This is referred to as figurative counting and we describe this strategy as counting-from-one. Thus the child counts from one to solve an additive task where the counters are not available to be seen. This strategy is sometimes referred to as 'count-all'. For two reasons we choose not to use this term. First, 'count-all' conflates perceptual and figurative counting. Whether the two collections of counters are screened or unscreened this is referred to as a count-all strategy. The difference is that the perceptual counter can use count-from-one to figure out how many counters in all, only when the two collections are visible. By way of contrast, the figurative counter can use counting-from-one to figure out how many counters in all, when the two collections are screened (not available to be seen). Second, the child who uses a counting-on strategy (see below) might still be said to have

counted all of the counters. From our perspective the significant aspect of the figurative counter is that they count from one to count the first collection, which from an adult perspective is redundant.

The Counting-on Child

The counting-on child looks at the first screen and says 'eight', and then looks at the second screen, and says 'nine, ten, eleven, twelve, thirteen'. This is referred to as counting-on to solve an additive task and is regarded as more advanced than figurative counting. Both counting-on and figurative counting are regarded as more advanced than perceptual counting. For the counting-on child, eight stands for a count – the act of counting the eight counters. The figurative counter needs to count from one to eight, in order for eight to stand for the act of counting the eight counters.

The Non-count-by-ones Child

This child uses a strategy that does not involve counting-by-ones. For example, the child first works out (without counting) the number to be added to eight to make ten (2), then partitions five into two and three, then adds three to ten (without counting) to make thirteen. This strategy is referred to as 'adding to ten', 'adding through ten', and 'bridging to ten'. This child is said to use a non-count-by-ones strategy, and this is regarded as a more sophisticated strategy than counting-on. This is one example of the range of non-count-by-ones strategies that children use in the range 1 to 20 (see Chapter 7).

Counting as Coordinating Words and Items

As indicated earlier, we make a distinction between counting and merely saying number words because in the case of counting the child coordinates each number word with an item. Like the perceptual counter, the figurative counter and the counting-on child (see above) are coordinating number words with items. The difference is that the perceptual counter is directly perceiving (seeing) the items (counters), whereas the figurative counter and the counting-on child imagine or visualize the items to be counted. For this reason figurative counting and counting-on as just described are regarded as cognitively and arithmetically more advanced than perceptual counting.

Emergent, Perceptual and Figurative Counting

This chapter focuses on the first three levels of counting, that is, emergent, perceptual and figurative counting. Perceptual and figurative counting have already been described (see above).

Emergent Counting

The term 'emergent' is used in cases where the child is not able to count perceptually. Thus the child is unable to count a collection of say, 12 or 15 counters. The child might not know the number word sequence or might not correctly coordinate each number word with an item to be counted. For example, the child might say 'four, five' while pointing at one counter only, or say 'se-ven' and coordinate one counter with 'se' and another with 'ven'.

Determining the Most Sophisticated Level

It is not uncommon for children to use a level of counting that is less advanced than they are capable of. As teachers, our task is to elicit the most advanced kind of counting that the child can use spontaneously and with certitude. Thus a child is classified as a perceptual counter only when we are convinced that the child is not able to use figurative counting or counting-on to solve a task such as 8 + 5 involving two screened collections. Typically, it is necessary to present the child with several tasks rather than just one, in order to elicit the most advanced kind of counting.

ASSESSMENT TASK GROUPS

List of Assessment Task Groups

A4.1: Comparing Small Collections
A4.2: Increase and Decrease in the Range 1 to 6
A4.3: Establishing the Numerosity of a Collection
A4.4: Establishing a Collection of Specified Numerosity
A4.5: Establishing the Numerosity of Two Collections
A4.6: Additive Tasks Involving Two Screened Collections
A4.7: Counting and Copying Temporal Sequences and Temporal Patterns

TASK GROUP A4.1: Comparing Small Collections

Materials: Cards with one, two … six dots (see Figure 4.1). Dots are randomly arranged (not in **regular spatial configurations**). About 10 cards for each number of dots (60 cards in all).

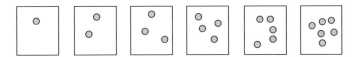

Figure 4.1 Comparing small collections cards

What to do and say: Place out two cards, for example, two dots and four dots. *Pick up the card which has more dots.* Repeat with other pairs of cards showing different numbers of dots.

Notes:

- This task is relatively easy for 5-year-olds and above. Accordingly, the task might reveal a lack of very beginning number knowledge.
- Children might spontaneously say a number to indicate how many dots on a card.
- Children who are not able to ascribe numerosity to a collection (Task A4.3) might nevertheless be successful on these tasks.
- An alternative phrasing is to use the term 'spot' rather than 'dot'.

TASK GROUP A4.2: Increase and Decrease in the Range 1 to 6

Materials: About 20 counters all of one color. A container (cup) used to conceal a small collection of counters.

What to do and say: Place out two counters. *How many counters?* Place the two counters in the cup and cover the cup. Place two more counters in the cup (four in all). *How many counters are there in the cup now?* Place one more counter in the cup (5). *How many now?* Remove two counters (3). *How many now?* Continue as follows: add two (5); remove one (4); add two (6); and so on.

Notes:

- These tasks assess the child's ability to determine the resultant number in a collection in the range 1 to 6, when one or two items are added or removed.
- In similar vein to Task Group A4.1, this task is relatively easy for 5-year-olds and above, and might also reveal a lack of very beginning number knowledge.

TASK GROUP A4.3: Establishing the Numerosity of a Collection

Materials: About 30 counters all of one color.

What to do and say: Place out a collection of 12 counters. *How many counters are there?* Similarly 15, 18 or 8 counters.

Notes:

- To succeed at these tasks children need to know the forward number word sequence up to the number of counters in the collection to be counted.
- Take note of whether the child spontaneously uses an organized approach to counting. For example, the child might have a 'pull-out' strategy, moving each counter in turn, away from the collection.
- Common errors are omitting a number word or incorrectly coordinating number words and items.

Photo 4.1   How many counters are there?

- Coordination errors include saying one word for more than one item, or saying more than one word for one item.
- Take note of whether the child is aware that the last number word is the answer to 'How many?'

TASK GROUP A4.4: Establishing a Collection of Specified Numerosity

Materials: About 50 counters all of one color.

What to do and say: Place out all of the counters in a pile. *Get me eight counters from this pile.* Similarly 13, 16 counters, and so on.

Notes:

- Refer to the notes for Task Group A4.3. Children's success on this Task Group corresponds closely with their success on Task Group A4.3.

Photo 4.2   Get me eight counters

TASK GROUP A4.5: Establishing the Numerosity of Two Collections

Materials: A collection of counters of one color (red) and a collection of another color (blue).

What to do and say: Place out seven red counters. *Here are seven counters.* Place out five blue counters. *Here are five blue counters. How many counters altogether?* Similarly with 8 and 3, 10 and 9, 5 and 3, and so on.

Photo 4.3 Establishing the numerosity of two collections

Notes:

- Some children have difficulty in conceiving of two collections alternatively as one collection whose items can be counted.
- Children who are successful on Task Groups A4.1 to A4.4, but have difficulty with these tasks might count each of the two collections separately from one but not count all of the items in the two collections together.

TASK GROUP A4.6: Additive Tasks Involving Two Screened Collections

Materials: A collection of counters of one color (red) and a collection of another color (blue); two screens of cardboard or cloth.

What to do and say: Briefly display and then screen six red counters. *Here are six red counters.* Briefly display and then screen three blue counters. *Here are three blue counters. How many counters altogether?* Similarly with collections such as 8 red and 2 blue, 11 red and 4 blue, 5 red and 2 blue, and so on.

Notes:

- The purpose of these tasks is to see if the child uses counting-on.
- Some children might solve these tasks by counting from one. They are apparently unable to use counting-on to solve these kinds of tasks.
- In the case of children who are not able to solve these tasks, the second collection (blue counters) can be unscreened.
- The general approach with these tasks is to have the number of counters in the second collection (blue counters) typically in the range 2 to 5, and the number in the first collection (red counters) larger than the number in the second collection (blue counters). The number in the first collection can be in the range 4 to 20 or beyond 20 as appropriate.

TASK GROUP A4.7: Counting and Copying Temporal Sequences and Temporal Patterns

Materials: None.

What to do and say: *I am going to make some claps and I want you to tell me how many times I clap.* Clap three times. *How many times did I clap?* Similarly with six claps, two claps, and so on.

This time I am going to make a pattern of claps and I want you to copy my pattern. Clap four times in a 2-2 pattern. *Can you copy my pattern? How many claps was that altogether?* Similarly with patterns such as: 3-3, 3-2, 2-2-2, and so on.

Notes:

- Ask the child to look away so that they do not observe you making the claps.
- Typically, children are less facile at counting **temporal sequences** than at counting collections, for example, counting a sequence of ten claps versus a collection of ten counters.
- Children might be able to copy a temporal pattern but not be able to work out how many items (claps) in the pattern.

 # INSTRUCTIONAL ACTIVITIES

List of Instructional Activities

IA4.1: Diffy Game
IA4.2: Number Row Count
IA4.3: Domino Addition
IA4.4: Addition Spinners
IA4.5: Counters in a Row
IA4.6: On the Mat
IA4.7: Toy Box
IA4.8: Chains
IA4.9: Give Me Five
IA4.10: Pass It On
IA4.11: Hide and Add
IA4.12: Rhythmic Patterns

ACTIVITY IA4.1: Diffy Game

Intended learning: To use counting to compare two quantities and find which is more.

Materials: Interlocking cubes, dice or spinner and counters.

Description: In pairs, the first child throws a 1 to 6 die and counts out that number of interlocking cubes and makes a tower. The second child rolls the die and counts and makes another tower of cubes. They compare the towers and decide which tower has more cubes. The child with the higher tower takes a counter to keep a score. If there is no difference in the towers no one takes a counter. The activity continues until one child has collected five/ten counters.

Photo 4.4   Which tower has more blocks?

Notes:

- Discuss the difference. Whose tower is higher? How much higher?
- Change the setting of cubes to counters and arrange the counters in a line, horizontally or vertically.

ACTIVITY IA4.2: Number Row Count

Intended learning: To count visible items forwards and backwards and say one more or one less, two more or two less and three more or three less.

Materials: Counters.

Description: Pairs or small group. By each putting out one counter in turn, the children build a row of counters (all of one color), counting as they go. Stop and ask: *How many counters will there be if I add one more?* Add one and check. Continue to add counters one by one within an appropriate range (e.g. 1 to 5, 1 to 12, 1 to 25). Similarly add or remove two counters each, then three. Begin with the row of counters already built and take turns to remove one counter each, counting as they go. Stop and ask: *How many will be left if I take away one more counter?* Take one away and check. Continue until all of the counters are removed. Similarly, remove two counters each, then three.

Note:

- Some children might need to count up from one to figure out the next number counting forwards or counting backwards.

ACTIVITY IA4.3: Domino Addition

Intended learning: To add with two collections where the first collection is screened and the number in the second collection is in the range 2 to 5.

Materials: Large blank domino with flaps that screen each side. A card can be used to screen one side of the domino.

Description: The teacher has a large blank domino. Four dots are placed in the left square of the domino (see Figure 4.2). The children are asked how many dots they can see. The teacher then uses the flap or card to screen the dots. The children are asked how many dots are under the flap.

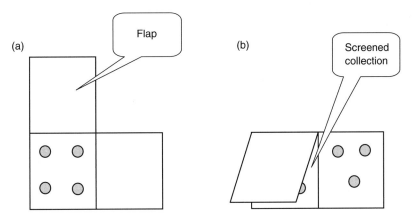

Figure 4.2 Domino Addition

If the children are unsure, the teacher can unscreen the dots to establish how many, and then screen them. The teacher then places three dots on the right-hand side of the domino and poses the task: *There are four dots under here and we have three more. How many dots do we have altogether?* The teacher allows some thinking time and re-poses the question if necessary. The activity can be continued using other numbers for example, 7 and 5, 8 and 3.

Notes:

- The numbers chosen for this activity should take account of children's facility with the FNWS.
- The range of numbers used can be varied. The number used on the left-hand side of the domino can vary in accordance with children's facility with the FNWS. The number on the right-hand side should be in the range 2 to 5, for example 17 + 5, 28 + 2, 46 + 3.
- When the first addend is beyond 10, a numeral card can be used instead of a collection of dots.
- When the first addend is large, it is not necessary to put out a corresponding number of dots. Ask children to pretend that there are a given number of dots under the flap.
- This activity is suitable for whole class (using an image projector) or small groups.
- Vary the activity by using other contexts which are familiar to the children, for example, a house and ants, nest and eggs, garages and cars.

ACTIVITY IA4.4: Addition Spinners

Intended learning: Addition involving screened collections of items where the second addend is in the range 2 to 5.

Materials:

- Spinner 1 – numerals 3, 4, 5, 6, 7, 8 (or other numerals chosen by the teacher).
- Spinner 2 – numerals 2, 2, 3, 3, 4, 5.
- Dice may be substituted for spinners.

Description: The teacher:

- spins the first spinner and counts out this number of counters (e.g. six) then screens them under a card (a regular or modified die could be used in place of the spinner)
- spins the second spinner with numerals 2, 2, 3, 3, 4, 5 (or other suitable numerals) and places this number of counters (e.g. three) next to the screen
- says: *There are six counters under here and three counters here. How many counters are there altogether?*
- allows time for the children to solve the task and might re-pose it, or briefly display the counters under the card
- continues the activity using different numbers generated by the spinners.

Notes:

- As children become familiar with the activity, counting out the counters from the first spinner is not needed and the range of numbers on the first spinner can be extended.
- The activity described above is intended for a whole class.
- Once children are familiar with the activity, it can be done individually or in pairs.
- The teacher may require children to record the numbers and their answers. A simple record sheet could be drawn up with columns headed First Spin, Second Spin and Total.
- Dice with dots or numerals can be used in place of the spinners.
- The numbers chosen for this activity should take account of children's facility with the FNWS.

ACTIVITY IA4.5: Counters in a Row

Intended learning: To count-on from a given number with visible items in a row.

Materials: Image projector, counters, strip of card (card stock), individual whiteboards and marker pens.

Description: An image projector and counters are used. The teacher counts out the counters laying them in a row. Children are asked to check the number of counters in the row (counting with the teacher if necessary). The teacher uses a strip of card (card stock) to screen the row of counters, then counts out three more counters continuing the row. The teacher poses the question: *There are eight counters under the card and we have three more counters. How many counters are there altogether?* The children write their answers on their whiteboards (or on scrap paper).

The teacher asks the children to come to the front and explain their answers. The teacher then uses the collections of counters on the screen to talk the children through the calculation, demonstrating counting-on from the number of screened counters.

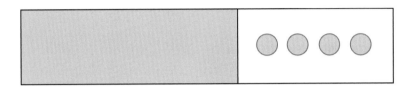

Figure 4.3   Counters in a row

Notes:

- The numbers chosen should take account of children's facility with the FNWS.
- The range of numbers used can be varied.
- The activity is suitable for whole class, small group or individuals.
- This activity can support children learning to count-on.

ACTIVITY IA4.6: On the Mat

Intended learning: Counting the number of children in a group.

Materials: Large mats.

Description: Children walk, run, skip or dance indoors or outdoors. Large mats (or circles) are placed (or drawn) in the area. On the signal, the children move to the nearest mat (or circle) and stand still. They count how many children are in the group. When they agree about the number of children they sit down holding up the correct number of fingers. The teacher asks a volunteer to check each group by pointing at each child in turn as the class counts together. Repeat.

Variations include:

- Fewer mats (or rings) will give larger collections of children to count.
- Children could stop when the music stops.
- The rule might be: no more than six on a mat.
- The teacher could state the number of children to be on each mat or each mat could display a different number saying how many children should sit there.
- One child from each group could be asked to collect a number card to indicate the number of children on the mat.

Notes:

- Children might not know the number word sequence.
- Children might not coordinate the number words with the children on the mat.
- Children might forget to include themselves in the count.
- Suitable for whole class or large groups.

ACTIVITY IA4.7: Toy Box

Intended learning: To establish the numerosity of a collection.

Materials: Collections of objects (toys), large die marked 0 and 1.

Description: Place a collection of small objects in the center of the table. One child rolls a large die labeled 0 and 1. If the die displays 1, the child takes one object. If the die displays 0, the child does not take anything. Take turns with each child building individual collections. When one child has a few objects in their collection ask: *How many do you have?* Encourage the child to touch and count each object, saying each number in turn. Ask: *How many altogether?* Emphasize that the last number in the count corresponds to the number of objects in the collection. Continue to play until one child has five objects.

- Vary the size of the objects counted (larger objects, smaller objects).
- Vary the objects in the collections, sometimes all the same, sometimes different.
- Vary the way the children collect the objects, for example arranging in a row, a ring or a container.
- Increase the number counted to a number in the range 6 to 10.
- Use a die numbered with 0, 1 and 2.

Notes:

- Children might have difficulty keeping track of the number words as they are counting.
- Children might not know the number word sequence very well.
- Children might have difficulty coordinating a number word with each item.
- Suitable for small groups.

ACTIVITY IA4.8: Chains

Intended learning: To establish the numerosity of a collection.

Materials: Colored bands or braids.

Description: Work in a large indoor or outdoor space. Provide five or six children with a colored band or braid. Children move as instructed by the teacher, for example: *Slither like a snake! Jump like a kangaroo! Hop like a rabbit!* At the teacher's signal everyone must freeze (stand still). Children wearing bands touch as many children as they can without moving their feet! The children who have been touched form a human chain. Each chain must count how many and shout out their number. The activity continues with each chain holding hands and moving together. When they freeze, each member of the chain can reach out to touch and collect new members. Continue until everyone (or almost everyone) joins a chain, and continue to count how many.

Notes:

- Chains should not be too long. Teachers need to be aware of the movement required by the chain.
- Define the area in which the children may move.
- Check the count! Fewer children with bands will give longer chains to count.
- Ask two chains to join together. *How many now?*
- Ask children to estimate before counting.
- Ask: *Who has more than 3? Who has fewer than 4? Which chain is longest? Which is the shortest?*
- Join chains together and ask a child to count how many children.
- The class can join in the count. Suitable for class or large group.

ACTIVITY IA4.9: Give Me Five

Intended learning: To establish the numerosity of a collection.

Materials: Ping-pong balls (or cubes) numbered 1 to 10, bag or box, objects to collect, hoops or containers.

Description: Group ten children into pairs. Place ping-pong balls numbered 1 to 10 in a bag or box. One pair of children pick out a ping-pong ball and say the number (with assistance if required). Each pair then goes to collect that number of named objects, for example, pencils, books, bean bags. They bring the items back and place them in a hoop or container. Each pair checks the other children's collections to see if they have the correct number of objects. The group then counts each collection in turn with one child pointing to each item in turn. Continue the activity with other numbers.

- Vary the activity by giving each pair a different number.
- Collect mixed items, for example, one pencil, one book, one bean bag.
- Place out containers with a differently numbered ping-pong ball in each.
- Children match the collections to the numbers.
- Extend the range of numbers.

- Use bundles of straws or towers of cubes to extend to 2-digit numbers, for example, ask children for 26 straws or cubes.
- Use a bead-string, numeral track or number line to show how many are collected.

Notes:

- Children might have difficulty keeping track of the number words as they are counting.
- Children might not know the number word sequence very well.
- Children might have difficulty coordinating a number word with each item.
- Suitable for whole class, small groups or pairs.

ACTIVITY IA4.10: Pass It On

Intended learning: To establish the numerosity of a collection.

Materials: Collections of objects, large die or spinner marked with 0, 1 and 2.

Description: Children sit in a circle. Each child has a collection of small objects (for example, five objects). One child rolls a large die labeled 0, 1, 2. If the die lands on 0, they do not pass anything on. The next child rolls the die. If it lands on 1 or 2 they pass on that number of objects to the child sitting on their left. The activity continues with each child taking a turn. When one child has a few in their collection, ask: *How many do you have?* Encourage children to touch and count each object, saying each number in turn. Ask: *How many altogether?* Emphasize that the last number in the count corresponds to the number of objects in the collection. The activity continues until one child has run out of objects or one child reaches a specified number of items (for example, ten).

- Vary the objects in the collections – sometimes all the same, sometimes different.
- Vary the way the children collect the objects, for example, placing in a row, in a ring, in a container.
- Increase the number counted to a number in the range 11 to 15.
- Use a die or spinner numbered with 0, 1, 2 and 3.

Notes:

- Children might have difficulty keeping track of the number words as they are counting.
- Children might not know the number word sequence very well.
- Children might have difficulty coordinating a number word with each item.
- Suitable for large or small groups.

ACTIVITY IA4.11: Hide and Add

Intended learning: To use counting-on in a partially screened addition task.

Materials: Two dot dice and a plastic cup, paper for recording.

Description: In pairs the children take turns to roll two dot dice and quickly cover one with a plastic cup. The challenge for the second child is to give the total. They can remove the cup to check and can record.

Notes:

- The regular configuration on the dice supports visualization.
- This activity can also be done with one numeral and one dot dice.
- This activity can be done with the whole class using giant dice.

ACTIVITY IA4.12: Rhythmic Patterns

Intended learning: To develop conceptually based temporal patterns which can be useful in keeping track when solving additive and **subtractive tasks**.

Materials: Maracas or similar percussion instrument.

Description: The teacher uses a percussion instrument (maracas or similar), for a rhythmic pattern for children to copy by clapping.
Examples:

A VIDEO DEMONSTRATING THIS ACTIVITY CAN BE ACCESSED ONLINE AT WWW. SAGEPUB.CO.UK/ WRIGHTTNC

- Clap to the right, clap to the left.
- Clap clap up high, clap clap down low.
- Clap to the right, clap clap clap to the left.

Ask children to join in when they are ready and repeat each pattern until everyone is joining in confidently, then switch to a different pattern.

- Keep the number of claps in each pattern within five initially.
- Children can tap knees, desk or head instead of clapping.
- Clap slowly, clap quickly.

Notes:

- Discuss the patterns. One clap then three claps, how many claps altogether?
- Make the pattern on a five-frame using two colors.

- Make the pattern on an arithmetic rack.
- Make more complex rhythmic patterns such as: clap to the right, clap to the left, five quick claps to the right.

Learning Trajectory

Table 4.1 Learning Trajectory: Early Counting and Addition

Topics	Page Ref.	Assessment Task Groups	Instructional Activities
Comparing small collections	54	A4.1	IA4.1
Increase and decrease in the range 1 to 6	55–57	A4.2	IA4.2 IA4.4 IA4.7
Establishing the numerosity of a collection	55–57	A4.3	IA4.2 IA4.5 IA4.6 IA4.8 IA4.9
Establishing a collection of specified numerosity	55–57	A4.4	IA4.9 IA4.10
Establishing the numerosity of two collections	55–57	A4.2 A4.5	IA4.3 IA4.5
Additive tasks involving two screened collections	55–57	A4.6	IA4.11
Temporal sequences and patterns	55–57	A4.7	IA4.12

5
Structuring Numbers 1 to 10

Summary

This chapter focuses on a new and important topic in early numeracy, that is, structuring numbers in the range 1 to 10. This topic relates to children's facility to combine and partition numbers without using counting-by-ones. Instead the child uses an emerging knowledge of doubles, and the five and ten structure of numbers, that is, using five and ten as reference points. Learning this topic provides a basis for a critically important objective – moving beyond a reliance on counting-by-ones.

 Key topics: 5.4, 5.5, 6.4, 6.5, 7.4, 7.5   Chapter: 4

Topic Overview

Combining and Partitioning Small Numbers

In Chapters 3 and 4, we explained several significant aspects of the developing number knowledge of children typical of 4–6-year-olds. These include numerosity, knowledge of number words and numerals (Chapter 3), and the development of early counting strategies (Chapter 4). Around the time that children have developed early counting strategies they also should learn to combine and partition small numbers without counting. This involves working first in the range 1 to 10, and then in the range 1 to 20. Instructional activities for combining and partitioning involve initially using settings consisting of regular spatial configurations, that is, spatial patterns of various kinds or finger patterns (see below), rather than using **formal arithmetic**, that is, bare numbers. For this reason we refer to these activities as combining and partitioning rather than, say, adding and subtracting.

> *Doubles to 10.* Typically the first combinations that children learn are the doubles of numbers in the range 1 to 5, that is, 1 and 1, 2 and 2, … 5 and 5.

> *Partitioning numbers 2 to 5.* Children can then learn the partitions of numbers in the range 2 to 5, that is, partitioning 2 into 1 + 1, 3 into 1 + 2, 2 + 1 and similarly for 4 and 5.

> *Five-pluses.* That is, additions of the form five-plus a number in the range 1 to 5.

Partitioning numbers 6 to 10. Children can then learn the partitions of numbers in the range 6 to 10. Six can be partitioned into 5 + 1, 4 + 2, 3 + 3, and so on, and similarly for 7 onward.

Doubles to 20. Although instruction at this stage is mainly limited to the range 1 to 10, children can also begin to learn the ten-pluses, that is, additions of the form 10 plus a number in the range 1 to 10, and the doubles of the numbers from 6 to 10.

Approaches to Teaching Combining and Partitioning

Instructional strategies for combining and partitioning numbers in the range 1 to 10 typically involve using spatial patterns and finger patterns. Spatial patterns can be flashed – displayed momentarily – using an image projector, and children can be asked about combining and partitioning the quantities shown in the spatial patterns. In the case of finger patterns, children can be asked to make finger patterns by placing their hands on top of their heads. In this way children are unable to observe their own patterns. Hands can be brought to the front for checking or correcting patterns. Spatial patterns and finger patterns are discussed in more detail below.

Spatial Patterns

Subitizing

Subitizing involves: (a) ascribing numerosity to a collection of items, typically a spatial configuration of dots, but not necessarily so; (b) doing so immediately; and (c) doing so without counting the items. Writers and researchers in psychology and education have discussed and examined the phenomenon of subitizing since the 1940s. In psychological experiments, examining subitizing typically involves using a projection device to flash spatial configurations of dots onto a screen, for a fraction of a second. When subitizing is examined in this way, adults typically can subitize collections of up to about five or six. Techniques involving flashing various collections of dots have been used extensively in research into infants' awareness of quantity.

For our purposes, activities with spatial configurations, particularly regular configurations, can be important in young children's number learning. For many years, activities involving dot patterns have had an important place in early number instruction. Activities that are considered useful range from activities involving the use of materials such as dice, dominoes and cards, to instructional procedures where patterns are flashed (momentarily displayed).

As discussed above, an important instructional goal for early number instruction is for children to be able to combine and partition small numbers without counting. Activities with spatial patterns can be one important avenue for developing children's knowledge with combining and partitioning. Teaching activities where the teacher briefly displays a spatial pattern, using an image projector, have been found to be beneficial for developing this knowledge. Initially, these activities can focus on developing children's familiarity with the standard dice patterns, for the numbers from one to six. Patterns where the dots appear in two horizontal rows can also be used. In similar vein, instruction can involve flashing patterns on a five-frame or a ten-frame and encouraging children to reason numerically about what they have seen.

Combining and Partitioning Using Spatial Patterns

Combining and partitioning can be introduced when children have developed familiarity with the patterns to six. Combining activities can involve using dots in two colors, for example, a five-pattern consisting of two red dots forming a two-pattern, and three blue dots forming a three-pattern. Children are asked to describe what they saw when the pattern was flashed. Similarly, partitioning can involve the teacher flashing a four-pattern, and asking the children to describe two numbers that make up the four-pattern. Partitioning activities of this kind can be extended to numbers in the range 6 to 10.

Finger Patterns

The use of finger patterns in association with activities such as counting, adding, subtracting, and so on, is very widespread, being used in many cultures and by adults as well as children. For a long time, use of finger patterns typically was ignored or actively discouraged in classrooms, and for many children, using fingers was quite a prominent activity but it was carried out surreptitiously with fingers moving rapidly but hidden under the desk.

Finger Patterns: Why and When?

The current view taken is that, in the early years, use of finger patterns should be encouraged because this can support the development of more sophisticated arithmetical strategies. In the middle and upper primary years, and beyond to adulthood, there are some instances where it makes sense to use finger patterns to support or augment arithmetical thinking. On the other hand, there are some ways that older children use fingers to support their mental arithmetic that are not regarded as being useful or productive. These typically involve children using long sequences based on counting-by-ones to work out additions and subtractions involving 2-digit numbers, or perhaps children counting-by-ones to solve multiplication or division problems. In cases such as these, children use a double count or a triple count that involves using their fingers to keep track. An example of a double count is to solve 17 − 15 by counting back from 17 by ones, while using fingers to keep track of 15 counts. An example of a triple count is to solve 19 + 34 by counting on by ones from 19 to 53, using fingers to keep track of the counts (34) while mentally keeping track of the number of tens (3) and ones (4). Another example of a triple count is to solve 4 × 8 by using: (a) the fingers on one hand to keep track of the ones in each four; (b) the fingers on the other hand to keep track of the number of fours (8); and (c) counting aloud to keep track of the total. Clearly, instructional goals should focus on progressing children from using these rather debilitating kinds of strategies to using strategies that do not involve counting-by-ones.

Numbers in the Range 1 to 5

Before doing combining and partitioning activities involving finger patterns, children need to be familiar with the basic patterns for numbers in the range 1 to 5 on each hand. Initially, some children will need to raise their fingers sequentially while looking at their fingers and counting to the required number. With practice most children can learn to raise fingers simultaneously and without looking at their hand, to make finger patterns on either hand, for numbers in the range 1 to 5.

Numbers in the Range 6 to 10 using 5 as a Reference

Children's knowledge of finger patterns for numbers in the range 1 to 5 can be extended to numbers in the range 6 to 10. The patterns for these numbers should be made with five fingers on one hand. Thus seven is made as five on one hand and two on the other, and so on, and these patterns can be learned as combinations involving 5 and a number in the range 1 to 5, that is the five-pluses. This supports the learning of five as a reference point (see below).

Adding Two Numbers in the Range 1 to 5

Finger patterns involving one number on each hand can also be learned for the doubles (1 + 1, 2 + 2, ... 5 + 5). This can be extended to all of the 25 combinations involving two numbers in the range 1 to 5, where one number is shown on each hand. Children should be encouraged to use finger patterns to work out the answers to these combinations, that is, without counting-from-one and without counting-by-ones. For example, in solving 4 + 3, raise the fifth finger on the 'four-hand' and lower one finger on the 'three-hand'. This results in the familiar pattern of 5 + 2 making 7.

Five and Ten as Reference Points in the Range 1 to 10

As indicated in the earlier sections, children's beginning knowledge about adding and subtracting numbers develops in two main strands. One of these concerns the development of counting strategies which culminate in the advanced counting-by-one strategies, that is, counting-on-from, counting-on-to, counting-back-from and counting-back-to (Chapter 6). The second strand concerns children's developing abilities to combine and partition numbers without counting. An important part of the second strand is to use five and ten as reference points.

Why Use Five and Ten as Reference Points?

Most adults and older children understand the tens and ones structure of numbers between 10 and 100. The natural thing is to think of a number such as 54 as comprising five tens and four ones. This structure is inherent in the numeration system because the system is a base-ten system. To use five as well as ten as a reference point is to think of numbers in terms of their tens and five structure. Thus 54 is five tens and one five less one; 17 is one ten, one five and two more; and 28 is three tens less two. In this way any number is no more than two from a reference point number (5, 10, 15, 20, and so on). Because of this, children who are fluent with five and ten as reference points are unlikely to rely on long sequences of counting-by-ones when adding or subtracting (so, too, with multiplication and division). This is the strong argument for teaching children from an early age to use five and ten as reference points. We can suppose that in countries and cultures where use of the abacus is prominent or use of the abacus has a strong historical tradition, using five and ten as reference points is virtually a natural occurrence.

Five as a Reference Point

The notion of five as a reference point takes two main forms. First, for the numbers less than five, children know these numbers in terms of their five-complement, that is, the number that goes with them to make five. Alternatively, we could say that the partitions of five are strongly emphasized in instruction, notwithstanding that children also need to know the partitions of all of the other numbers in the range 1 to 10. Second, for the numbers greater than five, children need to know these numbers in terms of their five-plus structure (five-plus-two for seven, five-plus-three for eight, and so on).

Adding through Five

Adding through five can be used to work out the **sum** of two numbers with the answer in the range 6 to 10. As an example, a child might work out 4 and 3, by saying 4 and 1 make 5, and 2 more is 7. Three and six is calculated by saying 3 and 2 more is 5, and 5 and 4 is 9, or by changing 3 and 6 into 4 and 5. A key point about these calculations is that they do not involve counting-by-ones.

Three steps   Typically, these calculations involve three kinds of steps. First, the child partitions five, using the first addend: 5 is 4 + □. Thus in working out 4 and 3, the first step is to partition five, knowing that 4 is the first number in the partition. Thus 5 is partitioned into 4 and 1. The second step is to partition the second addend three, using the second number in the partition of five (1). Thus three is partitioned into 1 and 2. The final step is to add the second number in the partition of three, that is 2, to 5. Thus 2 is added to 5 to make 7. Similarly, 3 and 6 could involve: (a) partitioning 5 into 2 and 3; (b) partitioning 6 into 2 and 4; and (c) adding 4 to 5 to obtain 9.

Automatized knowledge   In order to add through five the child needs to have automatized three segments of knowledge. **Automatized knowledge** is knowledge that is immediately available. This is also referred to as **habituated knowledge**. First, the child needs to be able to partition five. Second, the child needs to be able to partition any of the numbers 2 to 10. And third, the child needs to be able to add to five, any number in the range 1 to 5. Developing facility with adding and subtracting in the range 1 to 10 without counting-by-ones provides a very important basis for mentally adding and subtracting in the range 1 to 20 and beyond. Children who continue to use arithmetical strategies involving long counts are on a very different learning path from those who progressively develop facility with non-count-by-ones strategies, first in the range 1 to 10 and then in the range 1 to 20 and beyond. These are also known as grouping strategies.

ASSESSMENT TASK GROUPS

List of Assessment Task Groups

A5.1: Making Finger Patterns for Numbers in the Range 1 to 5
A5.2: Making Finger Patterns for Numbers in the Range 6 to 10
A5.3: Naming and Visualizing Domino Patterns 1 to 6
A5.4: Naming and Visualizing Pair-Wise Patterns on a Ten-Frame
A5.5: Naming and Visualizing Five-Wise Patterns on a Ten-Frame
A5.6: Partitions of 5 and 10
A5.7: Addition and Subtraction in the Range 1 to 10

TASK GROUP A5.1: Making Finger Patterns for Numbers in the Range 1 to 5

Photo 5.1   Show me three on your fingers

Materials: None.

What to do and say: *Show me three on your fingers.* Similarly, *2, 5, 1, 4. Now show me on your other hand: 3, 2, 5, 4, 1.*

Notes:

- Look for children who apparently need to look at their fingers. Also, look for children who raise fingers sequentially. Children who are facile with finger patterns will raise their fingers simultaneously and will not need to look at their fingers.
- Look for differences within one child, or across several children, in the ways they use their fingers on these tasks, for example, the particular fingers used to show one, two, and so on.
- Children's facility to make and read finger patterns is important when they use their fingers to keep track of counting. It is very common for children to use finger-based counting strategies when doing addition, subtraction, multiplication or division calculations.

TASK GROUP A5.2: Making Finger Patterns for Numbers in the Range 6 to 10

Photo 5.2   Make ten on your fingers

Materials: None.

What to do and say: *Can you show me six fingers?* Similarly, *9, 7, 10, 8.*

Notes:

- The notes for Task Group A5.1 are also relevant to this task group.
- Many children are less facile with finger patterns in the range 6 to 10 compared with 1 to 5.
- Children might raise five fingers on one hand simultaneously, and then raise the additional fingers sequentially.

TASK GROUP A5.3: Naming and Visualizing Domino Patterns 1 to 6

Materials: A card for each of the domino patterns from 1 to 6.

What to do and say: Flash cards in random order. *Tell me how many dots you see. What does the four pattern look like? Can you show me in the air?* Similarly with the other domino patterns.

Notes:

- Initially, children learn to name domino patterns in a pictorial sense (similar to the way they might learn to say 'dog' when shown a picture of a dog) rather than necessarily in a numerical sense.
- These kinds of spatial patterns can be an important basis for the development of number concepts. Children visualize spatial patterns to keep track of counting when doing addition, subtraction, multiplication or division calculations.
- As well, facility with spatial patterns is an important basis for strategies that do not involve counting-by-ones.

Photo 5.3   Tell me how many dots you see

TASK GROUP A5.4: Naming and Visualizing Pair-Wise Patterns on a Ten-Frame

Materials: A card showing a ten-frame with the **pair-wise pattern** for each number from 1 to 10 (ten cards in all).

What to do and say: Flash cards in random order. *Tell me how many dots you see. What does four look like on the ten-frame? Can you show me in the air?* Similarly with the other numbers.

Notes:

- The pair-wise patterns are made by progressively filling the columns of a 2 × 5 ten-frame (two rows and five columns).
- Children who take a few seconds to name a pattern, rather than answer immediately, might be visualizing the pattern and then counting the dots.
- Facility with these patterns is an important basis for strategies that do not involve counting-by-ones.

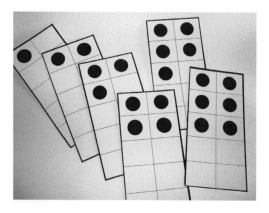

Photo 5.4   Pair-wise patterns on a ten-frame

Photo 5.5   Pair-wise eight
on a ten-frame

TASK GROUP A5.5: Naming and Visualizing Five-Wise Patterns on a Ten-Frame

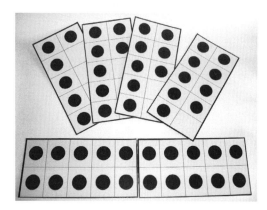

Photo 5.6   Five-wise patterns on a ten-frame

Photo 5.7   Seven as a five-wise pattern on a ten-frame

Materials: A card showing a ten-frame with the five-wise (**quinary**) pattern for each number from 1 to 10 (ten cards in all).

What to do and say: Flash cards in random order. *Tell me how many dots you see. What does six look like on the ten-frame? Can you show me in the air?* Similarly with the other numbers.

Notes:

- The notes for Task Group A5.4 are also relevant to this task group.
- The **five-wise patterns** are made by progressively filling the rows of a 2 × 5 ten-frame (two rows and five columns).

TASK GROUP A5.6: Partitions of 5 and 10

Materials: None.

What to do and say: *I will say a number and you say the number that goes with it to make five*: 3, 4, 2, 1. *I will say a number and you say the number that goes with it to make ten*: 9, 5, 8, 3, *and so on.*

Notes:

- Children usually have less difficulty when the unknown number is 1 or 2.
- After the child responds, they can be shown the number on a ten-frame. In this way a correct response can be confirmed and an incorrect response can be reconsidered.

Photo 5.8   Partitions of 5 and 10

TASK GROUP A5.7: Addition and Subtraction in the Range 1 to 10

Materials: Ten-frames showing the pair-wise patterns (see Task Group A5.4) and the five-wise patterns (see Task Group A5.5).

What to do and say: Flash the pair-wise pattern for six. *What number did you see? What is 6 and 2? Tell me how you worked that out?* Similarly, 4 + 3, 8 + 1, 5 + 3, and so on.

Flash the five-wise pattern for seven. *What number did you see? What is 7 and 2? Tell me how you worked that out?* Similarly, 4 + 2, 3 + 5, 6 + 3, and so on.

Flash the pair-wise pattern for six. *What number did you see? What is 6 take away 2? Tell me how you worked that out?* Similarly, 9 – 6, 7 – 4, 8 – 2, 6 – 4, and so on.

Flash the five-wise pattern for nine. *What number did you see? What is 9 take away 3? Tell me how you worked that out?* Similarly, 6 – 4, 8 – 3, 7 – 5, and so on.

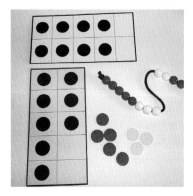

Photo 5.9 Addition and subtraction settings in the range 1 to 10

Notes:

- The general principle applied in these tasks is to flash the first stated number only. In the case of addition, the first addend is flashed. In the case of subtraction, the **minuend** is flashed.
- The purpose of these tasks is to gauge whether the children can use visualized patterns, rather than counting-on and counting-back, to solve addition and subtraction tasks.
- Children are likely to work flexibly with pair-wise, five-wise or other patterns.
- It is important to listen carefully to the child's explanation and to temper expectations that the child should use a particular strategy or pattern.

INSTRUCTIONAL ACTIVITIES

List of Instructional Activities

IA5.1: Bunny Ears
IA5.2: The Great Race
IA5.3: Quick Dots
IA5.4: Make Five Concentration
IA5.5 Five- and Ten-Frame Flashes
IA5.6: Memory Game
IA5.7: Domino Flashes
IA5.8: Domino Fish
IA5.9: Domino Snap
IA5.10: Make Ten Fish
IA5.11: Ten-Frame Bingo
IA5.12: Domino Five Up
IA5.13: Make Ten Ping Pong

ACTIVITY IA5.1: Bunny Ears

A VIDEO
DEMONSTRATING
THIS ACTIVITY
CAN BE ACCESSED
ONLINE AT WWW.
SAGEPUB.CO.UK/
WRIGHTTNC

Intended learning: To think figuratively about numbers in the range 1 to 10 and to partition numbers in the range 1 to 10 (for an explanation of figurative counting see the Topic Overview for Chapter 4).

Materials: None.

Description: Children make two fists with their hands and then raise these to the top of their head to represent two bunny's ears. The teacher then says a number, for example, six, and the child raises fingers on both hands to make the number. One child might raise four fingers on one hand and two on the other while another child might raise five fingers on one hand and one on the other. A third child might raise three fingers on each hand. The children must try to do this without looking at their hands, but some initially might find it difficult and have to check by looking. If it is decided to emphasize the five-plus combinations, children could be asked to make combinations 6 to 10 with five on one hand, for example 7 would be 5 and 2, and 9 would be 5 and 4. A simpler task involves children holding one hand above their heads and the teacher asks them to show 1 to 5 fingers.

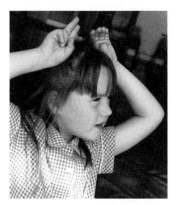

Photo 5.10 Bunny Ears for six shown as 4 and 2

Photo 5.11 Bunny Ears for six shown as 5 and 1

Notes:

- Young children might have problems in physically holding down fingers when they cannot look at them. If this is the case, allow them to check their finger pattern.
- This activity is suitable for pairs, small groups and whole class.
- Children should progress to keeping their hands above their heads, but still needing to count-on from five, while raising each finger.

- Finally, children should be able to flash the finger patterns for 6 through 10 without counting.
- Vary the activity by showing children a ten-frame card and asking children to show the Bunny Ears for that amount.
- Vary the activity by showing children a numeral card and asking children to show the Bunny Ears for that amount.
- Vary the activity by the teacher showing the Bunny Ears and asking the children to say the amount.

ACTIVITY IA5.2: The Great Race

Intended learning: To ascribe number to regular spatial patterns and match to a numeral in the range 1 to 6.

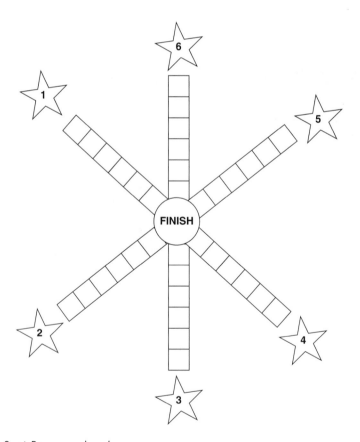

Figure 5.1   Great Race game board

Materials: Great Race game board, 1 to 6 dot die, six game markers to represent the racers (such as plastic bears).

Description: A racer is placed in each starting position. A 1 to 6 dot die is rolled to indicate which racer advances. For example, if the five-pattern is rolled, the racer in the lane with the numeral 5 advances one space. Continue rolling in succession until one of the racers reaches the finish (see Figure 5.1).

Notes:

- Initially children might need to count the spots on the die, but the goal is for children to recognize the pattern without counting.
- To promote visualization and subitizing, have one child roll the die and another child use a cup to cover the die after it is rolled.
- This game can be played individually or with partners taking turns rolling and advancing the indicated racer.
- Having all markers identical will help to ensure that the focus is on the numeral rather than other attributes such as color or size.

ACTIVITY IA5.3: Quick Dots

Intended learning: To subitize in the context of regular spatial configurations to nine and **irregular spatial configurations** to five.

Materials: Spatial configuration cards.

Description: Spatial configuration cards (see Figure 5.2) are flashed (displayed for approximately half a second). The children are asked how many dots they saw.

Notes:

- The ability to subitize helps children to develop mental structures for quantity. Subitizing can help advance the children's understanding of quantity to that of a composite unit, rather than as a numerical composite (See Chapter 10).
- Initially, children might visualize the pattern and then count the dots in their mental image. While this shows a strength in visualization, it is not subitizing.
- Children might learn the number for regular patterns in a pictorial sense, that is, they might link the number name for the pattern with a figural image which might not be linked with a numerical concept.
- Along with stating the amount shown, children should be encouraged to describe the arrangement of the dots, especially for larger numbers.
- Children should be able to name and create the pattern. A related activity is to ask children to create the pattern using counters when prompted with a spoken number word or displayed numeral.

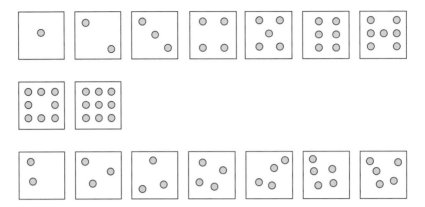

Figure 5.2 Pattern cards

ACTIVITY IA5.4: Make Five Concentration

Intended learning: To develop facility with combinations to five.

Materials: Five-frame cards showing the quantities 0 to 5.

Description: A set of twelve cards, two each of five-frames for 0 to 5 (see Figure 5.3), is arranged in an array, face down on the table. Children try to collect pairs of cards that add to five (make

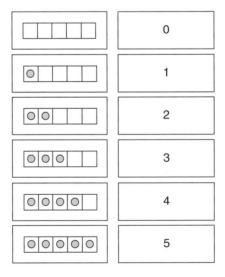

Figure 5.3 Five-frame cards

five). The first player turns over one card from the array and announces the number name of the pattern. The player then turns a second card face up, announces its number name and determines if the two cards total 5. For example, if a five-frame showing 3 is turned up it would need to be matched with a five-frame showing 2. If a match is made, the player keeps the cards. If a match is not made the cards are returned to their face-down position. Whether or not a match is made, play moves to the next player. Play continues until all cards have been matched. The winner is the child with the most cards.

Notes:

- The filled and empty cells in the five-frame provide visual support, which can help children work out what quantity is needed to make five.
- A more advanced version can be played using numerals 0 to 5 or a mix of five-frames and numerals.

ACTIVITY IA5.5: Five- and Ten-Frame Flashes

Intended learning: To develop facility with five and ten.

Materials: Five- and ten-frames, minibuses, counters.

Description: A five-frame is displayed using an image projector. The teacher asks: *How many squares are there?* Counters are placed in some of the squares without initially allowing the children to see. The five-frame is then flashed. The teacher asks: *How many dots? How many empty squares?* A five-seat minibus and smiley faces on transparent counters (see Figure 5.4) can be used in place of the five-frame.

Five-frame

Figure 5.4　Five-frame minibus

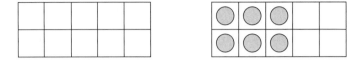

Ten-frame

Figure 5.5   Using ten-frame and ten-frame minibus

The same procedure is followed using a ten-frame or ten-seat minibus (see Figure 5.5). Doubles and five-plus patterns can be flashed.

Notes:

- A flash should be about half a second (not long enough for the items to be counted).
- This activity could be combined with finger patterns (Bunny Ears) (see Activity IA5.1).
- Children could also have their own five- and ten-frames and make combinations given by the teacher.
- This activity can be used with whole class, small groups or individual children.

ACTIVITY IA5.6: Memory Game

Intended learning: To increase children's figurative knowledge of numbers in the range 1 to 10.

Materials: Four sets of pair-wise dot cards and four sets of five-wise dot cards.

Description: Use two or four sets of dot cards, either pair-wise or five-wise patterns for 1 to 10 (see Figures 5.6 and 5.7.) Mix up the cards and place them face down on table. The children take turns in turning over two cards. If they find a matching pair, they keep the pair. The winner is the child with the most cards at the end of the game.

Notes:

- This activity is for pairs or small groups.
- This game can be played with a set of playing cards with the picture cards removed.

- To make the game easier for less able children, the range might be limited to 1 to 5, for example.
- Ask children to say the number that is the double of the number of dots on the card.
- To make the activity more challenging mix sets of pair-wise and five-wise dot cards so children need to match cards as shown in Figure 5.8.

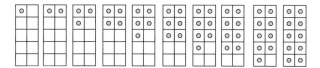

Figure 5.6   Pair-wise dot cards

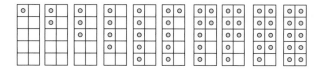

Figure 5.7   Five-wise dot cards

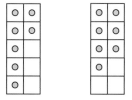

Figure 5.8   Five-wise and pair-wise dot cards for 7

ACTIVITY IA5.7: Domino Flashes

Intended learning: To ascribe number to domino patterns.

Materials: Domino patterns or large domino cards.

Description: Using an image projector (Figure 5.9), the teacher briefly displays (flashes) the pattern and children either say the number of dots they see or make the number on their fingers and display their finger pattern.

Note:

- This can be extended to other patterns such as the five-plus or doubles patterns.

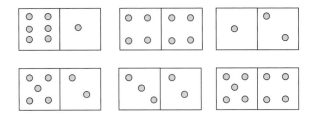

Figure 5.9 Domino cards

ACTIVITY IA5.8: Domino Fish

Intended learning: To extend knowledge of domino patterns.

Materials: Domino pattern cards, numeral cards.

Description: The activity is played the same as the game known as Fish. Instead of traditional playing cards, the teacher makes up cards containing the domino patterns (see Figure 5.9) and the matching numerals. Five cards are dealt to each player. The remaining cards are placed in a stack in the center of the players. Players try to make matching pairs of domino and numeral cards. Players take turns to ask another player for a particular card. If the player being asked does not have the required card they say: *Fish!* The player seeking the card takes the top card off the stack. The game continues until one player has no more cards. Players see how many pairs they have.

Note:

- This game can be extended to other patterns such as the five-plus or doubles patterns.

ACTIVITY IA5.9: Domino Snap

Intended learning: To extend knowledge of domino patterns.

Materials: Domino pattern cards large enough for children to manipulate, numeral cards.

Description: The activity is played the same as the game known as Snap. Instead of traditional playing cards, the teacher makes up cards containing the domino patterns (see Figure 5.9) and the matching numerals (as in Activity IA5.8). The cards are divided between two players and kept face down. Players take turns to put their top card on the stack. If this card matches the card on top of the stack, each player tries to put their hand on the stack saying 'Snap!', as they do it. The game proceeds until one player has all of the cards.

Note:

- This can be extended to other patterns such as the five-plus or doubles patterns.

ACTIVITY IA5.10: Make Ten Fish

Intended learning: To learn the partitions of ten.

Materials: At least four sets of numeral cards from 1 to 10.

Description: The activity is played the same as the game known as Fish. Instead of traditional playing cards, numeral cards 1 to 9 are used. These are clearer than playing cards. Five cards are dealt to each player. The remaining cards are placed in a stack in the center of the players. Players try to make matching pairs of cards adding to ten. Players take turns to ask another player for a particular card. If the player being asked does not have the required card they say *Fish!* The player seeking the card takes the top card off the stack. The game continues until one player has no more cards. Players see how many pairs they have.

Note:

- The game provides examples of **missing subtrahend tasks** (See Chapter 6) (for example, *I have six. How many more will make ten?*)

ACTIVITY IA5.11: Ten-Frame Bingo

Intended learning: Facility with combinations to ten.

Materials: Empty 3 by 2 grids, counters, large set of ten-frames.

Description:

- Children need an empty 3 by 2 grid and six counters each.
- They write six different numbers in the range 0 to 10 on their grid.
- The teacher shows or flashes a ten-frame. If the number needed to make ten appears on their grid, children place a counter on the number.
- The first to cover all six of their numbers calls *Bingo!*

Notes:

- Rather than flashing a ten-frame the teacher can show a numeral card.
- Rather than showing cards the teacher can say the number.

ACTIVITY IA5.12: Domino Five Up

A VIDEO DEMONSTRATING THIS ACTIVITY CAN BE ACCESSED ONLINE AT WWW. SAGEPUB.CO.UK/ WRIGHTTNC

Intended learning: To develop facility with combinations to five.

Materials: A set of floor dominos or multiple sets of table dominos.

Description:

- The game is played the same as traditional dominos but instead of matching equal dots children match tiles that add to five (3 and 2, 4 and 1).
- Remove all dominos showing a six-spot pattern.
- Large floor dominos or small desk sets can be used.

Note:

- The game can be changed to Domino Six Up or Seven Up. In these activities, all of the dominos showing a six-spot pattern in the set of dominos would be included.

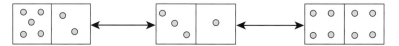

Figure 5.10   Domino Five Up

ACTIVITY IA5.13: Make Ten Ping Pong

Intended learning: To develop facility with partitions of ten.

Materials: No materials required.

Description:

- The teacher tells the children that she will say a number in the range 1 to 10 (e.g. 7) and the children's task is to say what number goes with the number she says to make ten (3). The teacher continues only saying a number in the range 1 to 10: *Four!* to which the children answer: *Six!* And so on. Thus the teacher does not repeat the instruction about saying what goes with the number she says to make ten.

Notes:

- This activity is suitable for small groups and the whole class, and can be adapted as an independent activity for a pair of children.
- The focus of the activity can be changed from make ten to many other standard addition or subtraction tasks, for example: make 20, add 5, take 5, add 10, take 10, double a number.

Learning Trajectory

Table 5.1   Learning Trajectory: Structuring Numbers 1 to 10

Topics	Page Ref.	Assessment Task Groups	Instructional Activities
Finger patterns 1 to 5	73	A5.1	IA5.1
Finger patterns 6 to 10	73	A5.2	IA5.1
Domino patterns 1 to 6	72–73	A5.3	IA5.2 IA5.3 IA5.6 IA5.7 IA5.8 IA5.9 Any dice game is useful
Pair-wise patterns		A5.4	IA5.6 IA5.7 IA5.8 IA5.9
Five-wise patterns		A5.5	IA5.6 IA5.7 IA5.8 IA5.9
Partitions of 5	73–75	A5.6	IA5.4 IA5.5 IA5.10 IA5.12
Partitions of 10	73–75	A5.6	IA5.4 IA5.10 IA5.11
Addition in range 1 to 10	74–75	A5.7	IA5.13
Subtraction in range 1 to 10	74–75	A5.7	IA5.13

6

Advanced Counting, Addition and Subtraction

Summary

This chapter continues on from Chapter 4 with a focus on the development of more advanced counting-by-ones strategies and the use of these strategies to solve addition and subtraction tasks. These are the strategies of counting-on, which includes counting-up-from and counting-up-to, and counting-back which includes counting-back-from and counting-back-to. The chapter explains clearly the place of these strategies in the overall development of early numeracy.

 Key topic: 7.3

Topic Overview

Advanced Counting-by-ones Strategies

In Chapter 4 we describe how the counting-on child would solve a task such as 8 + 5 presented with two screened collections. Children who can count-on in this way can develop (or perhaps already have developed) similar kinds of strategies for subtractive tasks. Collectively, these strategies for additive and subtractive tasks involving two screened collections are referred to as the four advanced counting-by-ones strategies and they have the following characteristics:

- They involve commencing the count from a number other than one, that is, they do not involve counting-from-one (in contrast to figurative and perceptual counting).
- They involve counting forwards or backwards by ones (in contrast to a non-count-by-ones strategy).
- They involve some means of keeping track of counting-by-ones, typically using fingers or implicit or explicit double counting.

There are four of these strategies in all, and each is typically associated with a particular kind of task.

These strategies are counting-up-from, counting-up-to, counting-back-from and counting-back-to. Each is summarized in Table 6.1 and explained below.

Table 6.1　Advanced counting-by-ones strategies, task types and solutions

Strategy type	Task type	Solution
Count-up-from	Additive: 8 + 5 = □	8 ... 9, 10, 11, 12, 13 altogether!
Count-up-to	Missing Addend: 8 + □ = 13	8 ... 9, 10, 11, 12, 13 ... 5 more!
Count-down-from	Removed Items: 13 − 5 = □	13 ... 12, 11, 10, 9, 8 left!
Count-down-to	Missing Subtrahend: 13 − □ = 8	13 ... 12, 11, 10, 9, 8 ... 5 taken away!

Note: Tasks are presented with screened collections of counters – as described below.

Counting-up-from

Counting-up-from typically is associated with children's solutions of additive tasks involving two screened collections, for example 8 + 5. The counting-on strategy is referred to specifically as counting-up-from. When solving 8 + 5, for example, the strategy involves counting up five from eight. Additive tasks are described in Task Group A6.1.

Counting-up-to

Counting-up-to typically is associated with children's solutions of missing addend tasks (a kind of subtractive task) where, for example, the child is told there are 8 counters in the first collection and 13 counters in all, and has to figure out how many are in the second collection. The counting-on strategy is referred to specifically as counting-up-to. The child starts at 8 and counts up to 13, and keeps track of the number of counts after 8, that is, 5 counts. Missing addend tasks are described in Task Group A6.2.

Counting-back-from

Counting-back-from typically is associated with children's solutions of a second kind of subtractive task, that is, the **removed items task**. In this case the child is told how many counters are in a collection, and then how many are removed from the collection. For example, there are 13 counters under the screen, and then 5 are removed, how many are left under the screen? The child uses a counting-back strategy which is referred to specifically as counting-back-from, that is, the child starts at 13, and counts back 5 from 13, to obtain the answer 8. Removed items tasks are described in Task Group A6.3.

Counting-back-to

Counting-back-to typically is associated with children's solutions of a third kind of subtractive task, that is, the missing subtrahend task. In this case the child is told how many counters are in a collection and how many remain after some are removed. For example, there are 13 counters under the screen, and then some are removed and 8 remain, how many were removed? The child uses a counting-back strategy which is referred to specifically as counting-back-to, that is, the child starts at 13, and counts back to 8, and keeps track of the number of counts after 13, that is 5. Missing subtrahend tasks are described in Task Group A6.4.

Counting-forward-from-one-three-times

A common approach to the initial teaching of addition and subtraction involves giving children word problems to solve and encouraging them to use materials such as counters to solve the problems. Often associated with this approach is the notion that it is important to let children use the materials to solve these problems for an extended sequence of lessons. In these situations children typically use a strategy that we refer to as counting-forward-from-one-three-times. This strategy is used for addition or subtraction problems.

Counting-forward-from-one-three-times for addition   For an addition problem the child counts out the number of counters corresponding to the first addend, then does the same thing for the second addend, and finally counts all of the counters from one.

Counting-forward-from-one-three-times for subtraction   In the case of a subtraction problem, the child counts out the number of counters corresponding to the minuend, then, using the collection just counted out, counts out and removes the number of counters corresponding to the **subtrahend**, and finally counts the remaining counters.

A critique   We are critical of this approach to instruction because in our view, it tends to perpetuate the use of what we would regard as primitive counting strategies, that is, strategies characterized by: (a) always counting with perceptual (visible) items; (b) always counting-by-ones; (c) always counting from one; and (d) always counting forwards. An additional, common characteristic of this approach is to have little regard for the relative size of the numbers that the children work with. This, too, we regard as problematic and we expand on this point below.

Screened Collections versus Word Problems

In the above sections we described four kinds of tasks, one additive and three subtractive, which can be presented using screened collections of counters. Although these tasks could alternatively be presented in word problem format rather than in a format involving screened collections, we would not advocate doing so. We believe that, at least in the initial period, the use of screened collections has benefits over the use of word problems. These benefits include that the children are provided with a consistent setting (collections of counters) which they can easily imagine (when the collections are screened). Also, the use of screened collections facilitates the development of the notion of verification, that is, children come to see that it is possible to check their answers when the collections have been unscreened. Our view is that the goal of early number instruction is for children to progress to formal arithmetic knowledge, and solving a wide range of word problems is not necessarily important for this progression. Additionally, word problems can entangle children in difficulties of reading and meaning.

Choosing Numbers for Additive and Subtractive Tasks

Because the strategies associated with these tasks (the four advanced counting-by-ones strategies described above) involve counting forward or backward, the particular choice of numbers that the teacher uses in posing such tasks is very important in our view.

Counting in the Range 2 to 5 Only

As a general rule, the number of counts the child makes using any particular strategy should be in the range 2 to 5 only. We refer to this as the **count number**. In terms of advancing children's number knowledge, we think it is unproductive to have children counting long sequences of numbers, and keeping track of their counts, which is inherent in these strategies. Thus, if the instructional goal is to develop these counting strategies, then, in our view, it would not be useful to present a missing addend task such as $6 + \square = 15$ (where it is understood that this is presented using screened collections or as a word problem). Similarly, a removed items task such as $22 - 13$ would not be useful. Nor would an addition task such as $8 + 13$ be useful if one's goal is to develop the counting-up-from strategy.

Using Advanced Counting-by-ones Strategies in the Range 20 to 100

As explained in the previous paragraph, the tasks that children solve using advanced counting-by-ones strategies should involve counts (count numbers) in the range 2 to 5 only. As long as this principle is kept in mind, these strategies can be used by children in the range 20 to 100. Thus a child might be asked to solve tasks such as the following: (a) an addition task, 38 red counters and 4 blue counters; (b) a removed items task, 37 counters are placed under a screen and 3 are removed; (c) a missing addend task, 88 red counters and some blue counters make 93 in all; and (d) a missing subtrahend task, 57 counters under a screen, some are removed and 55 remain. Tasks such as those just described could alternatively be presented as word problems. These kinds of tasks introduce children to addition and subtraction involving numbers throughout the range 20 to 100, and help to set the scene for addition and subtraction involving two 2-digit numbers (Chapters 8 and 9).

Finger Patterns and Advanced Counting-by-ones Strategies

Children who have well-developed finger patterns for numbers in the range 1 to 5 will use their fingers to keep track, as part of the advanced counting-by-ones strategies.

Using fingers to keep track on an additive task Thus a child might work out $8 + 5$ by counting on from 8 and raising a finger for each number word from 9 onward in turn for the number words from 9 to 13. The child stops at 13 because they have raised five fingers (they recognize the finger pattern for five). Thus when they raise the fifth finger, they know that they have made five counts, that is from 9 to 13. In this case, it is not necessary for the child to separately count the fingers from 1 to 5. Use of finger patterns in this way is relatively sophisticated. That the child raises the five fingers sequentially (versus simultaneously) does not indicate a lack of facility with finger patterns.

Using fingers to keep track on a missing subtrahend task   A second example of more facile use of finger patterns is: 11 counters are screened, and then some are removed and now there are only 7. How many counters were removed? The child counts back from 11 and raises a finger for each number word in turn, from 10 to 7. The child stops because they got to 7, and then looks at their finger pattern and says 'four', that is, the child can recognize the finger pattern for four, without having to count their fingers from one.

Interval- and discrete-based reasoning   When the child commences by saying 'ten' in coordination with raising one finger, we regard this as signifying a jump from 11 to 10. Similarly, saying 'nine' and raising a second finger signifies a jump from 10 to 9 and so on. Alternatively, the child might commence by saying 'eleven' in coordination with raising one finger. In this case we regard this as signifying one counter. Similarly, saying 'ten' and raising a second finger signifies a second counter and so on. In the first case the child's reasoning seems to involve focusing on the interval from one number to the next. We have labeled this **interval-based reasoning**. In the second case the child's reasoning seems to involve focusing on each counter in turn. We have labeled this **discrete-based reasoning**. In either case, and as with other strategies involving counting-by-ones, children will sometimes answer one more or one less than the correct answer. Determining whether the child is using interval-based or discrete-based reasoning is an important first step in addressing this issue.

Contrasting Three Solution Strategies Involving Finger Patterns

Three children are asked to solve the additive task 5 + 4 posed with two screened collections. All three children make use of their fingers to solve the task. The first child raises five fingers on one hand sequentially, then raises four fingers on the other hand sequentially, and then counts their raised fingers from 1 to 9. The second child counts from 1 to 5 and then continues their count from 6 to 9, and raises a finger in coordination with each of the number words from six to nine. The third child counts-on from 6 to 9, and raises a finger in coordination with each of the number words from six to nine. The first child is using perceptual counting, the second is using figurative counting and the third is using counting-on. Although the first child has solved an additive task involving two screened collections, they have done so by building perceptual replacements – their fingers replace the counters. In the case of the first child, what remains to be seen is whether they can solve an additive task when the first addend is greater than five, for example, 8 + 4. On such a task it is not feasible for the child to use their fingers to build simultaneously replacements for the two addends 8 and 4. For the third child, eight stands for having counted the first collection from 1 to 8, whereas the second child apparently needs to count from 1 to 8, in order for eight to stand for a count. These strategies are also described in Chapter 4.

 ASSESSMENT TASK GROUPS

List of Assessment Task Groups

A6.1: Additive Tasks Involving Two Screened Collections
A6.2: Missing Addend Tasks Involving Two Screened Collections
A6.3: Removed Items Tasks Involving a Screened Collection

A6.4: Missing Subtrahend Tasks Involving a Screened Collection
A6.5: Comparative Subtraction Involving Two Screened Collections
A6.6: Subtraction with Bare Numbers

TASK GROUP A6.1: Additive Tasks Involving Two Screened Collections

Materials: A collection of counters of one color (red) and a collection of another color (blue); two screens of cardboard or cloth.

What to do and say: Briefly display and then screen eight red counters. *Here are eight red counters.* Briefly display and then screen five blue counters. *Here are five blue counters. How many counters altogether?* Similarly with collections such as 9 red and 3 blue, 15 red and 2 blue, 11 red and 4 blue, and so on.

Notes:

- These tasks are of the same kind as those in Task Group 4.6.
- The purpose of these tasks is to gauge the child's ability to use counting-on. This strategy is referred to specifically as counting-up-from (for example, counting up three from eight). It is quite common for children to use their fingers to keep track of counting.
- Some children will use a strategy that involves little or no counting-by-ones.
- Some children might solve these tasks by counting from one. They are apparently unable to use counting-on to solve these kinds of tasks. In the case of children who are not able solve these tasks, the second collection (blue counters) can be unscreened.
- The general approach with these tasks is to have the number of counters in the second collection (blue counters) typically in the range 2 to 5, and the number in the first collection (red counters) larger than the number in the second collection (blue counters). The number in the first collection can be in the range 4 to 20 or beyond 20.

TASK GROUP A6.2: Missing Addend Tasks Involving Two Screened Collections

Materials: A collection of counters of one color (red) and a collection of another color (blue); one screen of cardboard or cloth.

What to do and say: Briefly display and then screen four red counters. *Here are four red counters. I am going to add some blue counters to those red counters.* Place two blue counters with the red counters without allowing the child to see them. *I added some blue counters to the four red counters and now there are six counters altogether. How many blue counters did I add?* Similarly as follows: $6 + \square = 10$, $9 + \square = 12$, $11 + \square = 13$, and so on.

Notes:

- The purpose of these tasks is to gauge the child's ability to use counting-on. This strategy is referred to specifically as counting-up-to (for example, begin at four and count up to six). It is quite common for children to use their fingers to keep track of counting.
- Some children will use a strategy that involves little or no counting-by-ones.
- It is common for children initially to misinterpret a missing addend task as an addition task, for example, $4 + O = 6$ is misinterpreted as $4 + 6$. In such cases the interviewer can present the task again and rephrase the task.

Photo 6.1   Here are four red counters

Photo 6.2   How many blue counters did I add?

- In similar vein to Task Group A6.1, the general approach with these missing addend tasks is to have the number of counters in the second collection (blue counters) typically in the range 2 to 5, and the number in the first collection (red counters) larger than the number in the second collection (blue counters). The number in the first collection can be in the range 4 to 20 or beyond 20.

TASK GROUP A6.3: Removed Items
Tasks Involving a Screened Collection

Materials: A collection of counters of one color (red); two screens of cardboard or cloth.

What to do and say: Briefly display and then screen seven red counters. *Here are seven red counters. I am going to take two counters away.* Remove two counters, briefly display them and screen them. *I took away two of the red counters. How many counters are left?* Similarly as follows: 10 remove 3, 12 remove 4, 16 remove 2, and so on.

Notes:

- The purpose of these tasks is to gauge the child's ability to use counting-back. This strategy is referred to specifically as counting-back-from (for example, count back two from seven). It is quite common for children to use their fingers to keep track of counting.
- Some children will use a strategy that involves little or no counting-by-ones.
- In similar vein to Task Group A6.1, the general approach with these removed items tasks is to have the number of removed items in the range 2 to 5.

TASK GROUP A6.4: Missing Subtrahend Tasks Involving a Screened Collection

Materials: A collection of counters of one color (red); two screens of cardboard or cloth.

What to do and say: Briefly display and then screen nine red counters. *Here are nine red counters. I am going to take some counters away.* Remove two counters and screen them without allowing the child to see them. *I had nine red counters, then I took away some of the counters and now there are only seven left. How many counters did I take away?* Similarly as follows: 11 − ☐ = 8, 13 − ☐ = 10, and so on.

Notes:

- The purpose of these tasks is to gauge the child's ability to use counting-back. This strategy is referred to specifically as counting-back-to (for example, begin at nine and count back to seven). It is quite common for children to use their fingers to keep track of counting.
- Children who use counting-back-from to solve removed items tasks (Task Group A6.3) might not be able to use counting-back-to to solve missing subtrahend tasks. Some children will use a strategy that involves little or no counting-by-ones. In similar vein to Task Group A6.1, the general approach with these tasks is to have the missing subtrahend in the range 2 to 5.

TASK GROUP A6.5: Comparative Subtraction Involving Two Screened Collections

Materials: A collection of counters of one color (red) and a collection of another color (blue); two screens of cardboard or cloth.

What to do and say: Briefly display and then screen seven red counters. *Here are seven red counters.* Briefly display and then screen four blue counters. *Here are four blue counters. If I put a blue counter* *on each of the red counters, how many red counters would not be covered with a blue counter?* Similarly as follows: 11 red and 7 blue, 13 red and 8 blue, 16 red and 13 blue, and so on.

Notes:

- Children might use counting-up-to or counting-back-to to solve these tasks. For example, 7 – 4 is solved by starting at four and counting-up-to seven or starting at seven and counting-back-to four.
- Some children will use a strategy that involves little or no counting-by-ones.
- In similar vein to Task Group A6.1, the general approach with these tasks is to have the unknown difference in the range 2 to 5.

TASK GROUP A6.6: Subtraction with Bare Numbers

Materials: Subtraction tasks written on a card in horizontal format. One card for each task.

What to do and say: Present the task 16 – 12. *Read this number task. Do you have a way to work this out? Try to work it out.* Similarly as follows: 14 – 10, 17 – 14, 27 – 22, and so on.

Notes:

- These tasks are typically more difficult than the subtractive tasks above (Task Groups A6.2 to A6.5).
- It can be informative to present these bare number tasks before presenting the subtractive tasks (Tasks Groups A6.2 to A6.5) in order to gauge if the child has relatively sophisticated strategies for subtraction, including strategies that involve little or no counting.
- In similar vein to Task Group A6.1, the general approach with these tasks is to have the unknown difference in the range 2 to 5.

 INSTRUCTIONAL ACTIVITIES

List of Instructional Activities

IA6.1: Class Count-On and Count-back
IA6.2: Hundred Chart Activities
IA6.3: Activities on a Bead Bar or Bead String
IA6.4: Bucket Count-On
IA6.5: Bucket Count-Back
IA6.6: Number Line Count-On

IA6.7: It's in the Bag
IA6.8: Team Mats
IA6.9: What's in the Box?
IA6.10: Under the Cloth
IA 6.11: Train Track
IA6.12: Frogs on the Lily Pads
IA6.13: Making Ice

ACTIVITY IA6.1: Class Count-On and Count-Back

Intended learning: To count on or back in the range 2 to 5, from a given number and consolidate forward and backward number word sequences.

Materials: Instruction cards.

Description: Explain to the children that they are going to count around the class or circle. The teacher turns her back and listens to the count. At an appropriate time the teacher shouts *Stop!* and turns around. The child who has said the last number is then given a card by the teacher with an instruction. For example: *Count back three. Add five. What is four more?* The child completes the instruction and the count continues around the class.

Notes:

- The teacher can limit the range of counting, for example, when the count reaches 20 children change to counting backwards.
- In the case of younger children, the teacher might have to read the instruction cards.

A VIDEO
DEMONSTRATING
THIS ACTIVITY
CAN BE ACCESSED
ONLINE AT WWW.
SAGEPUB.CO.UK/
WRIGHTTNC

ACTIVITY IA6.2: Hundred Chart Activities

Intended learning: To count forwards and backwards in the range 1 to 100, identifying numerals in this range, and counting on and back from given numbers.

Materials: Hundred chart, sets of cards for teacher and children.

Description: The teacher has a pack of ten cards. Each card has an instruction such as: *Count on two. Count back five.* The instructions involve numbers in the range 2 to 5. Tasks are posed using the hundred chart as a visual aid. The teacher chooses a number and asks a child to find it on the hundred chart. The teacher highlights the chosen number and asks the child to choose a card from the top of the pack. The child carries out the instruction on the card. The rest of the children are asked to carry out the instruction, providing answers verbally or on whiteboards. The child at the front demonstrates how they obtained the answer. Continue using other numbers. Children can work individually or in pairs with mini hundred charts and a set of instruction cards. They can generate their own number, write it down and then turn over a card, record the instruction and write the answer.

Notes:

- The numbers chosen for this activity should take account of children's facility with forward and backward sequences with the hundred chart.
- The activity can be made easier by using a 1 to 20 grid or a 1 to 50 grid, or more difficult by using a 101 to 200 grid.
- This activity is suitable for whole class, small groups and individuals.
- Children could use individual hundred charts.
- This activity helps children to see the position of numbers on a hundred chart. It also supports the development of place value knowledge because the numbers are arranged in tens.
- In the case of younger children, take account of children's ability to read the instruction cards.

ACTIVITY IA6.3: Activities on a Bead Bar or Bead String

Intended learning: To develop knowledge of quantity and position of numbers in the 1 to 100 range, and to count on and back in the range 2 to 5, from a given number.

Materials: Bead bar or string.

Description: The teacher uses a bead bar or bead string to pose questions to children. A 20s bar or 100s bar could be used. The beads are arranged in groups of ten in two different colors as shown in Figure 6.1.

The teacher asks a child to place a peg on the bar (or string) to show a number of beads, for example, 13. The teacher attaches a card to the peg displaying the numeral 13, and asks the children to add or subtract a number in the range 2 to 5. Children could answer orally or write

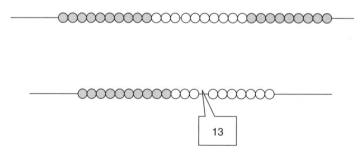

Figure 6.1   Bead string

answers on an individual whiteboard. The teacher discusses the responses and chooses a child to demonstrate the answer using the beads.

Notes:

- The numbers chosen for this activity should take account of the children's facility with forward and backward number word sequences.
- This activity is suitable for whole class, small group or individuals.
- Children could use individual bead strings.
- This activity helps children to see the quantity value of numbers and the position of numbers on a number line. It also supports the development of place value because the beads are arranged in tens.

ACTIVITY IA6.4: Bucket Count-On

Intended learning: To count on from the larger number when adding numbers in the range 1 to 4.

Materials: Opaque bucket, interlocking cubes.

Description: The teacher drops cubes into a bucket one by one, asking the children to count as each cube is dropped. After dropping, say, seven cubes, the teacher asks the children how many cubes in all. Now the teacher places one to four cubes on her fingers and asks the children how many cubes there are altogether now. For example, the teacher might say: *There are seven cubes in the bucket and three on my fingers. How many is that altogether?* Encourage the children to say the numbers in their heads. Then check by having everyone count-on together. Continue with other numbers.

A VIDEO DEMONSTRATING THIS ACTIVITY CAN BE ACCESSED ONLINE AT WWW. SAGEPUB.CO.UK/ WRIGHTTNC

Notes:

- This is a multi-sensory activity in that the children see and hear the cubes going into the bucket one by one.
- When selecting the first number take account of the children's counting ability in a particular range. For example, if children are able to count no more than ten, the number of cubes dropped into the bucket should be no more than six. If children are able to count to 100, then much larger numbers can be used.
- When children are familiar with the activity, numbers larger than 20 can be imagined rather than counted into the bucket. For example, the teacher says: *I'm going to pretend that there are 24 cubes in the bucket now and 2 on my fingers.* The teacher places 2 cubes on fingers for children to see. *How many cubes are there altogether?*
- This activity is suitable for whole class, small group or individuals.

ACTIVITY IA6.5: Bucket Count-Back

Intended learning: To subtract numbers in the range 1 to 4 by counting back.

Materials: Opaque bucket, interlocking cubes.

Description: The teacher drops cubes into a bucket one by one, and asks the children to count as each cube is dropped. Now the teacher removes from 1 to 4 cubes, displays them on their fingers, and asks how many cubes are left. For example, the teacher says: *There were 11 cubes in the bucket and I've taken 3 out. How many will be left in the bucket?* Encourage the children to say the numbers in their heads initially and then check by getting everyone to count back together: *10, 9, 8*. Have children check the number left in the bucket. Continue with other numbers.

Notes:

- This activity involves two senses. Children see and hear the cubes going into the bucket one by one.
- When selecting the first number take account of the children's counting ability. Some children might be working in the range 1 to 10 and others in the range 1 to 100.
- When children are familiar with the activity, numbers larger than 20 can be imagined rather than put into the bucket. For example: *I'm going to pretend that there are 24 cubes in the bucket now and I'm taking 2 out*. The teacher places 2 cubes on fingers for children to see. *How many cubes are left in the bucket?*
- The number of cubes removed should be in the range 1 to 4.
- This activity is suitable for whole class, small group or individuals.
- Alternative materials could be used.

ACTIVITY IA6.6: Number Line Count-On

Intended learning: To count on from the larger number when adding numbers in the range 1 to 4.

Materials: Pack of large-size numeral cards, blank die (for teacher to mark six faces as follows: 2, 2, 3, 3, 4, 4), small whiteboards, large whiteboard, dry wipe pens.

Description: The teacher has a pack of large-sized numeral cards, a die (or spinner) numbered 2, 2, 3, 3, 4, 4, and an empty number line drawn on the whiteboard. Children have individual whiteboards. The teacher turns over the first card in the pack and attaches it to the left-hand side of the empty number line (Figure 6.2).

Figure 6.2 Number line count-on (1)

The teacher asks a child to come to the front and throw the die. The teacher asks, *We are starting at 14, and we count on 3, where do we finish?* Allow time for children to solve the task and record on their individual whiteboards. The teacher then demonstrates the three jumps on her white-board, counting *15, 16, 17* and marking only 17 on the empty number line (Figure 6.3).

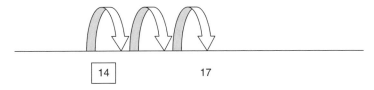

14   17

Figure 6.3   Number line count-on (2)

Continue using other numbers. Then ask the children to draw a line on their boards and write down the next number from the pack on their number line. The teacher throws the die and children count on and record the final number on their boards.

Notes:

- The numbers chosen for this activity should take account of the children's facility with numeral identification and the forward number word sequence.
- This activity is suitable for whole class, small group or individuals.
- It is not necessary for children to draw their empty number lines as a straight line.
- Encourage children to solve the task mentally, and then record on the empty number line, rather than use the empty number line in their initial solution.
- Teachers could use an electronic version (for example the National Numeracy Strategy interactive teaching program 'Number Line' in the UK) or another form of image projector.

ACTIVITY IA6.7: It's in the Bag

Intended learning: To count back from (down to) a given number.

Materials: Feely bag, cubes, numeral cards in selected range, spot dice.

Description: The teacher selects a child to choose a numeral card from 6 to 10 to generate the number of cubes used. The child puts the cubes one by one into the feely bag while counting. A second child rolls the spot die marked 1 to 5 to see how many to remove, and then removes them one by one – thus encouraging a count-down-from solution. The teacher asks, *How many are left in the bag?* After the children answer, the teacher displays the cubes so the children can check.

   A follow up activity is to have the children working in threes. For example, one child puts the cubes into the bag, one takes them out and one solves the task and checks.

A VIDEO DEMONSTRATING THIS ACTIVITY CAN BE ACCESSED ONLINE AT WWW. SAGEPUB.CO.UK/ WRIGHTTNC

Notes:

- This activity can be changed to a missing subtrahend activity: the first child selects from numeral cards 6 to 10 to generate the number of cubes to put in the feely bag and a second child secretly removes a number of cubes without the other children seeing. The second child then tells the others how many are left in the bag and asks, *How many have I taken?* The second child then reveals the cubes removed from the bag so the third child can check.
- Extend the range of numbers on the numeral cards. Use a numeral die rather than a spot die.
- Change the activity to include addition. Continue adding or removing two each time, then sometimes one and sometimes three. Increase to three, four or five.
- Change the setting to coins in a money box or letters in a post box.
- Children can write a number sentence to record the task.
- This activity is suitable for whole class or small group.

ACTIVITY IA6.8: Team Mats

Intended learning: To solve missing addend tasks by counting-up-to.

Materials: Mats for children to sit on, numeral cards.

Description: Work in a large space such as a school hall. Divide the class into two or three teams. Each team has two large mats. The teacher gives one team a numeral card, say four. Four from that team sit on one of their mats. The teacher then gives the same team a larger numeral, say seven. The teacher asks, *How many more children do we need to make seven?* Children from the other teams work out how many more children are needed to sit on the second mat, making seven in all. The teacher now gives a turn to the other team (or teams). The total is in the range 1 to 10 and the missing addend is in the range 2 to 5.

Notes:

- This activity can be varied according to how much space is available.
- A variation is to change this to a missing subtrahend game. The teacher gives the team the total first, say nine. Nine from that team sit on one of their mats. The teacher then gives the team a smaller number, say six. Children from the other teams work out how many children must move to the other mat.
- In this activity the children themselves become the objects to count and this can be quite an enjoyable activity.

ACTIVITY IA6.9: What's in the Box?

A VIDEO DEMONSTRATING THIS ACTIVITY CAN BE ACCESSED ONLINE AT WWW.SAGEPUB.CO.UK/ WRIGHTTNC

Intended learning: To solve missing addend tasks by counting-up-to.

Materials: Cubes, a box with two compartments and lids, numeral cards, individual whiteboards.

Description: Use a box with two compartments and a lid for each compartment. A card with the numeral 9 is placed on the side of the box (this is the total number of items needed). The teacher counts six cubes into one compartment of the box and closes the lid. The aim of the activity is to place in the second compartment the number of cubes needed to make the number on the side of the box. Ask the children how many cubes are needed. Have children place the cubes in the compartment in order to check their answer. Ask the children how they could record the activity on their whiteboard. Continue using other numbers. The missing addend should be in the range 2 to 5.

Children can work in pairs or small groups with one child turning over the numeral cards (two collections, each set a different color) in order to generate the numbers to be used. The second child places the cubes in the box and places the numeral card corresponding to the total on the side or on top of the box. The other children try to solve the task.

Notes:

- A large blank domino and screen can be used in place of the box.
- The range of numbers can extend from 10 to 15, to 20.

ACTIVITY IA6.10: Under the Cloth

Intended learning: To solve missing subtrahend tasks by counting back or counting on.

Materials: Cubes or other materials, cloth large enough to screen the cubes.

Description: The teacher counts out a group of cubes or other objects (for example, teddy bears) for the children to see. The teacher screens the cubes and asks the children to close their eyes. The teacher then removes a small number (in the range 1 to 5) and puts them out of sight. The teacher asks the children to open their eyes and unscreens the cubes. Then the teacher says: *There were 12 cubes under the cloth. I have taken some away and now there are 8 cubes under the cloth. How many cubes did I take away?* The children are given time to work out their answers and then asked to explain their strategies. The cubes are unscreened and the activity is explained if necessary. Continue with other numbers.

Notes:

- Missing subtrahend tasks typically are more difficult than missing addend or removed item tasks involving similar numbers.
- Children can solve the above task by counting back from 12 to 8 or counting up from 8 to 12. Discussing different strategies will help children to understand that the task involves finding the difference between the two numbers.
- The minuend should be in the range where the children can count forwards and backwards.
- It is important to keep the missing subtrahend small (in the range 1 to 5) even when using minuends beyond 20.
- When using minuends beyond 20, interlocking cubes arranged in sets of 10 could be used.
- This activity is suitable for whole class, small group, pairs or individuals.

- An alternative is to use an upturned, opaque container with 10 cubes on top. Some of the cubes are then hidden under the container and children try to guess how many are hidden.
- An alternative suited to the whole class is to use an image projector and counters.

ACTIVITY IA6.11: Train Track

Intended learning: To solve missing subtrahend tasks by counting back or counting on.

Materials: Counter or cubes, strip of card (train carriage), box with cut out for the tunnel.

Description: The teacher places eight cubes (or counters) on a strip of card (train carriage). Part of the carriage moves into a tunnel. The teacher describes what has taken place. *There are eight people on the train. We can see five people, how many people are in the tunnel?* Ask the children to explain their answers. Allow them to move the train to check their answers Continue using different numbers. Ask the children how they would record what they have been doing using a whiteboard?

Note:

- The teacher can introduce the idea of notating the activity, using a number sentence, for example, $8 + 5 = 13$.

ACTIVITY IA6.12: Frogs on the Lily Pads

Intended learning: To use counting-on or counting-back to solve comparison tasks.

Materials: Large circles, green head bands.

Description: Place out eight large circles in a line on the floor and give five green head bands to the children who are to be frogs. Ask the frogs to stand in a line and then to jump onto the lily pads. Now ask the class: *Do we have enough frogs? How many lily pads do not have frogs?* Now that the class is familiar with the task, ask the class to turn around so that they cannot see the lily pads. Place out nine lily pads in a line and line up six frogs. Without the children seeing the lily pads and frogs, ask: *How many lily pads will not have a frog?* Encourage the children to explain their answers. Finally, ask the children to turn around and tell the frogs to find a lily pad. Similarly, with other numbers keeping the difference between 2 and 5.

Notes:

- Because the children turn around so they cannot see the lily pads and frogs, they cannot solve the task by counting the lily pads that don't have a frog.
- This activity is suitable for a large group or a class and requires a large space. If a large space is not available the activity can be acted out on a table.

ACTIVITY IA6.13: Making Ice

Intended learning: To use counting-on or counting-back to solve comparison tasks.

Materials: Collection of small pots or cups, lollipop sticks, screens.

Description: Place out nine small pots in a line and six lollipop sticks in a second line. Cover the collection. Ask: *Do we have enough sticks for the number of lollipops we are going to make?* Ask a child how they came to their answer and allow them to check. Similarly, with other numbers keeping the difference between 2 and 5. The children can work in threes. The first child turns over two numeral cards, the second puts out the number of pots and lollipop sticks and then screens the collection. The third child solves the task. The roles can be interchanged so each child has a chance to solve the task.

Notes:

- When the pots and sticks are screened children cannot solve the task by counting the number of empty pots.
- The range of numbers can be increased to up to 15.

Learning Trajectory

Notes:

- In this chapter, the basic tasks are additive and subtractive tasks involving screened collections.
- Many of the activities described below involve variations of these tasks.
- The first group of activities reviews knowledge of forward and backward number word sequences which is pre-requisite knowledge for additive and subtractive tasks involving screened collections.
- Many of the activities outlined in Chapter 3 can be revisited to review forward and backward number word sequences.

- Teachers should aim to provide tasks that will support learning to count on and count back to solve additive and subtractive tasks rather than using strategies involving counting-from-one.
- Some children might use non-count-by-ones strategies to solve additive and subtractive tasks. These strategies are discussed in Chapter 7.

Table 6.2 Learning Trajectory: Advanced Counting, Addition and Subtraction

Topics	Page Ref.	Assessment Task Groups	Instructional Activities
Forward and backward number word sequences in the range 1 to 100			IA6.1 IA6.2 IA6.6
Additive tasks involving two screened collections	92–94	A6.1	IA6.3 IA6.4
Missing addend tasks involving two screened collections	92–96	A6.2	IA6.8 IA6.9
Removed item tasks involving a screened collection	92–96	A6.3	IA6.5 IA6.7 IA6.9
Missing subtrahend tasks involving a screened collection	92–96	A6.4	IA6.10 IA6.11
Comparative subtraction involving two screened collections	92–96	A6.5	IA6.12 IA6.13
Subtraction with bare numbers	92–96	A6.6	

7
Structuring Numbers 1 to 20

Summary

This chapter extends the focus of Chapter 5 to the topic of structuring numbers in the range 1 to 20. This topic relates to the development and use of non-counting strategies in the range 1 to 20, and provides a crucial basis for the development of mental strategies for addition and subtraction involving 2-digit numbers. This chapter presents new approaches to teaching involving use of materials such as the arithmetic rack or the double ten-frame.

 Key topic: 8.5   Chapter: 4

Topic Overview

In earlier chapters we describe how children's beginning knowledge about adding and subtracting numbers develops in two main strands. One of these concerns the development of counting strategies which culminate in the advanced counting-by-ones strategies, that is, counting-on-from, counting-on-to, counting-back-from and counting-back-to (Chapters 4 and 6). The second strand concerns children's developing abilities to combine and partition numbers without counting, first in the range 1 to 10 (Chapter 5). Children who are fluent at combining and partitioning numbers in the range 1 to 10, are ready to extend this to the range 1 to 20. This is referred to as structuring numbers 1 to 20, and is the focus of this chapter. Further information on instruction related to structuring numbers 1 to 20 is available in Wright et al. (2012) *Developing Number Knowledge: Assessment, Teaching & Intervention with 7–11-year-olds* (see Bibliography).

Using the Arithmetic Rack

The arithmetic rack (Figure 7.1) is a device for teaching children structuring numbers in the range 1 to 20. Ideally, each child has a rack and the teacher has a large rack for use with the whole class or a group of children. Learning with the arithmetic rack involves three main steps:

- making and reading numbers 1 to 20
- adding two numbers
- subtraction involving two numbers.

Double Ten-frame

The double ten-frame (Figure 7.2) is an alternative to the arithmetic rack. The activities described here for the arithmetic rack can be adapted for use with a double ten-frame.

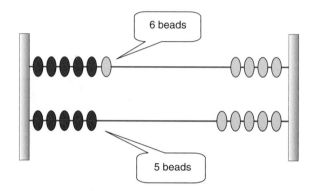

Figure 7.1   Arithmetic rack showing 11

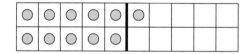

Figure 7.2   Double ten-frame showing 11

Making and Reading Numbers 1 to 20

Children learn to make patterns for the numbers in the following groups: 1 to 5, 6 to 10, 11 to 15, 16 to 20. The goal is for children to be able to make the patterns in one or two quick movements rather than moving beads one at a time. Most patterns can be made in two or three main ways. One way relies on the five and ten structure of the rack and the other relies on the doubles structure. We adopt a convention of, from the child's perspective, starting with all of the beads at the right hand end of the rack and moving the beads to the left to make a pattern. In this way, when one scans from left to right to look at, for example, a five-wise pattern for 11 (see Figure 7.1), the pattern appears as ten and one more rather than one and ten more.

Numbers 1 to 5 on the Rack

The number 1 is made by moving one bead on the upper row to the left. The numbers 2, 3 … 5 are made in two ways. One way involves moving two, three … five beads on the upper row to the left. These are referred to as five-wise patterns. The other way shows each even number as a double and each odd number as a 'near double' (for example, 5 as 3 and 2). In this way 2 is shown as one bead on the upper row and one on the lower row, 3 is two beads on the upper row and one bead on the lower row, and so on. These are referred to as pair-wise patterns.

Numbers 6 to 10 on the Rack

Each of the numbers 6, 7 and 8 is made in three main ways and it is important that children become fluent with these. For example, 7 is made: (a) with seven beads on the upper row (five red and two green) – referred to as a ten-wise pattern; (b) with five beads on the upper row and two beads on the lower row referred to as a five-wise pattern; and (c) as a near double with four beads on the upper row and three on the lower row – referred to as a pair-wise pattern. However, 9 and 10 are made in two main ways: (a) using the upper row only – ten-wise; or (b) using five on the upper row and four or five respectively on the lower row – five-wise/pair-wise.

Numbers 11 to 14 on the Rack

In similar vein, 11 is made in two main ways, and 12 to 14 are made in three main ways and children should also become fluent with these. For example, 13 is made: (a) with ten beads on the upper row and three on the lower row – ten-wise; (b) with eight beads on the upper row and five on the lower row – five-wise; and (c) as a near double with seven beads on the upper row and six on the lower row – pair-wise.

Numbers 15 to 20 on the Rack

The numbers from 15 to 18 are made in two main ways. For example, 16 is made: (a) with ten beads on the upper row and six on the lower row – ten-wise/five-wise; and (b) with eight beads on each row. Finally, 19 and 20 are made with ten beads on the upper row and nine or ten beads respectively, on the lower row.

Interchanging the Rows

Children should also learn that the number of beads on each row can be interchanged. Thus 7, for example, could be made: (a) with seven beads on the lower row; (b) with two beads on the upper row and five beads on the lower row; and (c) as a near double with three beads on the upper row and four on the lower row. Similarly, 13, for example, could be made: (a) with three beads on the upper row and ten on the lower row; (b) with five beads on the upper row and eight on the lower row; and (c) as a near double with six beads on the upper row and seven on the lower row.

Reading Numbers on the Rack

The teacher screens the rack from the children and makes a number. The number is flashed (briefly displayed) and the children's task is to say the number displayed on the rack.

Adding Two Numbers with the Sum in the Range 1 to 20

The rack is used to calculate addition of two numbers in the range 1 to 10. The first addend is made on the upper row and the second addend

Photo 7.1 Adding two numbers on the arithmetic rack

is made on the lower row. Instruction should allow for flexibility in the way children calculate rather than imposing a strict procedure to follow. Children learn that sometimes it is helpful to exchange beads on the upper row for an equal number of beads on the lower row. In other instances they can determine the sum without the need to move any beads. In many instances there are several ways the sum can be determined and children are encouraged to describe a variety of ways.

Doubles: 1 + 1 to 5 + 5

These should be straightforward because the children have already learned the doubles structure of the even numbers. In this case the children begin with the two addends (for example, 3 + 3), and have to realize that this can be regarded as the doubles structure for six.

Five-plus a Number in the Range 1 to 5

For 5 + 3 for example, five beads are moved on the upper row and three on the lower row. Again, this can be regarded alternatively as 5 + 3 and also as 8.

Two Addends in the Range 1 to 5

These additions should be straightforward because the children have already learned to combine and partition numbers in the range 1 to 10, and this familiar knowledge can be consolidated in the context of the arithmetic rack.

Doubles: 6 + 6 to 10 + 10

These additions will be straightforward because the children have learned the doubles structure of the numbers 12, 14, and so on. Thus the children begin with the two addends, for example 7 + 7, and realize that this can be regarded as 7 + 7 and also as 14. Children can also learn to transform these into alternative structures through transformations such as the following:

6 + 6 becomes 10 + 2

7 + 7 becomes 10 + 4

8 + 8 becomes 10 + 6

9 + 9 becomes 10 + 8

Ten-plus a Number in the Range 1 to 10

For 10 + 6 for example, ten beads are moved on the upper row and six on the lower row. The structure can be regarded alternatively as 10 + 6 and 16.

Five-plus an Addend in the Range 6 to 9

For 5 + 8 for example, five beads are moved on the upper row and eight on the lower row. The structure can be regarded alternatively as 5 + 8 and also as 13. For 8 + 5, eight beads are moved on the upper row and five on the lower row. The structure can be regarded alternatively as 8 + 5 and 13.

One Addend in the Range 6 to 9 and One Addend in the Range 1 to 4

Additions of this kind can be solved by transformations such as the following:

6 + 4 becomes 5 + 5 – swap one bead

8 + 3 becomes 10 + 1 – swap two beads

9 + 4 becomes 10 + 3 – swap one bead

7 + 4 becomes 5 + 5 + 1 or 6 + 5 – swap one bead

6 + 2 becomes 5 + 3 – swap one bead

8 + 1 becomes 9 – swap one bead

7 + 3 becomes 5 + 5 – swap two beads

9 + 2 becomes 10 + 1 – swap one bead

8 + 4 becomes 7 + 5 – swap one bead

7 + 2 becomes 5 + 4 – swap two beads, and so on.

Sums which are the commutations (turnarounds) of these can be solved similarly. Thus 4 + 6 is solved similarly to 6 + 4, and so on.

Two Different Addends in the range 6 to 9

Additions of this kind can involve transformations such as the following:

6 + 7 becomes 5 + 5 + 3 or 10 + 3 – swap one bead

8 + 9 becomes 7 + 10 – swap one bead

9 + 6 becomes 10 + 5 – swap one bead

7 + 8 becomes 5 + 5 + 5 or 10 + 5 – swap two beads

6 + 8 becomes 5 + 5 + 4 or 10 + 4 – swap one bead

7 + 9 becomes 6 + 10 – swap one bead

The other six sums of this kind are 7 + 6, 9 + 8, 6 + 9, 8 + 7, 8 + 6 and 9 + 7. Each of these is the commutation (turnaround) of one of those above. Thus 7 + 6 corresponds with 6 + 7, and so on.

One Addend in the Range 11 to 19 and One Addend in the Range 1 to 10

In this case one of the addends is a teen and the sum is 20 or less. Some examples are 14 + 3, 12 + 7, 15 + 4. These are best calculated by linking to the corresponding sum involving two addends in the range 1 to 10. Thus 4 + 3 is used to solve 14 + 3, 2 + 7 is used to solve 12 + 7, and 5 + 4 is used to solve 15 + 4.

Subtraction in the Range 1 to 20

Subtraction using the rack can take the forms of take away, **difference** or adding up. Also, the rack can first be used to consolidate subtraction in the range 1 to 10.

Subtraction with the Minuend Less Than or Equal to 10

Children have already learned to partition numbers in the range 1 to 10. The rack can be used to calculate or show partitions. Partitions in the range 1 to 10 can be calculated in two main ways, using both rows or using the upper row, and so on. Using both rows, partitions of eight can be calculated as follows: make eight using six on the upper row; make eight using three on the upper row, and so on. Using the upper row only, partitions of eight can be shown by moving eight beads to the left, and then partitioning those beads, for example, take two beads away. How many are left?

Subtracting with Minuend in the Range 11 to 20

This includes subtractions such as 11 – 4, 17 – 8, 15 – 7, 12 – 9. In these cases the minuend is in the range 11 to 20 and both the known subtrahend and the unknown difference are less than 10. These subtractions can be thought of in three main ways: take away, finding the difference and adding up.

Subtraction as Take Away

The example 11 – 4 can be calculated as follows: make 11 as ten beads on the upper row and one bead on the lower row. Take away one bead on the lower row and three beads on the upper row. Thus 11 – 4 becomes 11 – 1 – 3 becomes 10 – 3 becomes 7. This is referred to as going through 10. Alternatively, children might use the near doubles structure for 11 of six on the upper row and five on the lower row, then subtract 4 from 5 leaving 1 to add to the 6. Thus 11 – 4 becomes 6 + 5 – 4 becomes 6 + 1 becomes 7.

The example 16 – 7 can be calculated as follows: make 16 as ten beads on the upper row and six beads on the lower row. Take away six beads on the lower row and one bead on the upper row. Thus 16 – 7 becomes 16 – 6 – 1 becomes 10 – 1 becomes 9. As above, this is called going through 10. Alternatively, children might use the doubles structure for 16. Thus 16 – 7 becomes 8 + 8 – 7 becomes 8 + 1 becomes 9.

Subtraction as Finding the Difference

The example 12 – 9 is calculated as follows: make 12 as ten beads on the upper row and two beads on the lower row. Take away two beads on the lower row and one bead on the upper row to leave 9. Thus 12 – 9 is thought of as 12 – □ = 9, and this involves going through 10 (12 – 2 – 1 makes 9).

The example 13 – 8 is calculated as follows: make 13 as ten beads on the upper row and three beads on the lower row. Take away three beads on the lower row and two beads on the upper row to leave 8. Thus 13 – 8 is thought of as 13 – □ = 8. This also involves going through 10 (13 – 3 – 2 makes 8).

Subtraction as Adding Up

The example 15 – 7 is calculated as follows: make 7 as seven beads on the upper row. Calculate $7 + \square = 15$. This might be thought of as $7 + 3 + 5$ makes 15, that is, going through 10. Alternatively a child might think of $7 + 7 + 1$, that is, using the double structure of 14 rather than adding up through 10.

The example 11 – 8 is calculated as follows: make 8 as eight beads on the upper row. Calculate $8 + o = 11$, as $8 + 2 + 1$, that is, going through 10.

Subtraction as Partitioning

As well as the three ways of thinking of subtraction (as just described), any subtraction can also be regarded as partitioning a number when one of the partitions is given. Thus 15 – 7 can be regarded as finding what goes with 7 to make 15. Partitioning in this way can build on partitioning in the range 1 to 10 as described in Chapter 5.

From Using the Rack to Mental Strategies

The above sections describe for addition and subtraction a progression from calculating involving smaller numbers and more familiar structures to that involving larger numbers and less familiar structures. Another important progression is from using the rack to mental strategies. This involves four main steps. For addition, these steps are:

- making both addends on the rack and exchanging beads as necessary
- making the first addend only, and looking at the rack to determine the addition
- making the first addend only, and then screening the rack
- addition without making either addend on the rack and where the rack is removed from the children's view.

For subtraction, these steps are:

- making the minuend on the rack and exchanging beads as necessary to determine the subtraction
- making the minuend only, and looking at the rack to determine the subtraction
- making the minuend only, and then screening the rack
- subtraction without making the minuend on the rack and where the rack is removed from the children's view.

Working Flexibly with Doubles and Near Doubles, and Five and Ten

Children can work towards flexibly using doubles and near doubles, and five and ten for addition and subtraction in the range 1 to 20. Children can also develop awareness of the principle that the order of adding two numbers does not affect the sum of the two numbers ($6 + 8$ can be worked out by adding 6 to 8 or 8 to 6). This is known as the commutativity of addition. Alternatively, addition is **commutative**. This is sometimes referred to as 'turn arounds'.

As indicated earlier there are particular segments of knowledge that children should automatize, in order to develop good facility with addition and subtraction in the range 1 to 20. These are: (a) knowing the doubles from 1 + 1 to 5 + 5; (b) learning the partitions of the numbers from 2 to 5; (c) learning to partition 10 into 9 + 1 and 8 + 2; (d) learning the commutative property; (e) learning the partitions of the numbers from 6 to 10; and (f) learning the doubles from 6 + 6 to 10 + 10.

Instruction should focus on using these segments of knowledge as a basis for addition and subtraction in the range 1 to 20. For example, a child might work out 6 + 7 by partitioning 6 into 5 and 1, and 7 into 5 and 2, and then adding two 5s to 10, and 2 and 1 to 3, making 13 in all. The task of 8 + 9 might involve partitioning 8 and 9 into 5 and 3 and 5 and 4 respectively, and then adding two 5s to make 10, and adding 4 and 3 by adding through 5 to make 7, making 17 in all. The task of 13 − 8 might involve adding 2 to 8 to make 10 and 3 to 10 to make 13, making 5 added in all.

ASSESSMENT TASK GROUPS

List of Assessment Task Groups

A7.1: Naming and Visualizing Pair-Wise Patterns for 1 to 10
A7.2: Naming and Visualizing Five-Wise Patterns for 1 to 10
A7.3: Naming and Visualizing Pair-Wise Patterns for 11 to 20
A7.4: Naming and Visualizing Five-Wise and Ten-Wise Patterns for 11 to 14
A7.5: Naming and Visualizing Ten-Wise Patterns for 15 to 20
A7.6: Addition using Doubles, Fives and Tens – Addends Less than 11
A7.7: Subtraction using Doubles, Fives and Tens – Subtrahend and Difference Less than 11
A7.8: Addition using Doubles, Fives and Tens – One Addend Greater than 10
A7.9: Subtraction using Doubles, Fives and Tens – Subtrahend or Difference Greater than 10

TASK GROUP A7.1: Naming and Visualizing Pair-Wise Patterns for 1 to 10

Materials: Arithmetic rack, screen.

What to do and say: Make a pair-wise pattern for 7 and screen the pattern. *I am going to show you a number on the rack. Tell me what number you see.* Flash the pattern for 7. Similarly for the other numbers.

What does 5 look like on the arithmetic rack when I am building pairs? Can you tell me? What does 5 look like if I try to make it using pairs? Similarly for the other numbers.

Notes:

- These tasks are of the same kind as those in Task Group 5.4.
- On the visualization task, if the child describes a five-wise pattern ask additional questions designed to support them to visualize a pair-wise pattern.
- A double ten-frame structure can be used in place of an arithmetic rack. Using a double ten-frame structure will require a separate ten-frame for each number.
- For 9, the pair-wise pattern and the five-wise pattern using two rows are identical. Similarly for 10.
- As a general rule, the arrangements of numbers on the upper and lower rows can be interchanged. For example, a pair-wise pattern for 7 is made with four on the upper row and might also be made with four on the lower row. To avoid unnecessary complexity here, these are not regarded as distinct forms. At the same time children should experience both of these forms.

TASK GROUP A7.2: Naming and Visualizing Five-Wise Patterns for 1 to 10

Materials: Arithmetic rack, screen.

What to do and say: Using two rows with five on the upper row, make a five-wise pattern for 6 and screen the pattern. *I am going to show you a number on the rack. Tell me what number you see.* Flash the pattern for 6. Similarly for other numbers in the range 1 to 10.

Using the upper row only, make a five-wise pattern for 7. *This time I will use the top row only. What number did you see?* Flash the pattern for 7.

What does 8 look like on the arithmetic rack when I am building fives using two rows? Can you tell me? What does 8 look like if I try to make it using a five? Similarly with the other numbers.

What does 9 look like on the arithmetic rack when I use the upper row only? Similarly with the other numbers.

Notes:

- These tasks are of the same kind as those in Task Group 5.5.
- On the visualization task, if the child describes a pair-wise pattern ask additional questions designed to support them to visualize a five-wise pattern.
- For the numbers from 1 to 5, the five-wise patterns can be made one way only, that is, using the upper row.
- For the numbers from 6 to 10, it is important that children learn both: (a) the five-wise patterns, using five on the upper row, and the remainder on the lower row, and (b) the ten-wise patterns, using the upper row only.
- As a general rule, the arrangements of numbers on the upper and lower rows can be interchanged. For example, a five-wise pattern for 7 is made with five on the upper row and might also be made with five on the lower row. To avoid unnecessary complexity here, these are not regarded as distinct forms. At the same time children should experience both of these forms.

TASK GROUP A7.3: Naming and Visualizing Pair-Wise Patterns for 11 to 20

Photo 7.2   Showing 14 on the arithmetic rack

Photo 7.3   Naming and visualizing pair-wise patterns for 11–20

Materials: Arithmetic rack, screen.

What to do and say: Make a pair-wise pattern for 15 and screen the pattern. *I am going to show you a number on the rack. Tell me what number you see.* Flash the pattern for 15. Similarly for other numbers in the range 11 to 20.

What does 12 look like on the arithmetic rack when I am building pairs? Can you tell me? Similarly with the other numbers in the range 11 to 20.

Notes:

- Refer to the notes for Task Group A7.1 above.
- For 19, the pair-wise, five-wise and ten-wise patterns are identical. Similarly for 20.

TASK GROUP A7.4: Naming and Visualizing Five-Wise and Ten-Wise Patterns for 11 to 14

Materials: Arithmetic rack, screen.

What to do and say: Using two rows with seven on the upper row and five on the lower row, make a five-wise pattern for 12 and screen the pattern. *I am going to show you a number on the rack. Tell me what number you see.* Flash the pattern for 12. Similarly for 11, 13 and 14.

Using two rows with ten on the upper row and three on the lower row, make a ten-wise pattern for 13 and screen the pattern. *I am going to show you a number on the rack. Tell me what number you see.* Flash the pattern for 13. Similarly for 11, 12 and 14.

What does 14 look like on the arithmetic rack when I am building fives using two rows? Can you tell me? What does 14 look like if I try to make it using fives? Similarly for 11, 12 and 13.

What does 11 look like on the arithmetic rack when I use ten on the upper row? Similarly for 12, 13 and 14.

Notes:

- Refer to the notes for Task Group A7.2 above.
- For the numbers from 11 to 14, it is important that children learn: (a) the five-wise patterns (five only on the lower row); and (b) the ten-wise patterns (ten on the upper row).

Task Group A7.5: Naming and Visualizing Ten-Wise Patterns for 15 to 20

Materials: Arithmetic rack, screen.

What to do and say: Using ten on the upper row, make a ten-wise pattern for 18 and screen the pattern. *I am going to show you a number on the rack. Tell me what number you see.* Flash the pattern for 18. Similarly for the other numbers.

What does 16 look like on the arithmetic rack when I use ten on the upper row? Similarly for the other numbers.

Note:

- For the numbers from 15 to 20, the five-wise patterns and the ten-wise patterns take the same form. Nevertheless, these patterns can be described both in terms of their ten structure: 16 has ten and six, and their five structure: 16 has three fives and one.

TASK GROUP A7.6: Addition Using Doubles, Fives and Tens – Addends Less than 11

Materials: Arithmetic rack, screen, addition tasks written on a card in horizontal format (one card for each task).

What to do and say: Using the upper row, make a five-wise structure for 9. Flash the structure. *What number did you see?* Display the following task on a card: 9 + 3. *Use the rack to work this out. How did you do it?*

Using the upper row, make a five-wise structure for 7. Flash the structure. *What number did you see?* Display the following task on a card: 7 + 5. *Use the rack to work this out. How did you do it?*

Make a pair-wise structure for 8. Flash the structure. *What number did you see?* Display the following task on a card: 8 + 6. *Use the rack to work this out. How did you do it?*

Similarly with additions such as: 9 + 2, 4 + 7, 10 + 3, 5 + 9, and so on.

Notes:

- Children are likely to work flexibly with pair-wise, five-wise and other patterns.
- It is important to listen carefully to the child's explanation and to temper expectations that the child should use a particular strategy or pattern.

TASK GROUP A7.7: Subtraction Using Doubles, Fives and Tens – Subtrahend and Difference Less than 11

Materials: Arithmetic rack, screen, subtraction and missing addend tasks written on a card in horizontal format. One card for each task.

What to do and say: Make a ten-wise structure for 14. Flash the structure. *What number did you see?* Display the following task on a card: 14 – 5. *Use the rack to work this out. How did you do it?*

Make a five-wise structure for 12. Flash the structure. *What number did you see?* Display the following task on a card: 12 – 7. *Use the rack to work this out. How did you do it?*

Make a pair-wise structure for 17. Flash the structure. *What number did you see?* Display the following task on a card: 17 – 8. *Use the rack to work this out. How did you do it?*

Make a five-wise structure for 8. Flash the structure. *What number did you see?* Display the following task on a card: 8 + ☐ = 11. *Use the rack to work this out. How did you do it?*

Make a five-wise structure for 6. Flash the structure. *What number did you see?* Display the following task on a card: 6 + ☐ = 15. *Use the rack to work this out. How did you do it?*

Make a pair-wise structure for 8. Flash the structure. *What number did you see?* Display the following task on a card 8 + ☐ = 12. *Use the rack to work this out. How did you do it?*

Similarly with other subtraction and missing addend tasks.

Note:

• The notes for Task Group A7.6 are also relevant to this task group. In the case of subtraction and missing addend tasks, children are likely to use a relatively wide range of strategies.

TASK GROUP A7.8: Addition Using Doubles, Fives and Tens – One Addend Greater than 10

Materials: Arithmetic rack, screen, addition tasks written on a card in horizontal format. One card for each task.

What to do and say: Make a ten-wise structure for 11. Flash the structure. *What number did you see?* Display the following task on a card: 11 + 3. *Use the rack to work this out. How did you do it?*

Make a five-wise structure for 14. Flash the structure. *What number did you see?* Display the following task on a card: 14 + 5. *Use the rack to work this out. How did you do it?*

Make a pair-wise structure for 12. Flash the structure. *What number did you see?* Display the following task on a card: 12 + 7. *Use the rack to work this out. How did you do it?*

Similarly with additions such as: 16 + 2, 13 + 4, 17 + 3, and so on.

Notes:

- The notes for Task Group A7.6 are also relevant to this task group.
- Children might use a known sum in the range 1 to 10. For example, 4 + 4 is used to work out 14 + 4.

TASK GROUP A7.9: Subtraction Using Doubles, Fives and Tens – Subtrahend or Difference Greater than 10

Materials: Arithmetic rack, screen, subtraction and missing addend tasks written on a card in horizontal format. One card for each task.

What to do and say: Make a ten-wise structure for 19. Flash the structure. *What number did you see?* Display the following task on a card: 19 – 5. *Use the rack to work this out. How did you do it?*

Make a five-wise structure for 13. Flash the structure. *What number did you see?* Display the following task on a card: 13 – 2. *Use the rack to work this out. How did you do it?*

Make a pair-wise structure for 16. Flash the structure. *What number did you see?* Display the following task on a card: 16 – 3. *Use the rack to work this out. How did you do it?*

Make a ten-wise structure for 11. Flash the structure. *What number did you see?* Display the following task on a card: 11 + *o* = 16. *Use the rack to work this out. How did you do it?*

Make a five-wise structure for 12. Flash the structure. *What number did you see?* Display the following task on a card: 12 + *o* = 19. *Use the rack to work this out. How did you do it?*

Make a pair-wise structure for 14. Flash the structure. *What number did you see?* Display the following task on a card: 14 + *o* = 18. *Use the rack to work this out. How did you do it?*

Similarly with other subtraction and missing addend tasks.

Notes:

- The notes for Task Groups A7.6 and A7.7 are also relevant to this task group.
- Children might use a known difference in the range 1 to 10. For example, 6 – 3 is used to work out 16 – 3.

INSTRUCTIONAL ACTIVITIES

List of Instructional Activities

IA7.1: Double Decker Bus Flashes
IA7.2: Getting On and Off the Bus
IA7.3: Dot Snap
IA7.4: Making Combinations to Twenty Fish

IA7.5: Using Ten-Plus Combinations
IA7.6: Five and Ten Game
IA7.7: Chocolate Boxes
IA7.8: Double Ten-Frame Facts
IA7.9: Bead Board
IA7.10: Clear the Board

ACTIVITY IA7.1: Double Decker Bus Flashes

Intended learning: To learn addition in the range 1 to 20.

Materials: Image projector with a double ten bus, children's double ten buses, counters (each set of 20 should be of one color).

Description: An empty bus is displayed on an image projector (see Figure 7.3). The class is asked what they observe. The purpose is for them to see that the upper and lower rows each have ten windows. There is a heavier line after the fifth window in both upper and lower rows. Examples of activities:

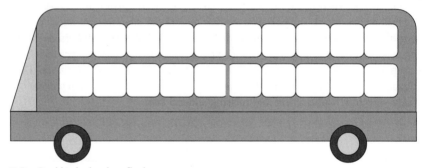

Figure 7.3   Double decker bus flashes

- Doubles combinations are flashed (for example, 4 on the upper row and 4 on the lower row).
- Ten-plus combinations are flashed (for example, 10 on the lower row and 3 on upper row). Children are asked how many people are on the bus?
- Pairs of children are given a bus and 20 counters. They are asked to show numbers of people on the bus. After each task, the teacher asks each pair to explain how the people were arranged on their bus.
- How many ways can 12 people be arranged on the bus? Have the children list their results.

To emphasize the ten-plus combinations the teacher could indicate that the driver always likes the lower row filled before people are allowed upstairs to the upper row. Using this idea, give these tasks:

- Ask each pair to show arrangements of between 10 and 20 people (for example, 16 would be 10 and 6).
- Ask each pair to seat between 10 and 20 people on the bus. Discuss these arrangements. Now have each pair change the counters to show a ten-plus combination (that is, fill the lower row first).

Notes:

- It is important to discuss the combinations made by the children.
- The ten-plus combinations help to build knowledge of the ten and ones aspect of teen numbers.

ACTIVITY IA7.2: Getting On and Off the Bus

Intended learning: To learn addition and subtraction in the range 1 to 20.

Materials: Image projector with a double ten bus, children's double ten buses, counters (each set of 20 should be one color).

Description: Using an image projector, demonstrate people getting on the bus. For example: *There are 9 people on the bus. If another 4 get on, how many will there be altogether?* Discuss the different ways of working this out. When the children are familiar with these tasks, modify the task by briefly displaying and then screening the projection – the bus has gone behind a building (Figure 7.4). Similarly with people getting off the bus.

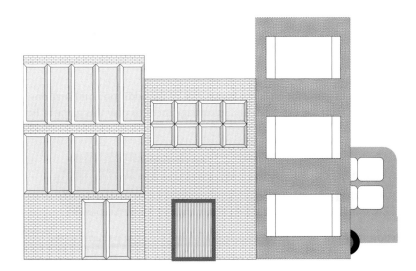

Figure 7.4   Getting on and off the bus (screened)

Note:

- This is an excellent setting to emphasize adding and subtracting through ten. For example 8 + 5. Two more are needed to make up 10 (the lower row is filled), leaving 3 more to go upstairs (10 and 3) making a total of 13.

ACTIVITY IA7.3: Dot Snap

Intended learning: To learn addition in the range 1 to 20.

Materials: Double ten dot cards, numeral cards 10 to 20.

Description: This is played the same as the traditional game known as Snap. Double ten dot cards are used instead of playing cards or numeral cards. A mixture of dot and numeral cards could be used (Figure 7.5). A stack of cards is shuffled and divided between two players who take turns to place their top card face up in the middle. If this card matches the card already showing on the growing center stack, the players try to be the first to put their hand on the stack and call *Snap!* The player who does this, gets all the cards in the stack. The game proceeds until one player has all of the cards.

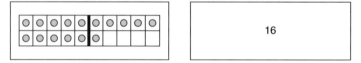

Figure 7.5   Double ten cards and numeral cards

Notes:

- This is an excellent game for building knowledge of the addition combinations to 20.
- Provide children with a set of cards and encourage them to play this game at home.

ACTIVITY IA7.4: Making Combinations to Twenty Fish

Intended learning: To visualize pairs-wise, five-wise and ten-wise patterns in the range 10 to 20.

Materials: At least two sets of pair-wise, five-wise and ten-wise pattern cards 10 to 20, other pattern cards as required.

Description: The activity is played the same as the game known as Fish. Instead of traditional playing cards, dot pattern cards for numbers in the range 10 to 20 are used. Five cards are dealt to each player. The remaining cards are placed in a stack in the center of the players. Players try to make matching pairs of cards, for example a double 8 with a 10 + 6 as displayed in Figure 7.6.

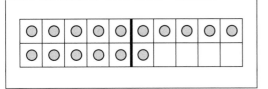 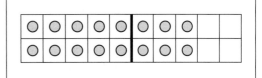

Figure 7.6 Making combinations to Twenty Fish (1)

Players take turns to ask another player for a particular card. If the player being asked does not have the required card they say *Fish!* The player seeking the card takes the top card off the stack. The game continues until one player has no more cards. Players count to see how many pairs they have.

Notes:

- Numeral cards could also be used and matched with the dot pattern cards.
- Cards displaying combinations like 9 dots and 6 dots (see Figure 7.7) also could be used.
- As a variation, players could form sets of three cards instead of pairs.

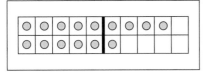 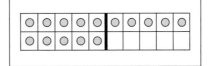

Figure 7.7 Making combinations to Twenty Fish (2)

ACTIVITY IA7.5: Using Ten-Plus Combinations

Intended learning: To use ten-plus combinations to solve other additions.

Materials: Bus and counters for the image projector, children's bus sheets (as shown above in Figures 7.8 and 7.9).

Description: The teacher displays a nine-plus combination using a double ten bus with an image projector, for example, nine on the lower row and six on the upper row (see Figure 7.8).

How many are on the bus? What happens if one person comes down from the upper row to fill the vacant seat on the lower row? How many are on the bus now?

Other upper and lower bus combinations are used. The children note these on a sheet (Figure 7.9) and change them to ten-plus combinations.

Figure 7.8   How many on the bus?

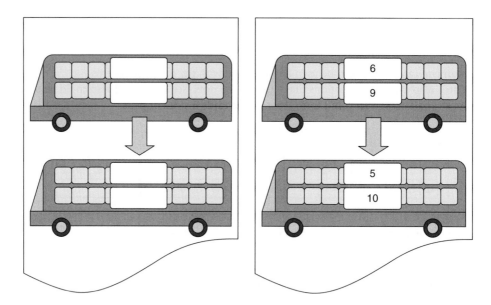

Figure 7.9   Ten-plus combinations

Note:

- As children become familiar with this task, try giving the combinations verbally without using the bus.

ACTIVITY IA7.6: Five and Ten Game

Intended learning: To solve addition tasks involving five and ten.

Materials: A five and ten die and a one to six (traditional) die, game sheet.

Description: Players take turns to: (a) roll the five and ten die (for example, a 10 is face up) and write the number rolled on the game sheet; (b) roll the one to six die (for example, a 4 is face up) and write this number on the game sheet; and (c) add these two numbers and put the answer on the game sheet (Figure 7.10). The game progresses until the game sheet is full.

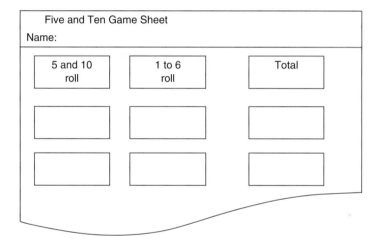

Figure 7.10   Five and Ten game sheet

Notes:

- This activity is suitable for pairs or individuals.
- The die can have five and ten dot patterns and numerals as children become more proficient.
- This activity can be extended to any decuple (20, 30, etc.) or centuple (100, 200, etc.).

ACTIVITY IA7.7: Chocolate Boxes

Intended learning: Using ten to solve additions involving eight and nine.

Materials: Green and blue chocolate box cards (seen in Figure 7.12), die (if required).

Description: Initially the teacher displays a double ten chocolate box on an image projector (see Figure 7.11).

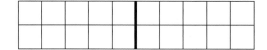

Figure 7.11   Chocolate box

Children are asked: *How many squares?* The dark line demarcating the fives can be indicated. Some chocolates (counters) can be put in the box in a variety of arrangements and the children are asked to tell how many chocolates and how many empty spaces, and so on.

Cards like those illustrated in Figure 7.12 are made up and used to play this game. Players take turns to: (a) select a card from the blue stack (8 and 9 combinations); (b) select a card from the green stack showing 1 to 6 dots (or roll a one to six die); and (c) add the two numbers by making a ten in the chocolate box. The other player can check the answer using a chocolate box and counters if required. If correct, the player keeps these cards. If incorrect, the cards are placed at the bottom of their stacks. When the activity is finished, the players count to see how many cards they have.

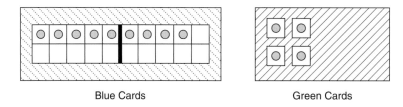

Blue Cards   Green Cards

Figure 7.12   Chocolate box cards

Notes:

- This activity is suitable for pairs.
- It can be used as a whole-class activity by arranging children into pairs, with each pair playing the game.
- After the game is finished, see if children can solve these additions without using the cards: *What is nine and four? What is eight and six?*

ACTIVITY IA7.8: Double Ten-Frame Facts

Intended learning: To use spatial arrangements involving fives, tens and doubles to work out addition facts to 20.

Materials: Double ten-frame cards.

Description: Double ten-frame cards with dots in some of the cells (Figure 7.13) are flashed to the class. The teacher asks: *How many dots in the upper row? How many dots in the lower row? How many dots altogether? How many more dots to make 20?*

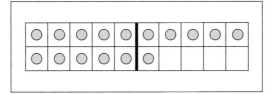

Figure 7.13   Double ten-frame patterns

Notes:

- Double ten-frame cards can be used in the same ways as traditional flash cards.
- This activity is suitable for whole class or small groups. Children can work in pairs on this activity.
- Ten-frame cards with a full ten are easier for children.
- A good idea is to work with particular subsets of ten-frame cards, for example, cards with doubles, cards with nine on the upper row, cards with eight on the upper row.
- The correct responses to the four questions can be written on the back of each card so that children can monitor the responses of others.

ACTIVITY IA7.9: Bead Board

Intended learning: To use five and ten as reference points in arithmetical situations.

Materials: Ten bead board.

Description: The bead board (Figure 7.14) is a small, inexpensive version of the arithmetic rack. This setting provides structure for numbers to 20 with an emphasis on references to five

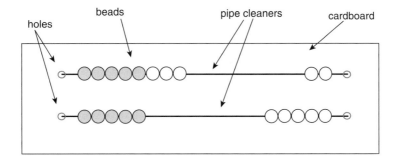

Bead board

Figure 7.14   Bead board

and ten. The bead board can be used for a variety of activities. Children can be asked to name numbers displayed on the bead board or, conversely, children can be asked to display numbers on the bead board. Children can use the bead board to solve additive and subtractive tasks, and to investigate number relationships, such as commutativity and the inverse relationship between addition and subtraction.

Notes:

- Bead boards can be provided to children for specific tasks.
- Bead boards could be accessible for children, as needed.
- To make a bead board, string beads in two colors onto pipe cleaners, slip pipe cleaners into slits in a rectangle of matte board and twist together in the back.

ACTIVITY IA7.10: Clear the Board

A VIDEO
DEMONSTRATING
THIS ACTIVITY
CAN BE ACCESSED
ONLINE AT WWW.
SAGEPUB.CO.UK/
WRIGHTTNC

Intended learning: To learn the addition combinations to 12.

Materials: Clear the Board sheet, counters (the number is decided by the teacher), two dice.

Description: This activity is suitable for whole class, groups or pairs. Each player has ten counters (number can be varied) and a Clear the Board sheet. Players place all of their counters anywhere on the board (no more than four can be placed in any one column). Players in turn roll the two dice adding the numbers together to give a total (for example if a 3 and a 5 are rolled, the total is 8). If a player has counters in a column (e.g. the 8 column), one counter is removed from the column. The next player then has a turn. The game proceeds until a player has removed all the counters from their board.

Notes:

- This game supports children in learning to partition numbers.
- Using traditional dice supports children in learning to identify the dot patterns.

Clear the Board sheet

2	3	4	5	6	7	8	9	10	11	12

Figure 7.15 Clear the Board sheet

Learning Trajectories

Notes:

- Addition and subtraction are presented as separate learning trajectories. This is not intended to indicate that the whole trajectory for addition should be completed before starting the trajectory for subtraction. Rather, each topic in the addition trajectory should be followed as soon as possible by the corresponding topic in the subtraction trajectory.
- These activities mainly involve using the arithmetic rack setting.
- As stated in the Chapter 7 Topic Overview, a double ten-frame can be used in place of the arithmetic rack.
- The notes in the Chapter 7 Topic Overview and the Assessment Task Groups are particularly useful for developing instructional tasks and activities for this topic.
- Many of the Instructional Activities in Chapter 5 involving card games (Fish, Snap, Memory) can be adapted for the range 1 to 20 in this chapter.
- The link between addition and subtraction can be reinforced by giving the related subtraction task after an addition task. For example, after $10 + 4$, give $14 - 4$.

Table 7.1 Learning Trajectory: Structuring Numbers 1 to 20 – Addition

Topics	Page Ref.	Assessment Task Groups	Instructional Activities
Introducing the Arithmetic Rack and/or Double Ten Frame	111–115		IA7.1 IA7.9 IA7.10
Making and reading numbers 1 to 5 on the AR/DTF	111–115	A7.1 A7.2	IA7.1 IA7.3
Making and reading numbers 6 to 10 on the AR/DTF	111–115	A7.1 A7.2	IA7.1 IA7.3
Making and reading numbers 11 to 14 on the AR/DTF	111–115	A7.3 A7.4	IA7.1 IA7.3
Making and reading numbers 15 to 20 on the AR/DTF	111–115	A7.3 A7.4	IA7.1 IA7.3
Doubles $1 + 1$ to $5 + 5$	111–115	A7.1	IA7.3 IA5.4, IA5.8 Modify the cards
Five plus a number	111–115	A7.2	IA7.3 IA5.4, IA5.8 Modify the cards
Two addends in range 1 to 5	111–115		IA7.3 IA5.4, IA5.8 Modify the cards
Doubles $6 + 6$ to $10 + 10$	111–115	A7.3	IA7.3 IA7.4 IA5.4, IA5.8 Modify the cards

(Continued)

Table 7.1   (Continued)

Topics	Page Ref.	Assessment Task Groups	Instructional Activities
Using 5 when adding	111–115		IA7.2
		A7.2	IA7.3
			IA5.4, IA5.8 Modify the cards
			IA7.6
Near 10 additions	111–115		IA7.7
Two addends in range 1 to 10	111–115	A7.6	IA7.3
			IA7.4
			IA7.8
Working flexibly with doubles and near doubles	111–115	A7.6 A7.8	IA5.4, IA5.8 Use cards with numerals 1 to 10
Additions to 20		A7.6 A7.8	IA7.3 IA7.4 IA7.8
Progressing from the arithmetic rack to mental strategies for addition	111–115		

Table 7.2   Learning Trajectory: Structuring Numbers 1 to 20 – Subtraction

Topic	Page Ref.	Assessment Task Groups	Instructional Activities
Using the arithmetic rack to review partitions	116–118	A7.1 A7.2 A7.3 A7.4	IA7.1 Use an arithmetic rack or double ten bus
Take away subtraction tasks	116–118	A7.7 A7.9	IA7.2 Getting off the bus
Missing addend and missing subtrahend tasks	116–118	A7.7 A7.9	IA7.2 IA7.4 Modify the cards
Working flexibly with doubles and near doubles	116–118	A7.7 A7.9	IA7.3 IA7.4
Using addition knowledge to solve subtraction tasks	116–118	A7.7 A7.9	IA7.2
Progressing from the arithmetic rack to mental strategies for addition and subtraction	116–118		IA7.3 IA7.4

8

Two-digit Addition and Subtraction: Jump Strategies

Summary

This chapter focuses on the development of a range of strategies which are referred to as jump strategies – in the case of addition, the child begins from one addend and goes forward in jumps of tens and ones accordingly to the second addend. The chapter includes detailed descriptions of approaches to the development of these strategies for addition and subtraction. The topic of conceptual place value (see Chapter 2) is apposite to this chapter.

 Key topics: 8.3, 8.4, 9.1, 9.2, 9.5   Chapters: 5, 6

Topic Overview

Chapter 7 focuses on the development in children of a range of flexible strategies for addition and subtraction in the range 1 to 20. We refer to these as non-count-by-ones strategies and they are also known as grouping strategies. The emphasis is on procedures that do not involve counting-by-ones. Included among these are strategies in which 5 or 10 is used as a reference point, strategies involving doubles, and strategies involving various ways of partitioning numbers. Chapter 6 refers to extending the use of advanced counting-by-ones strategies in the range of 20 to 100, keeping in mind that this should involve counting in the range 2 to 5 only. Children who have developed facile non-count-by-ones strategies for adding and subtracting in the range 1 to 20, and who can use the advanced counting-by-ones strategies in the range 1 to 100, are ready to develop mental strategies for addition and subtraction involving two 2-digit numbers.

In Chapter 2 we describe two different kinds of mental strategies used by children when adding or subtracting two 2-digit numbers. These kinds of strategies are referred to as jump and split. In the rest of this chapter we provide an overview of an approach that fosters the development of jump strategies. Chapter 9 focuses on an approach that fosters the development of split strategies. We take the view that instruction can focus on one or both of these approaches, and that the focus on jump strategies can precede the focus on split strategies or vice versa. Further information on instruction related to jump strategies is available in Wright et al. (2012) *Developing Number Knowledge: Assessment, Teaching & Intervention with 7–11-year-olds* (see Bibliography).

Fostering the Development of Jump Strategies

As described in Chapter 2, in the case of addition, jump strategies involve working from one of the numbers and partitioning the second in order to make several jumps forward. In the case of subtraction, jump strategies involve making several jumps backward or alternatively, jumping forward from the smaller number to the larger, and keeping track to work out the total jump. Jump strategies have the advantage that they are not significantly more difficult to use when the addition of the numbers in the ones exceeds nine. For example, working out 26 + 38 is not necessarily much more difficult than working out 26 + 32. Being facile with addition and subtraction in the range 1 to 20 is a prerequisite for learning jump strategies. Thus, children learning to use jump strategies should not be limited to strategies involving counting-by-ones and should not incorporate counting-by-ones into their developing jump strategies.

The reader is invited to work out the following examples using a jump strategy:

33 + 21	56 + 23	46 + 38	37 + 43
47 – 11	86 – 24	92 – 83	63 – 37

The Role of the Empty Number Line

The empty number line is an instructional device that is regarded as particularly suited to fostering the development of jump strategies. Children use the ENL to make a written record that serves to summarize their particular strategy. In this way children make a record for themselves, for future reference, about how they solved particular tasks. Also, children can use an ENL in this way to communicate their method to their colleagues and the teacher. Recording strategies in this way is referred to as 'notating'. Examples of the use of the ENL to notate jump strategies are provided in Figure 8.1.

Other Means of Notating Jump Strategies

Two other means of notating jump strategies are arrow notation and horizontal number sentences. The use of arrow notation is shown in the section later in this chapter headed 'Fostering the Development of a Range of Strategies'. Using horizontal number sentences involves writing a horizontal number sentence to describe each step in the strategy. A significant strength of notating with horizontal number sentences is that it can be used for virtually any strategy. This is discussed further in Chapter 9.

ENL as a Notating Device versus ENL as a Means of Solving a Task

The view taken in this book is that the most productive way for children to use the ENL is as a means of notating a mental strategy. Therefore, children should be strongly encouraged to solve tasks mentally, write their answers, and finally to use the ENL to notate their method. This contrasts with the use of the ENL in a procedural way to solve the task. This approach is problematic, we believe, because children will develop a reliance on using the ENL to solve addition and subtraction tasks. The important goal for children is the development of flexible mental strategies. The goal is not to develop an alternative written method for solving addition and subtraction tasks.

Alternative Means of Notating for Split Strategies

Although this chapter focuses on jump strategies and the use of the ENL for notating jump strategies, teachers should be particularly mindful that, in spite of instruction aimed at fostering jump strategies, children might sometimes use a split strategy and a few children might have a continuing, strong preference for split strategies. As a general rule, it is not productive to use an ENL to notate a split strategy. The alternative is

Photo 8.1   Notating a jump strategy

to use horizontal number sentences or branching notation to notate the child's strategy. Notating split strategies in these ways is described in Chapter 9.

Jump versus Split

Becoming facile with jump strategies is particularly useful because jump strategies tend to be more versatile and flexible than split strategies. This relates in part to the point made above, that is, that some children will find split strategies difficult in cases where the combination (addition or subtraction) in the ones is beyond the range 1 to 10, that is, calculations that, in terms of the traditional algorithm, involve **regrouping** (carrying) in the case of addition, or regrouping (renaming, borrowing) in the case of subtraction. It is quite common for children who mainly develop and use split strategies to have particular difficulty when they first encounter subtraction with regrouping. What typically happens in the case of these children is that they do the following: $62 - 25$: $60 - 20 = 40$; $5 - 2 = 3$; answer 43.

Some Children's Initial Preference for Split Strategies

Children who have difficulty with mental strategies will tend to find the initial split strategy easier to use than the corresponding jump strategy. Thus a child having general difficulty with this topic, when working out $43 + 35$, for example, will probably find it easier to use a split strategy than a jump strategy. One reason for this is that using a jump strategy involves incrementing (for addition) or decrementing (for subtraction) off the decuple (a multiple of 10 such as 10, 20, 30 …). Thus a child might have difficulty using a jump strategy to work out $47 + 32$ because they have difficulty with saying, for example, 47, 57, 67, 77, and simultaneously keeping track of the increments. In order to stop at 77, it is necessary to monitor the increments of ten, and to realize that three increments have been made (corresponding to adding 30 to 47). Instruction focusing on incrementing and decrementing 2-digit numbers on and off the decuple is described below. This topic, and the topic of learning to add and subtract through a decuple, constitute important building blocks for the development of jump strategies.

53 + 36

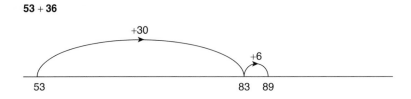

38 + 24

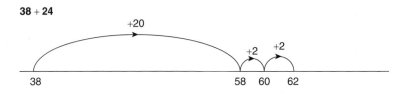

87 – 22

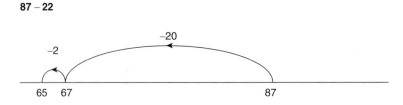

64 – 27

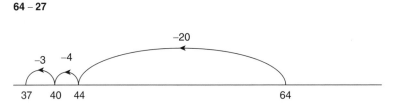

Figure 8.1 Using the empty number line to record strategies

Learning to Add and Subtract through a Decuple

Children who are facile at adding and subtracting in the range 1 to 20 are ready to extend this to the range 1 to 100. Learning to add and subtract through a decuple is an important initial step for addition and subtraction involving two 2-digit numbers. The following are two groups of tasks related to this topic, which are important because they can constitute one or more steps of the jump strategy.

Adding and Subtracting Involving a Decuple and a Number from 1 to 9

This includes cases such as:

a) 60 + 5, 40 + 6. For example, 60 + 5 might arise as the final step when using a jump strategy to work out 38 + 27.

b) 52 − *o* = 50, 74 − *o* = 70. For example, 74 − □ = 70 might arise as an interim step when using a jump strategy to work out 94 − 26.

c) 27 + *o* = 30, 58 + *o* = 60. For example, 58 + □ = 60 might arise as an interim step when using a jump strategy to work out 38 + 27.

d) 80 − 6, 50 − 5. For example, 50 − 5 might arise as the final step when using a jump strategy to work out 72 − 27.

Adding and Subtracting Involving a Non-decuple and a Number from 1 to 9

This includes cases such as:

a) 62 + 5, 43 + 6. For example, 62 + 5 might arise as the final step when using a jump strategy to work out 32 + 35.

b) 56 − 3, 48 − 5. For example, 48 − 5 might arise as the final step when using a jump strategy to work out 98 − 55.

c) 67 + 8, 88 + 4. For example, 88 + 4 might arise as the final step when using a jump strategy to work out 68 + 24.

d) 53 − 6, 41 − 5. For example, 41 − 5 might arise as the final step when using a jump strategy to work out 71 − 35.

Learning to Increment and Decrement 2-digit Numbers

Learning to increment and decrement 2-digit numbers by 10 is an important first step in developing strategies for addition and subtraction involving 2-digit numbers. This topic consists of two main steps. These are incrementing and decrementing on the decuple and incrementing and decrementing off the decuple. The decuples are the numbers 10, 20, 30, ..., that is, the multiples of 10.

Incrementing and Decrementing on the Decuple

Incrementing by 10 on the decuple involves being able to say immediately the number that is 10 more than a given decuple. This corresponds with being able to say the next highest decuple after a given decuple. Similarly, decrementing by 10 on the decuple corresponds to saying the next lowest decuple.

Incrementing and Decrementing off the Decuple

Incrementing by 10 off the decuple refers to incrementing a non-decuple by 10, that is, saying immediately the number that is 10 more than a given non-decuple; for example, saying immediately the number that is 10 more than 72 (82). Similarly, an example of decrementing off the decuple is to say immediately the number that is 10 less than 47 (37).

Incrementing and Decrementing versus Counting-by-ones

While the tasks of incrementing and decrementing on and off the decuple seem rather trivial and easily learned, significant numbers of children in the middle and upper elementary years and beyond seem unable to do these, at least in the context of trying to solve 2-digit addition and subtraction tasks, and to solve these mentally rather than use a standard written method, that is, a standard algorithm. Children who might be expected to increment or decrement by 10, and cannot do so, typically will use counting-on or counting-back by ones to solve the task in question. For example, to work out what is 10 more than 72, they will count-on from 72 and keep track of their counts, and stop when they have made 10 counts, that is, they will stop at 82.

Incrementing and Decrementing by Several Tens

Children who can increment or decrement by 10 can easily extend this to incrementing or decrementing by several tens; that is, they can learn to work out, for example, 54 and three more tens or 54 and 30 more. Instructional strategies for children to learn to increment and decrement by 10 and by several tens are based on the use of one or more of the materials commonly used as a basis for learning about 2-digit numbers, such as ten-strips or **bundling sticks**.

Incrementing and Decrementing Flexibly by Tens and Ones

Children should also learn to increment and decrement flexibly by tens and ones. As an example of incrementing, the child might start from 14 and add 10, then add 15 to the answer, add 32 to that answer, and so on. As an example of decrementing, the child might start from 96 and take 10, then take 13 from the answer, then take 25 from the answer, and so on. Tasks of this kind can be presented initially using ten-strips. This can progress to tasks presented verbally or in written form without the use of materials such as ten-strips.

Fostering the Development of a Range of Strategies

Over a series of lessons where children are encouraged to use jump and split strategies (see Chapter 9), the children can develop to the point where they can flexibly use either strategy according to their own particular preference. This can also involve development and use of a range of mental strategies. The following are some of the other strategies children frequently use. Many of these are quite similar to jump strategies. Also, except for the strategies involving transforming (see below), these can also be notated on an ENL.

Split-jump for Addition

The first step of this strategy involves splitting and working with the tens part of each number, the second step involves adding on the ones part of one number and finally adding on the ones part of the other number.

37 + 45: 30 + 40 is → 70, 70 + 7 → 77, 77 + 3 → 80, 80 + 2 → 82.

Split-jump for Subtraction

Again, the first step of this strategy involves splitting and working with the tens part of each number, the second step involves adding on the ones part of the minuend. Finally, the ones part of one subtrahend is subtracted.

75 − 26: 70 − 20 → 50, 50 + 5 → 55, 55 − 5 → 50, 50 − 1 → 49

Subtraction by Adding Up

This involves starting from the subtrahend, adding numbers until the minuend is reached, and keeping track of the numbers added.

63 − 48: 48 + 10 → 58, 58 + 2 → 60, 60 + 3 → 63, making 15 in all.

Addition by Jumping to 10

38 + 47: 38 + 2 → 40, 40 + 40 → 80, 80 + 5 → 85

Subtraction by Jumping to 10

64 − 49: 64 − 4 → 60, 60 − 40 → 20, 20 − 5 → 15

Addition by Transforming

48 + 27: transform to 50 + 25

Subtraction by Transforming

96 − 39: transform to 97 − 40

Addition by Compensation

24 + 49: 24 + 49 → 24 + 50 − 1, that is, 74 − 1 → 73

Subtraction by Compensation

73 − 48: 73 − 48 → 73 − 50 + 2 → 23 + 2 → 25

ASSESSMENT TASK GROUPS

List of Assessment Task Groups

A8.1: Forward and Backward Number Word Sequences by Tens, on and off the Decuple
A8.2: Adding from a Decuple and Subtracting to a Decuple
A8.3: Adding to a Decuple and Subtracting from a Decuple
A8.4: Incrementing and Decrementing by Tens on and off the Decuple
A8.5: Incrementing Flexibly by Tens and Ones
A8.6: Adding Tens to a 2-Digit Number and Subtracting Tens from a 2-Digit Number
A8.7: Adding Two 2-Digit Numbers without and with Regrouping
A8.8: Subtraction Involving Two 2-Digit Numbers without and with Regrouping
A8.9: Addition and Subtraction using Transforming, Compensating and Other Strategies

TASK GROUP A8.1: Forward and Backward Number Word Sequences by Tens, on and off the Decuple

Materials: None.

What to do and say: On the decuple: *Count by ten. Start from 90 and go backwards.* Off the decuple: *Start from 24 and count by tens. Start from 97 and go backwards by tens.*

Notes:

- If the child has difficulty, say the first two or three number words. For example: *Count by tens – 10, 20, ... ? Start from 24. From 34.*
- In the case of saying the forward sequence off the decuple, the first three words (four, fourteen, twenty-four) can be difficult for children because there is not a simple verbal pattern compared with twenty-four, thirty-four, forty-four.
- These tasks differ from those in Task Group A8.4 because in Task Group A8.4 the children are incrementing and decrementing in the context of base-ten materials.
- Developing facility with these tasks is important for the development of jump strategies for addition and subtraction involving two 2-digit numbers.

Task Group A8.2: Adding from a Decuple and Subtracting to a Decuple

Materials: Writing paper and pens/pencils.

What to do and say: Adding from a decuple. Use tasks such as the following: 40 + 7, 20 + 5, 90 + 3, and so on. Draw an ENL and mark 40 on the line (use a vertical stroke and write '40' under the stroke). Write the task 40 + 7 below the ENL. *What is 40 plus 7? Use this ENL to show that.* Similarly for 20 + 5, 90 + 3, and so on.

Subtracting to a decuple. Use tasks such as the following: 63 – □ = 60, 86 – □ = 80, 39 – □ = 30, and so on. Draw an ENL and mark 63 (as in Task Group A8.1). *What is the next tens number (decuple) below 63?* Write the task 63 – □ = 60 below the ENL. *What taken from 63 leaves 60? Use this ENL to show that.* Similarly for 86 – □ = 80, 39 – □ = 30, and so on.

Notes:

- Some children need explicit instruction in naming the decuple after or before a non-decuple, for example, 57: *What is the decuple after 57 (60)? What is the decuple before 57 (50)?*
- In the case of the decuple before, some children will incorrectly respond with the next decuple going back, for example, *What is the decuple before 57?* The child answers 40.
- Some children will confuse decuple after or before with ten more or ten less respectively. *What is the decuple after 57?* The child answers 67. *What is the decuple before 32?* The child answers 22.
- In order to solve these tasks children should have knowledge of the use of the ENL to notate addition and subtraction.
- Adding from a decuple and subtracting to a decuple are important building blocks for the development of mental strategies for addition and subtraction involving two 2-digit numbers.
- Observe closely to see if the child uses counting-by-ones to keep track.

TASK GROUP A8.3: Adding to a Decuple and Subtracting from a Decuple

Materials: Writing paper and pens/pencils.

What to do and say: Adding to a decuple with addend in the range 1 to 5. Use tasks such as the following: 38 + □ = 40, 75 + □ = 80, 26 + □ = 30, and so on. Draw an ENL and mark 38 (as in Task Group A8.1). Write the task 38 + □ = 40 below the ENL. *What is the next tens number (decuple) after 38? What number added to 38 makes 40? Use this ENL to show that.* Similarly for 75 + □ = 80, 26 + □ = 30, and so on.

Subtracting from a decuple with subtrahend in the range 1 to 5. Use tasks such as the following: 30 – 4, 60 – 2, 90 – 5, and so on. Draw an ENL and mark 30. Write the task 30 – 4 below the ENL. *What is 30 – 4? Use this ENL to show that.* Similarly for 60 – 2, 90 – 5, and so on.

Adding to a decuple with addend in the range 6 to 9. Use tasks such as the following: 54 + □ = 60, 21 + □ = 30, 83 + □ = 90, and so on. Draw an ENL and mark 54. *What is the next tens number (decuple) after 54?* Write the task 54 + □ = 60 below the ENL. *What number added to 54 makes 60? Use this ENL to show that.* Similarly for 75 + □ = 80, 26 + □ = 30, and so on.

Subtracting from a decuple with subtrahend in the range 6 to 9. Use tasks such as the following: 60 – 7, 40 – 9, 60 – 6, and so on. Draw an ENL and mark 60. Write the task 60 – 7 below the ENL. *What is 30 – 4? Use this ENL to show that.* Similarly for 40 – 9, 60 – 6, and so on.

Notes:

- In order to solve these tasks children should have knowledge of the use of the ENL to notate addition and subtraction.
- Adding to a decuple and subtracting from a decuple are important building blocks for the development of mental strategies for addition and subtraction involving two 2-digit numbers.
- Observe closely to see if the child uses counting-by-ones to keep track.

TASK GROUP A8.4: Incrementing and Decrementing by Tens on and off the Decuple

Photo 8.2   Incrementing by tens off the decuple

Materials: Ten-strips (strips of cardboard of length 10 cm containing 10 dots – 5 black and 5 grey), four-strips, and so on (like a ten-strip but with only 4 dots), a screen of cardboard or cloth.

What to do and say: Incrementing on the decuple. Place out three ten-strips. *How many dots are there? How many tens are there?* Screen the three ten-strips. Place another ten-strip under the screen. *How many dots are there now? How many tens are there?* Continue up to 100, adding one or two ten-strips at a time.

Decrementing on the decuple. Place out nine ten-strips. *How many dots are there? How many tens are there?* Screen the nine ten-strips. Take one ten from under the screen. *How many dots are there now? How many tens are there?* Continue down to zero, taking one or two ten-strips at a time.

Incrementing off the decuple. Place out two ten-strips and a four-strip. *How many dots are there?* Screen the 24 dots. Place another ten-strip under the screen. *How many dots are there now?* Continue up to 104, adding one or two ten-strips at a time.

Decrementing off the decuple. Place out nine ten-strips and a six-strip. *How many dots are there?* Screen the 96 dots. Take one ten-strip from under the screen. *How many dots are there now?* Continue down to 6, taking one or two ten-strips at a time.

Notes:

- Observe closely to see if the child uses counting-by-ones. For example, 30 and ten more *(31, 32, 33, … 40)* and, 96 take away ten *(95, 94, 93, … 86)*.
- Children who use counting-by-ones are likely to use their fingers to keep track of ten counts.

TASK GROUP A8.5: Incrementing Flexibly by Tens and Ones

Materials: Piece of cardboard about 40 cm long containing the following sets: a ten-strip; a six-strip; two ten-strips; a ten-strip and a two-strip; two ten-strips and a four-strip aligned on the piece of cardboard as follows: 10; 6; 10 and 10; 10 and 2; 10 and 10 and 4. Two screens about 30 cm in length as seen in Figure 8.2.

Photo 8.3   Subtraction task

What to do and say: Screen all of the number strips. Move the screen to the right, thereby unscreening the first ten-strip. *How many dots are there (10)?* Uncover the six-strip. *How many dots altogether now (16)?* Uncover the next two ten-strips. *How many altogether now (36)?* Use the second strip to screen the first 36 dots, and then unscreen the next ten-strip and the two-strip. *How many altogether now (48)?* Now unscreen the remaining two ten-strips and the four-strip. *How many altogether now (72)? How many more would I need to make 100?*

Notes:

- This task has six parts. Children might use counting-by-ones during any of these parts.
- Some children might increment by tens on the first two or three parts of the task, and then count by ones for the latter parts.

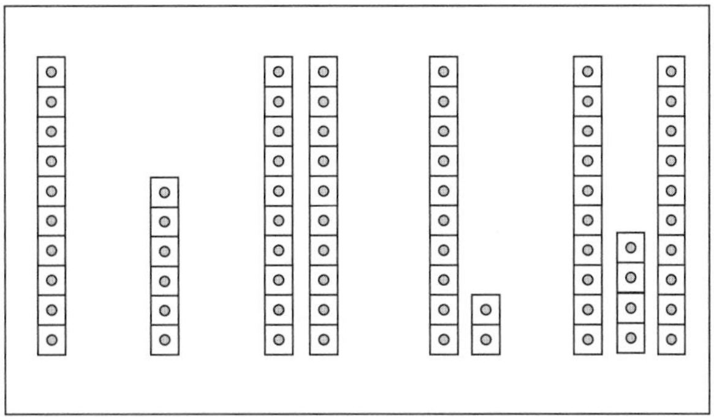

Figure 8.2   Incrementing by tens and ones

TASK GROUP A8.6: Adding Tens to a 2-Digit Number and Subtracting Tens from a 2-Digit Number

Photo 8.4   Subtracting 10 from a 2-digit number

Materials: Writing paper and pens and pencils.

What to do and say: Adding 10 to a 2-digit number. Use tasks such as the following: 42 + 10, 67 + 10, 24 + 10, and so on. Draw an ENL and mark 42. Write the task 42 + 10 below the ENL. *What is 42 plus 10? Use this ENL to show that.* Similarly for 67 + 10, 24 + 10, and so on.

Subtracting 10 from a 2-digit number. Use tasks such as the following: 73 − 10, 58 − 10, 95 − 10, and so on. Draw an ENL and mark 73. Write the task 73 − 10 below the ENL. *What is 73 take away 10? Use this ENL to show that.* Similarly for 58 − 10, 95 − 10, and so on.

Adding larger decuples to a 2-digit number. Use tasks such as the following: 64 + 20, 23 + 50, 62 + 30, and so on. Draw an ENL and mark 64. Write the task 64 + 20 below the ENL. *What is 64 plus 20? Use this ENL to show that.* Similarly for 23 + 50, 62 + 30, and so on.

Subtracting larger decuples from a 2-digit number. Use tasks such as the following: 72 − 20, 91 − 70, 45 − 30, and so on. Draw an ENL and mark 72. Write the task 72 − 20 below the ENL. *What is 72 take away 20? Use this ENL to show that.* Similarly for 91 − 70, 45 − 30, and so on.

Notes:

- These are also important building blocks for the development of mental strategies for addition and subtraction involving two 2-digit numbers.
- For tasks involving larger decuples (20, 30, and so on, rather than 10) gauge to what extent the child increments or decrements one 10 at a time (versus working with the larger decuple).
- Children who increment or decrement one 10 at a time might use counting-by-ones to keep track of the number of tens, particularly in the case of larger decuples (40, 50, 60, and so on).

TASK GROUP A8.7: Adding Two 2-Digit Numbers without and with Regrouping

Materials: Writing paper and pens/pencils.

What to do and say: Addition without regrouping. Use tasks such as the following: 52 + 24, 65 + 33, 37 + 42, and so on. Draw an ENL and mark 52. Write the task 52 + 24 below the ENL. *What is 52 plus 24? Use this ENL to show that.* Similarly for 65 + 33, 37 + 42, and so on.

Addition with regrouping. Use tasks such as the following: 59 + 34, 38 + 25, 64 + 28, and so on. Draw an ENL and mark 59. Write the task 59 + 34 below the ENL. *What is 59 plus 34? Use this ENL to show that.* Similarly for 38 + 25, 64 + 28, and so on.

Notes:

- Children are likely to work left to right, although some might work right to left (working with the ones first then the tens). Working right to left is much more likely if the child has received formal or informal instruction in the standard written algorithm.
- It is important to gauge whether the child's tendency is to use a jump strategy, a split strategy or some other strategy, or whether the child uses a range of strategy types (jump, split, split-jump, and so on).
- The ENL is particularly suited to notating jump strategies and similar strategies (for example, jumping to ten – see earlier in this chapter). In the case of addition with regrouping, some children might use a jumping to ten strategy (59 + 34: 60 + 33 = 93)
- If the child has a strong tendency to use split strategies, the interviewer should indicate to the child an alternative means of notating involving a sequence of number sentences (52 + 24: 50 + 20 → 70, 2 + 4 → 6, 70 + 6 = 76) rather than the ENL.
- Observe closely to see if, when using a jump strategy, the child uses counting-by-ones to keep track of the tens or the ones (52, 62, 72, then 73, 74, 75, 76!). Using counting-by-ones might also be indicated in the child's notating on the ENL.
- Rather than use an advanced strategy (jump, split, split-jump, and so on) some children will use counting-by-ones (52, 53, 54, 55 ... 76). This involves a triple count: keeping track of the ones in each ten, the number of tens counted (2), and the overall total. Children who use counting-by-ones are likely to use their ten fingers to keep track of the ones in each ten.

TASK GROUP A8.8: Subtraction Involving Two 2-Digit Numbers without and with Regrouping

Materials: Writing paper and pens/pencils.

What to do and say: Subtraction without regrouping. Use tasks such as the following: 87 – 32, 45 – 24, 99 – 65, and so on. Draw an ENL and mark 87. Write the task 87 – 32 below the ENL. *What is 87 take away 32? Use this ENL to show that.* Similarly for 45 – 24, 99 – 65, and so on.

Subtraction with regrouping. Use tasks such as the following: 62 – 28, 81 – 29, 73 – 34, and so on. Draw an ENL and mark 62. Write the task 62 – 28 below the ENL. *What is 62 take away 28? Use this ENL to show that.* Similarly for 81 – 29, 73 – 34, and so on.

Notes:

- Many of the notes for Task Group A8.7 apply to this task group as well.
- As with addition (Task Group A8.7), the ENL is particularly suited to notating jump strategies and similar strategies.

- Examples of strategies similar to jump strategies which can be notated on the ENL include: jumping to ten in the case of regrouping (62 – 28: 60, 40, 34); adding up (99 – 65: 65, 95, 99 → 34); and compensating (82 – 39: 42, 43).
- Children who have a strong tendency to use split strategies might have significant difficulties with subtraction with regrouping.
- A very common error is the following: 62 – 28: 60 – 20 = 40; 8 – 2 = 6; 40 + 6 = 46. Also 60 – 20 = 40; 12 – 8 = 4; 40 + 4 = 44.

TASK GROUP A8.9: Addition and Subtraction using Transforming, Compensating and Other Strategies

Materials: Writing paper and pens/pencils.

What to do and say: Addition. Use tasks such as the following: 32 + 34, 48 + 29, 17 + 58, 28 + 29, and so on. Draw an ENL and mark 32. Write the task 32 + 34 below the ENL. *What is 32 plus 34? Use this ENL or write number sentences to show how you work it out.* Similarly for 48 + 29, 17 + 58, and so on.

Subtraction: Use tasks such as the following: 72 – 68, 51 – 25, 77 – 29, and so on. Draw an ENL and mark 72. Write the task 72 – 68 below the ENL. *What is 72 take away 68? Use this ENL or write number sentences to show how you work it out.* Similarly for 51 – 25, 77 – 29, and so on.

Notes:

- Close observation of children's solutions is an excellent way to learn about the diverse range of strategies used by children.
- Examples of transforming: 32 + 34 is the same as 33 + 33 → 66! 77 – 29 is the same as 78 – 30 → 48.
- Examples of compensating: 17 + 58, I will add on 60 and take off 2 → 77 → 75! 77 – 29, I will take off 30 and add on 1 → 47 → 48.
- Examples of using a known sum: 28 + 29, I know 30 + 30 = 60, so 28 + 29 is 60 –3 → 57; 51–25, I know 25 + 25 = 50, so 51 – 25 is 26.
- Example of subtraction by adding up: 72 – 68, 68 + 2 is 70, 70 + 2 is 72 → 4.

 INSTRUCTIONAL ACTIVITIES

List of Instructional Activities

IA8.1: Walk-about Sequences
IA8.2: Bead String with Ten Catcher
IA8.3: Leap Frog
IA8.4: Jump to 100
IA8.5: Jump from 100

IA8.6: Target Number
IA8.7: Jump Addition and Subtraction Worksheets
IA8.8: Jump Addition and Subtraction Cards
IA8.9: Jump Addition and Subtraction Spinners
IA8.10: What's the Question?
IA8.11: Race to 50

ACTIVITY IA8.1: Walk-about Sequences

Intended learning: To practice the forward and backward number word sequences by ten on and off the decuple.

Materials: None.

Description: The teacher begins the activity by walking around the room while saying the number word sequence aloud. At some point, she points to a child. That child will continue the sequence and also walk around the room. When the teacher says *Stop!* the child saying the sequences points to the nearest child. That child then continues saying the sequence and walking. The activity can be done with any number word sequence. Similarly, from various starting points.

Notes:

- A number chart can be used for additional learning support.
- This activity is suitable for whole-class warm-up or an indoor recess activity.
- The child could choose when to point to the next person.
- For a challenge, extend the sequence beyond 100.

ACTIVITY IA8.2: Bead String with Ten Catcher

Intended learning: To add ten and tens to any number.

Materials: String of 100 beads in alternating colors of lots of ten, tube or cloth for cover, chalk or white board for recording strategies.

Description: Use a bead string with alternating colors for each set of 10 beads. Briefly show the first collection and then cover with a tube or piece of cloth: (a) use a ten catcher to slide a second collection beside the first as illustrated; (b) leave the second collection uncovered. Ask: *How many in all? How did you know?*

Variation: both collections can be screened.

Notes:

- This activity is suitable for whole class, small group or individuals.
- Choose tasks that progress in terms of their level of difficulty.

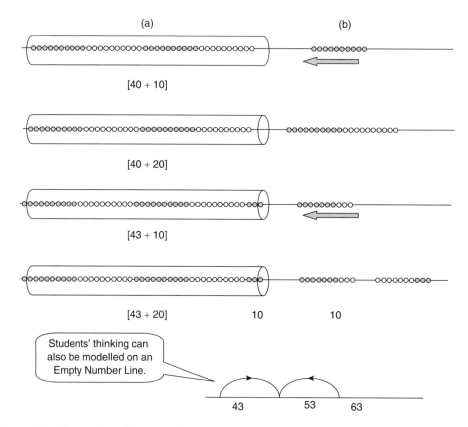

Figure 8.3   Bead string with ten catcher

 ACTIVITY IA8.3: Leap Frog

Intended learning: To develop knowledge of 2-digit addition and subtraction with and without regrouping.

Materials: Spinners and game boards (Figures 8.4–8.9), two paper clips (for spinners), counters to use as markers, recording sheets, paper and pencils

Description: The activities below involve pairs of children using two spinners to generate two numbers. Each child takes turns to:

- Spin Spinner A which generates the first number.
- Spin Spinner B which generates the number to be added or subtracted.
- Solve the addition or subtraction.
- Place a counter on a square with this number on their game board.
- The aim is to get a row of counters in a line (horizontally, vertically or diagonally).

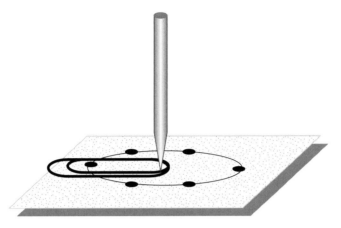

Figure 8.4 Spinner made from pencil and paper clip

Five examples:
Leap Frog 1: Addition or subtraction involving a 1-digit number and a 2-digit number.

43	1149	31	35	65
52	39	45	21	33
55	41	39	44	20
32	66	53	40	45
21	39	33	65	55

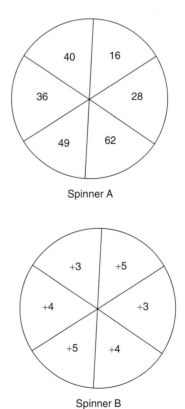

Figure 8.5 Leap Frog 1

Leap Frog 2: Addition or subtraction involving a decuple (e.g. 20, 30) and a 2-digit number.

29	19	9	79	89
69	59	29	19	79
9	69	89	9	39
39	29	9	79	89
39	59	69	19	9

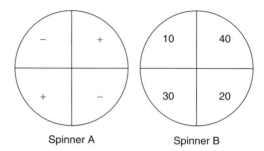

Spinner A is spun to determine an addition or subtraction.
Spinner B gives the number added or subtracted from 49.

Figure 8.6   Leap Frog 2

Leap Frog 3: Addition or subtraction involving a near-tens number (e.g. 11) and a 2-digit number.

43	21	14	35	21
39	15	43	21	43
21	35	39	14	15
14	21	35	15	39
40	43	15	35	14

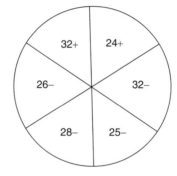

Only one spinner needed. Either 11 is added or
subtracted to the numbers on the spinners as indicated.

Figure 8.7   Leap Frog 3

Leap Frog 4: Addition or subtraction without regrouping, involving two 2-digit numbers.

90	23	51	38	22
28	48	92	63	92
33	63	42	37	104
52	75	22	62	28
78	13	37	90	75

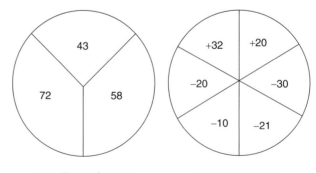

Leap Frog A Spinner   Leap Frog B Spinner

Figure 8.8   Leap Frog 4

Leap Frog 5: Addition or subtraction with regrouping, involving two 2-digit numbers.

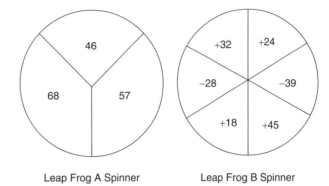

78	40	18	113	89
100	29	91	7	18
18	81	64	89	70
86	7	102	81	29
75	91	40	64	92

Leap Frog A Spinner   Leap Frog B Spinner

Figure 8.9 Leap Frog 5

Notes:

- Teachers can vary the spinners to suit the needs of the children. Some of the possibilities are shown below. For example, the second spinner could display only additions or only subtractions.
- Children can engage in the activity by themselves.
- The addition or subtraction task can be recorded or a record sheet can be produced to accompany the activity.

ACTIVITY IA8.4: Jump to 100

Intended learning: To add two 2-digit numbers using a jump strategy and to record the strategy using an empty number line.

Materials: Hundred chart, two paper clips (for spinners), different tokens or markers such as dried beans for each player or team, paper and pencils.

Description: There are two players. Player 1 spins the spinner and places a counter on that number on the hundred chart. Player 1 spins the spinner again and uses the jump method to add this number to the first number and moves the counter to this total. Player 2 follows these same steps. Players alternate turns until both players have gone past 100. As a variation, children can record the numbers on a record sheet as shown in Figure 8.12. They can show their strategies on an empty number line which is also on the record sheet.

For example, Player 1 spins the two spinners and gets 23. Player 1 records this on the record sheet and puts a counter on 23 on the hundred chart. Player 1 spins again and gets 34. This is recorded on the record sheet and the player uses a jump strategy to solve the addition and moves the counter to this number on the hundred chart (Figures 8.10–8.11).

Record 23 + 34 = 57.

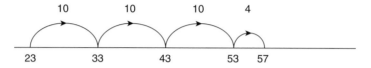

Figure 8.10   Using the empty number line to record the solution to 23 + 34

Hundred Chart									
1	2	3	4	5	6	7	8	9	10
11	12	13	14	15	16	17	18	19	20
21	22	23	24	25	26	27	28	29	30
31	32	33	34	35	36	37	38	39	40
41	42	43	44	45	46	47	48	49	50
51	52	53	54	55	56	57	58	59	60
61	62	63	64	65	66	67	68	69	70
71	72	73	74	75	76	77	78	79	80
81	82	83	84	85	86	87	88	89	90
91	92	93	94	95	96	97	98	99	100

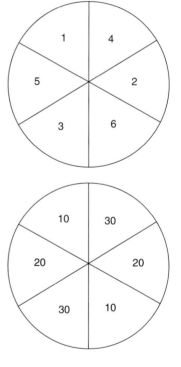

Figure 8.11   Hundred chart and spinners

Notes:

- Spinners are made by holding a pencil point through a paper clip to the center of the spinner. Flick the paper clip to spin (see Figure 8.4).
- This activity is suitable for small groups or pairs.
- The game can be extended beyond 100.

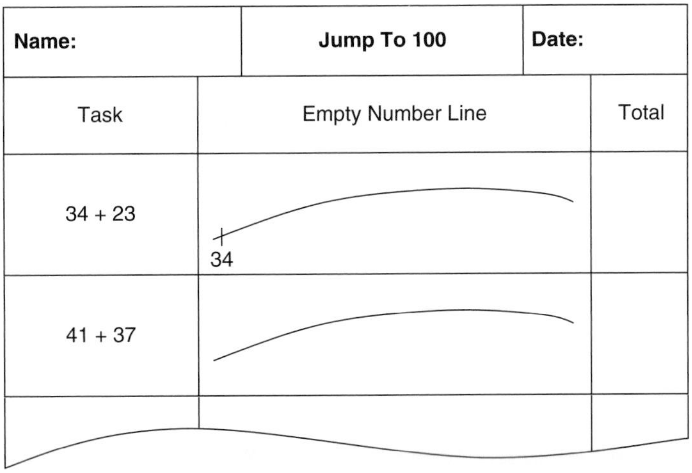

Name:	Jump To 100	Date:
Task	Empty Number Line	Total
34 + 23	34	
41 + 37		

Figure 8.12   Jump to 100 record sheet

ACTIVITY IA8.5: Jump from 100

Intended learning: Subtraction involving two 2-digit numbers using the jump method with the support of a hundred chart.

Materials: Hundred chart and spinners, two paper clips (for spinners), different tokens or markers such as dried beans for each player or team, pencil and paper.

Description: Use the hundred chart (see Activity IA8.4) and spinners to generate 2-digit subtraction tasks. Record each task that is generated as a separate horizontal number sentence. Pairs may be substituted for individual players. Player A places a marker on 100. Each spinner is spun to make the number that is to be subtracted. The number Player A is on and the number spun are recorded. Use the jump method to move the marker to find the solution. The difference of the two numbers is recorded. Player B repeats these steps. Players alternate turns until both players have reached zero (or a number determined by the teacher). For example: Player A is on 58 and spins 30 and 4. Record 58 – 34. Start at 58 and jump up three rows and left four columns. Record 58 – 34 = 24.

Notes:

* As an alternative have children use an empty number line to show their strategies.

A VIDEO DEMONSTRATING THIS ACTIVITY CAN BE ACCESSED ONLINE AT WWW. SAGEPUB.CO.UK/ WRIGHTTNC

ACTIVITY IA8.6: Target Number

Intended learning: To jump by tens on a hundred chart.

Materials: Hundred chart transparency, children's hundred charts and counters.

Description: A hundred chart is placed on an image projector. The teacher selects a target number (53, for example) and places a counter on this square. The teacher underlines a starting number (e.g. 89) and also puts a counter on this square. Children are selected individually to come to the front and show how the starting counter can be moved to get to the target number. The different strategies are discussed, with the children deciding how many were added or subtracted on each move. The whole class could then participate in this activity. Individuals or pairs of children could have their own hundred chart to try to find the quickest way to get the target number.

Notes:

• When the strategies are being discussed, note those children who count by ones and those who count by tens.

ACTIVITY IA8.7: Jump Addition and Subtraction Worksheets

Intended learning: To practice using a jump strategy to solve addition and subtraction tasks and show solutions on an empty number line.

Materials: A series of sheets prepared by the teacher. See the Chapter 8 learning trajectory for a sequence of addition and subtraction tasks.

Description: Worksheets are prepared similar to those displayed below. These can be targeted to each child's level of knowledge.

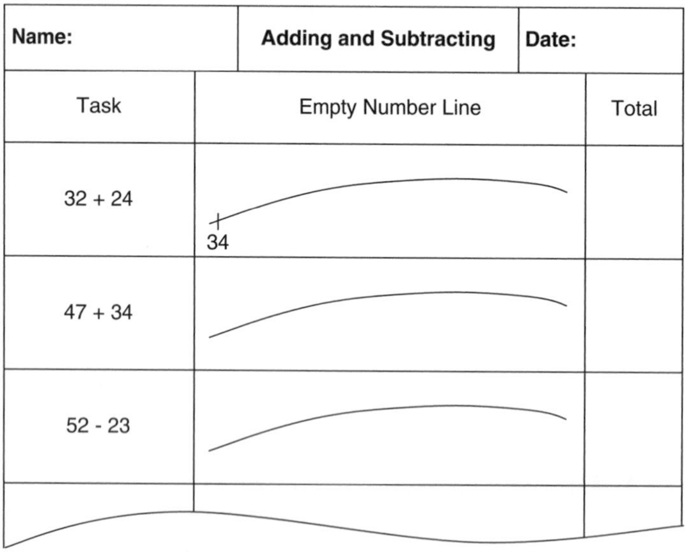

Name:	Adding and Subtracting	Date:
Task	Empty Number Line	Total
32 + 24	⊢ 34	
47 + 34		
52 - 23		

Figure 8.13   Adding and subtracting record sheet

Notes:

- Have the children mentally solve the tasks and then notate their strategies on an empty number line.
- Leave adequate time for class discussion of children's strategies. Have them demonstrate their strategies to the class using an empty number line and ask if anyone used a different strategy.

ACTIVITY IA8.8: Jump Addition and Subtraction Cards

Intended learning: To practice using a jump strategy to solve addition and subtraction tasks and notate strategies on an empty number line.

Materials: Cards with addition tasks and cards with subtraction tasks, record sheet or paper.

Description: The child selects a card containing an addition or subtraction task, records this on paper or on a record sheet, shows how this can be solved using a jump strategy, and notates the strategy on an empty number line.

Notes:

- Some examples of tasks are: adding 1-digit numbers, adding or subtracting whole tens.
- The tasks can be customized to children's current levels of knowledge

ACTIVITY IA8.9: Jump Addition and Subtraction Spinners

Intended learning: To practice using a jump strategy to solve addition and subtraction tasks and showing strategies on an empty number line.

Materials: Red spinner with numbers between 41 and 79, green spinner with numbers between 12 and 38.

Description: The child spins the red spinner and records this number on a record sheet, spins the green spinner and records this number on a record sheet, shows how this can be solved using a jump strategy, and records the strategy on an empty number line.

Notes:

- The teacher chooses either addition or subtraction spinners.
- This activity is similar to Activity IA8.8 but the spinners provide more variation in the tasks.

ACTIVITY IA8.10: What's the Question?

Intended learning: To identify jump strategies used in solving addition and subtraction tasks.

Materials: Prepared sheets containing completed solutions on an empty number line as shown in Figure 8.14.

Description: Prepare worksheets showing some completed empty number lines. Children write down what the original task was. After children complete the tasks, the teacher guides a discussion asking children to state the strategies displayed on the empty number lines.

Notes:

- During the discussion the teacher could choose some children to draw some solutions on an empty number line and the remaining children can be asked to determine the original task.

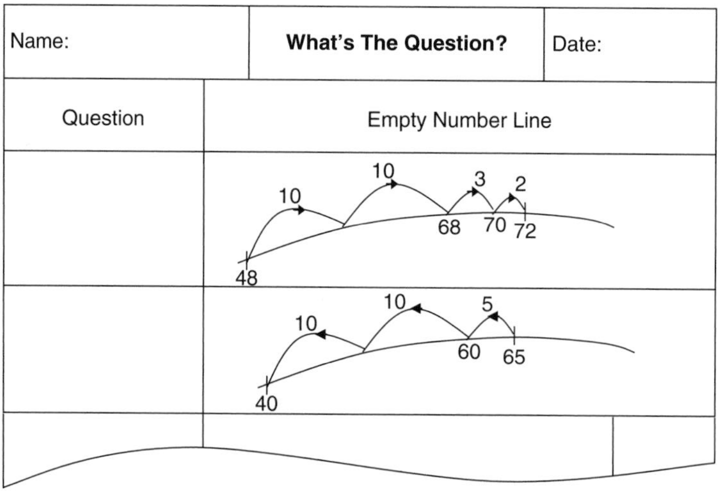

Figure 8.14   What's the Question? record sheet

ACTIVITY IA8.11: Race to 50

Intended learning: To develop strategies for addition, missing addend and missing subtrahend tasks.

Materials: Hundred chart, one counter per player, two spinners:

- Spinner A for example: 10, 11, 12, 20, 21, 22, 30, 31, 32
- Spinner B for example: 1, 2, 3, 4, 5, 6, 7, 8

Description: Organize children into pairs. The object is to reach 50 on a hundred chart by adding the number generated by the spinner. If after several turns they go past 50, they need to subtract the number generated by their spinner to get closer to the target of 50. The number spun is added or subtracted to the player's score and the player's counter is moved to this new score. Each player chooses which of the two spinners to spin according to whether a small number or a larger number is required. For example, if they were at 42 they only need 8 to reach 50 so they would choose the spinner with small numbers (Spinner B). The game can stop when one player reaches 50 or after both players get to 50.

Notes:

- Children are encouraged to work out the additions or subtractions before they move their counter.
- The numbers on the spinners can be customized to children's current levels of knowledge.

Learning Trajectory

Table 8.1 Learning Trajectory: 2-Digit Addition and Subtraction – Jump Strategies

Topics	Page Ref.	Assessment Task Groups	Instructional Activities
Forward and backward number word sequences by tens on and off the decuple	139–140	A8.1	IA8.1
Adding from a decuple and subtracting to a decuple	138	A8.2	IA8.2 IA8.3 Adjust spinner numbers
Adding to a decuple and subtracting from a decuple	138	A8.3	IA8.3 Adjust spinner numbers
Incrementing and decrementing by tens off a decuple	139–40	A8.4	IA8.3 Adjust spinner numbers
Adding a 1-digit number to a 2-digit number without bridging the decuple	138–139		IA8.3 Adjust spinner numbers
Adding a 1-digit number to a 2-digit number involving partitioning and bridging the decuple	138–139		IA8.3 Adjust spinner numbers
Subtracting a 1-digit number from a 2-digit number without bridging the decuple	138–139		IA8.3 Adjust spinner numbers

(Continued)

Table 8.1   (Continued)

Topics	Page Ref.	Assessment Task Groups	Instructional Activities
Subtracting a 1-digit number from a 2-digit number involving partitioning and bridging the decuple	138–139		IA8.3 Adjust spinner numbers
Incrementing flexibly by tens and ones with tens strips	138–140	A8.5	
Introducing the empty number line (ENL)	136		
Adding tens to a 2-digit number	140	A8.6	IA8.3 Adjust spinner numbers
Subtracting tens from a 2-digit number	140	A8.6	IA8.3 Adjust spinner numbers
Adding two 2-digit numbers without regrouping	140–141	A8.7	IA8.4
Subtraction involving two 2-digit numbers without regrouping	140–141	A8.8	IA8.5
Adding two 2-digit numbers with regrouping	140–141	A8.7	IA8.4 IA8.6 IA8.7 IA8.8 IA8.9 IA8.10
Subtraction involving two 2-digit numbers with regrouping	140–141	A8.8	IA8.5 IA8.6 IA8.7 IA8.8 IA8.9 IA8.10
Addition and subtraction involving two 2-digit numbers using other strategies	140–141	A8.9	IA8.11

9

Two-digit Addition and Subtraction: Split Strategies

Summary

This chapter focuses on the development of a range of strategies which are referred to as split strategies. In the case of addition, the child splits each of the two addends into tens and ones and then separately combines, tens with tens and ones with ones. The chapter includes detailed descriptions of approaches to the development of these strategies for addition and subtraction.

 Key topics: 9.3, 9.4, 9.5   Chapters: 5, 6

Topic Overview

Chapter 8 focused on the development of jump strategies and related kinds of strategies for adding and subtracting involving two 2-digit numbers. This chapter focuses on the development of split strategies. As indicated in Chapter 8, base-ten materials are considered important for the development of split strategies, and this chapter includes a focus on the use of base-ten materials. This chapter also includes the topic of higher decade addition and subtraction, a forerunner to 2-digit addition and subtraction. Also included is a focus on extending strategies for adding and subtracting involving two 2-digit numbers, to working with two 3-digit numbers.

In Chapter 2 we describe two different kinds of mental strategies used by children when adding or subtracting involving two 2-digit numbers. These kinds of strategies are referred to as jump and split. Chapter 8 focused on an approach that fosters the development of jump strategies. This chapter focuses on an approach that fosters the development of split strategies. We take the view that instruction can focus on one or both of these approaches, and that the focus on jump strategies can precede the focus on split strategies or vice versa. Further information on instruction related to split strategies is available in Wright et al. (2012) *Developing Number Knowledge: Assessment, Teaching & Intervention with 7–11-year-olds* (see Bibliography).

Higher Decade Addition and Subtraction

Higher decade addition and subtraction involves a 2-digit number and a number in the range 1 to 10. This is because each addition or subtraction of this kind can be linked to a corresponding addition or subtraction respectively, in the range 1 to 10 or 1 to 20. For example, 43 + 5 can be linked to 3 + 5, 75 – 2 can be linked to 5 – 2, 76 + 9 can be linked to 6 + 9, and 52 – 7 can be linked to 12 – 7. Thus solving a higher decade addition or subtraction task can involve using the corresponding addition or subtraction respectively. For example, 3 + 4 is used to work out 53 + 4, 7 + 8 is used to work out 37 + 8, 7 – 2 is used to work out 87 – 2 and 14 – 9 is used to work out 44 – 9. Second, by starting with addition (or subtraction) in the range 1 to 10 or 1 to 20, a sequence of additions (or subtractions) can be determined. For example, 3 + 4, 13 + 4, 23 + 4, and so on; 7 + 8, 17 + 8, 27 + 8, and so on; 7 – 2, 17 – 2, 27 – 2, and so on; 14 – 9, 24 – 9, 34 – 9, and so on. Children can come to see the simple pattern in these kinds of sequences involving addition or subtraction.

Within the Decade – Addition

This involves cases such as 47 + 2, 83 + 5, 64 + 4, and so on. Children should be able to solve these tasks using the corresponding addition in the range 1 to 10, for example, using 7 + 2 to work out 47 + 2. Tasks of this kind can be an important building block for adding two 2-digit numbers. For example, when a child works out 27 + 22 by first adding 27 and 20, the next step involves adding 47 and 2.

Within the Decade – Subtraction

This involves cases such as 49 – 2, 88 – 5, 68 – 4, and so on. Children should be able to solve these tasks using the corresponding subtraction in the range 1 to 10, for example, using 9 – 2 to work out 49 – 2. Tasks of this kind can be an important building block for subtraction involving two 2-digit numbers. For example, when a child works out 69 – 22 by first working out 69 – 20, the next step involves working out 49 – 2.

Beyond the Decade – Addition

This involves cases such as 46 + 7, 77 + 5, 29 + 6, and so on. Two ways that children might work out this problem are: (a) using the corresponding addition in the range 1 to 20, for example, using 6 + 7 to work out 46 + 7; and (b) working the addition out directly without using 6 + 7, for example, first solving 46 + □ = 50, then partitioning 7 into 4 and 3, and finally adding 50 and 3. Tasks of this kind can be an important building block for adding two 2-digit numbers. For example, when a child works out 26 + 27 by first adding 26 and 20, the next step involves adding 46 and 7.

Beyond the Decade – Subtraction

This involves cases such as 53 – 7, 82 – 5, 35 – 6, and so on. Two ways that children might work out this problem are: (a) using the corresponding subtraction in the range 1 to 20, for example, using 13 – 7 to work out 53 – 7; and (b) first solving 53 – □ = 50, and then partitioning 7 into 3 and 4, and finally solving 50 – 4. Tasks of this kind can be an important building block for subtracting two 2-digit numbers. For example, when a child works out 73 – 27 by first working out 73 – 20, the next step involves working out 53 – 7.

Sequences in Higher Decade Addition and Subtraction

Children can work with and notate sequences such as the following:

5 + 2 = 7, 15 + 2 = 17, 25 + 2 = 27, 35 + 2 = 37, and so on.

8 – 3 = 5, 18 – 3 = 15, 28 – 3 = 25, 38 – 3 = 35, and so on.

8 + 4 = 12, 18 + 4 = 22, 28 + 4 = 32, 38 + 4 = 42, and so on.

11 – 6 = 5, 21 – 6 = 15, 31 – 6 = 25, 41 – 6 = 35, and so on.

Working with these sequences can help children make connections from a higher decade addition or subtraction to a corresponding addition or subtraction in the range 1 to 10 or 1 to 20.

Fostering the Development of Split Strategies

As described in Chapter 2, split strategies involve calculating separately with tens and ones. First, the child calculates with the tens, then with the ones, and finally the resultant tens and ones are combined. The split strategy is easier to use when the calculation in the ones does not involve numbers larger than 9. Here are some examples in the case of addition: 42 + 25, 36 + 21, 36 + 53, and in the case of subtraction: 86 – 32, 44 – 23, 97 – 55.

Prior Knowledge for the Split Strategy

An important point to keep in mind is that when children are working these examples, they should be facile with adding and subtracting in the range 1 to 10. When a child works out 36 + 53, they should be able to calculate each of 30 + 50 (using 3 + 5), and 6 + 3 almost instantaneously, and similarly calculate 80 + 9 almost instantaneously. The child who is using strategies involving counting-by-ones to calculate 3 + 5 and 6 + 3 is not ready to learn 2-digit addition to 100. This applies similarly in the case of subtraction. In using a split strategy to work out 86 – 32, the child should be able to calculate each of 80 – 30 and 6 – 2 almost instantaneously.

Base-ten Blocks and Bundling Sticks

Settings such as bundling sticks or base-ten blocks are very useful for fostering the development of split strategies. These can be used by the teacher working with a group or whole class using an image projector. Also, the teacher can gradually develop situations in which the materials are screened (hidden from view) to encourage visualization on the part of the children. An important point is that simply giving base-ten materials to each child with instructions to work examples such as those above is unlikely to foster split strategies. In this situation our instructional goal is to foster mental strategies. When children are given the materials they are likely to use several strategies that are not conducive to developing more facile strategies. Strategies that tend to be counterproductive at this point include: counting a collection of blocks from one, counting-by-ones, and counting blocks that can be seen.

Means of Notating for Split Strategies

In Chapter 8 we described three means of notating in the case of jump strategies. These are the empty number line, arrow notation and horizontal number sentences. As well, we described how horizontal number sentences involve writing a number sentence for each step in the strategy and can be used for virtually any strategy. This includes jump, split, split-jump, and a variation of the split strategy involving working from right to left. Because of its similarity to the standard written algorithm we refer to this strategy as a quasi-vertical algorithm strategy. Use of horizontal number sentences to notate this strategy is shown below.

36 + 47:   7 + 6 = 13

13 = 10 + 3

40 + 10 = 50

50 + 30 = 80

80 + 3 = 83

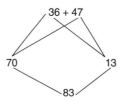

Figure 9.1 Using drop-down notation to notate a split strategy

Figure 9.1 shows an alternative method of notating split strategies. This is referred to as splitting, branching or drop-down notation.

Extending to 3-digit Addition, Subtraction and Place Value

Children who have developed facile and flexible jump (Chapter 8) and split strategies for adding and subtracting two 2-digit numbers are ready to extend these strategies to working with 3-digit numbers. In order to do so, children need: (a) to be facile with number word sequences and numerals in the range 100 to 1,000, and (b) to be able to increment and decrement 3-digit numbers, by 10 and by 100. These two topics are now described.

Number Words and Numerals to 1,000

This refers to learning to name and write 3-digit numerals and learning to say number word sequences forward and backward in the range 100 to 1,000. The latter topic refers to saying the sequence forward or backward from a given 3-digit number, or knowing what comes after or before a given 3-digit number. Some examples are: (a) being able to count on or back from 810, 701, 297, and so on; (b) knowing what comes after 246, 310, 700, 899, and so on; and

(c) knowing what comes before 416, 800, 920, and so on. Developing children's knowledge of number word sequences and numerals in the range 100 to 1,000 should be developed in parallel with the development of jump and split strategies in the range 1 to 100.

Incrementing and Decrementing by Tens
Extending to 3-digit addition and subtraction involves several steps: first, the strategies of **incrementing and decrementing by tens** on and off the decuple in the range 1 to 100 can be extended beyond 100. For example, (a) going forward by tens from 350, from 287, and from 790; (b) going backward by tens from 650, from 289, and from 800.

Incrementing and Decrementing by Hundreds
Second, children can learn to increment and decrement by hundreds both on and off the decuple and on and off the hundred. For example, (a) going forwards by hundreds from 100, from 260, from 407, from 165; (b) going backwards by hundreds from 1,000, from 920, from 608, and from 482. Becoming facile with number word sequences in this way provides a basis for using strategies akin to jump and split strategies to do addition or subtraction involving two 3-digit numbers. For example, children might solve tasks such as the following using (a) a split strategy and (b) a jump strategy:

634 + 211	459 + 203	175 + 282	367 + 255
889 – 236	372 – 106	416 – 121	723 – 235

Developing Strategies for 3-digit Addition and Subtraction
In similar vein to the case of 2-digit addition and subtraction, children's development of flexible jump and split strategies involving 3-digit addition and subtraction will support a corresponding development of an understanding of place value to 1,000. Thus, as in the case of 2-digit numbers, place value knowledge is developed in conjunction with, rather than prior to, the development of flexible strategies for adding and subtracting. Also as before, base-ten materials (hundreds, tens and ones) are particularly suited to the development of split strategies. Further, situations which invoke low-level counting strategies should generally be avoided. As before, this can be done by displaying and then screening base-ten materials to encourage visualization or imaging on the part of the children. Again, as described in Chapter 8, the empty number line can be used to support the development of jump strategies. The ENL enables children to notate, discuss, explain and reflect on their strategies.

 ASSESSMENT TASK GROUPS

List of Assessment Task Groups

A9.1: Higher Decade Addition and Subtraction without and with Bridging the Decuple
A9.2: Partitioning and Combining Involving 2-Digit Numbers
A9.3: Combining and Partitioning Involving Non-Canonical (Non-Standard) Forms
A9.4: Addition Involving Two 2-Digit Numbers without and with Regrouping
A9.5: Subtraction Involving Two 2-Digit Numbers without and with Regrouping

TASK GROUP A9.1: Higher Decade Addition and Subtraction without and with Bridging the Decuple

Materials: Base-ten materials (for example, popsicle sticks bundled into tens and singles), a cardboard screen.

What to do and say: Addition without bridging. Place out 6 tens and 2 ones. *How many sticks altogether?* Screen the 62 sticks. Add 2 sticks. *How many sticks are there now?* Continue with tasks such as the following: 35 + 4, 82 + 6, 53 + 4, and so on. Continue to use base-ten materials to present the tasks.

Subtraction without bridging: Place out 5 tens and 7 ones. *How many sticks altogether?* Screen the 57 sticks. Remove 3 sticks. *How many sticks are there now?* Continue with tasks such as the following: 88 – 4, 23 – 2, 96 – 3, and so on, using base-ten materials to present the tasks.

Addition with bridging. Place out 4 tens and 9 ones. *How many sticks altogether?* Screen the 49 sticks. Add 6 sticks. *How many sticks are there now?* Continue with tasks such as the following: 86 + 6, 35 + 8, 67 + 4, and so on, using base-ten materials.

Subtraction with bridging. Place out 8 tens and 4 ones. *How many sticks altogether?* Screen the 84 sticks. Remove 6 sticks. *How many sticks are there now?* Continue with tasks such as the following: 63 – 9, 25 – 8, 72 – 5, and so on, using base-ten materials.

Notes:

- For more advanced children an alternative is to present these tasks in the form of number sentences in horizontal format.
- In the cases of addition and subtraction without bridging, children might use a known fact in the range 1 to 10. For example, 62 + 2: 2 and 2 are 4 so 62 and 2 are 64. And, 96 – 3: 6 take away 3 is 3 so 96 take away 3 is 93.
- In the cases of addition and subtraction with bridging, children might use a strategy involving going through ten. For example, 49 + 5: 1 more is 50, and 4 more makes 54. And 72 – 5: 72 take away 2 is 70, and 70 take away 3 is 67.
- In the cases of addition and subtraction with bridging, some children might use a known fact in the range 1 to 20. For example, 49 + 5: 9 + 5 is 14, so 49 + 5 is 54. And 72 – 5: 12 take away 5 is 7, so 72 take away 5 is 67.
- In the case of addition with bridging, a preliminary step such as the following could be used: 49 + 5, 49 and one more is 50.
- Some children might use counting-by-ones on these tasks. For example, 82 + 6: 83, 84, 85, 86, 87, 88. And 72 – 5: 71, 70, 69, 68, 67.
- Children who use counting-by-ones are likely to use their fingers to keep track of their counts.

TASK GROUP A9.2: Partitioning and Combining Involving 2-Digit Numbers

Materials: Base-ten materials (for example, popsicle sticks bundled into tens and singles), a screen.

What to do and say: Partitioning. Ask the child to look away. Place 4 tens and 3 ones under the screen. *Under here there are 43 sticks. How many tens are there? How many ones are there?* Remove the screen. *Check to see if you are correct.* Similarly with 2 tens and 4 ones, 5 tens and 1 one, and so on.

   Combining. Ask the child to look away. Place 3 tens and 2 ones under the screen. *Under here there are 3 tens. How many sticks would that be? There are also 2 ones, how many sticks altogether?* Similarly with 6 tens and 2 ones, 4 tens and 8 ones, and so on.

Notes:

- This task group is important because these kinds of tasks can arise in children's mental computation involving adding or subtracting two 2-digit numbers. Tasks like these can also arise in multiplication and division.
- These tasks are particularly important in cases where children tend to use split strategies for adding or subtracting two 2-digit numbers. Split strategies involve working separately with the tens and ones.
- On the combining task, observe closely to see if the child uses counting-by-ones. For example, 40 and 8: 40, 41, 42, … 48.

TASK GROUP A9.3: Combining and Partitioning Involving Non-Canonical (Non-Standard) forms

Materials: Base-ten materials (popsicle sticks) of one color (red), base-ten materials of another color (green), two screens.

What to do and say: Combining. Using red, place out 4 tens. *How many tens are there? How many red sticks are there?* Screen the 40 red sticks. Using green, place out 1 ten and 6 ones. *How many green sticks are there?* Screen the 16 green sticks. *I have 40 red under here and 16 green under here. How many altogether?* Similarly with combinations such as: 50 red and 12 green, 30 red and 18 green, and so on.

   Partitioning. Ask the child to look away. Place 5 red tens, 1 green ten and 3 green ones under a screen. *Under this screen I have 63 sticks: 13 are green and the remainder are red. How many red sticks are there?* Similarly with combinations such as 20 red and 15 green, 70 red and 11 green, and so on.

Place 7 red tens, 1 green ten and 7 green ones under a screen. *Under this screen I have 87 sticks: 70 are red and the remainder are green. How many green sticks are there?* Similarly with combinations such as: 40 red and 16 green, 20 red and 13 green, and so on.

Notes:

- Partitioning 64 into 60 and 4, for example, can be regarded as a standard partition for 64. Partitioning 64 into 50 and 14 is referred to as a **non-canonical** (non-standard) partition of 64.
- Children should be facile with, not only working with the standard partition for any 2-digit number, but also working with the non-canonical partitions of 2-digit numbers.
- Combining non-canonical forms arises in the case of addition with two 2-digit numbers involving regrouping (carrying). For example, combining 70 and 13 might arise when 35 + 48 is solved using a split strategy.
- Partitioning non-canonical forms arises in the case of subtraction with two 2-digit numbers involving regrouping (borrowing). For example, partitioning 72 into 60 and 12 might arise when 72 – 35 is solved by a split strategy.
- These tasks are particularly important in cases where children tend to use split strategies for adding or subtracting two 2-digit numbers. Split strategies involve working separately with the tens and ones.
- Observe closely to see if the child uses counting-by-ones. For example, 40 + 16 → 41, 42, 43, … 56. And, 63 – 13 → 62, 61, 60, 59, … 50.

TASK GROUP A9.4: Addition Involving Two 2-Digit Numbers without and with Regrouping

Materials: Base-ten materials (popsicle sticks) of one color (red), base-ten materials of another color (green), two screens.

What to do and say: Without regrouping. Using red, place 45 under one screen. Using green, place 22 under another screen. *I have 45 red under here and 22 green under here. How many altogether?* Similarly for 54 + 35, 63 + 22, 31 + 57, and so on.

With regrouping. Using red, place 28 under one screen. Using green, place 37 under another screen. *I have 28 red under here and 37 green under here. How many altogether?* Similarly for 67 + 24, 35 + 28, 49 + 35, and so on.

Notes:

- Observe closely to see if the child uses: (a) a jump strategy: 45 + 22: 65, 67! (b) a split strategy: 45 + 22: 40 + 20 is 60, 5 + 2 is 7, 67 or (c) counting-by-ones: 45 + 22: 46, 47, 48, … 67.
- Use of base-ten materials (as used in these tasks) can tend to elicit split strategies rather than jump strategies.

TASK GROUP A9.5: Subtraction Involving Two 2-Digit Numbers without and with Regrouping

Materials: Base-ten materials (popsicle sticks), a screen.

What to do and say: Without regrouping. Place 68 under the screen. *I have 68 under here. Look away.* Take away 21. *I took away 21. How many are left?* Similarly for 96 – 34, 87 – 36, 46 – 23, and so on.

   With regrouping. Place 52 under the screen. *I have 52 under here. If I took away 29, how many would be left?* Similarly for 85 – 37, 62 – 46, 91 – 66, and so on.

Notes:

- Observe closely to see if the child uses: (a) a jump strategy: 68 – 21: 48, 47! (b) a split strategy: 68 – 21: 60 – 20 is 40, 8 – 1 is 7, 47 or (c) counting-by-ones: 68 – 21: 67, 66, 65, … 47.
- Use of base-ten materials (as used in these tasks) can tend to elicit split strategies rather than jump strategies.
- Children using split strategies might be successful in the case of subtraction without regrouping but not in the case of subtraction with regrouping.
- A very common error in the case of subtraction with regrouping using a split strategy is as follows: 52 – 29: 50 – 20 is 30, 9 – 2 is 7, 37: instead of 23. Another error is: 52 – 29: 50 – 20 is 30, 12 – 9 is 3, 33: instead of 23.

INSTRUCTIONAL ACTIVITIES

List of Instructional Activities

IA9.1: Follow the Pattern
IA9.2: Counting by Tens
IA9.3: Ten More or Ten Less
IA9.4: Add or Subtract Tens
IA9.5: Playing with Money
IA9.6: Addition Tasks with Screened Materials
IA9.7: Subtraction Tasks with Screened Materials
IA9.8: Split the Subtrahend (Decuples)
IA9.9: Making Bundles of Ten
IA9.10: Make and Break Numbers

ACTIVITY IA9.1: Follow the Pattern

Intended learning: To use known facts in higher decade addition.

Materials: Worksheets with number patterns for the children to continue.

Description: Children continue patterns provided by the teacher. Example: 3 + 4 = 7, 13 + 4 = 17, 23 + 4 = 27. Children are given the first three number sentences but must then try to see the pattern and continue it. Subtraction number sentences could also be used. Example: 6 − 4 = 2, 16 − 4 = 12, 26 − 4 = 22. Some children might need their own hundred chart to help them initially. Examples should also include bridging the decuple in addition: 7 + 8 = 15, 17 + 8 = 25, 27 + 8 = 35; and in subtraction: 11 − 3 = 8, 21 − 3 = 18, 31 − 3 = 28.

Notes:

- This activity is only suitable for children who are able to sequence and identify numbers in the range 1 to 100.
- More able children can work with patterns using 3- or 4-digit numbers (e.g. 296 − 8 = 288, 286 − 8 = 278, 276 − 8 = 268), including patterns that bridge a centuple (e.g. 406 − 7 = 399, 907 − 9 = 898, 701 − 3 = 698).
- This activity will also support the development of place value knowledge.

ACTIVITY IA9.2: Counting by Tens

Intended learning: To link counting forward by tens to addition of tens, and counting backward by tens to subtraction of tens on and off the decuple.

Materials: Base-ten materials and a large screen.

Description: Use base-ten material (bundling sticks, Unifix cubes, base-ten blocks, etc.) to count forward or backward by tens. Begin with one 10 on an image projector (or on the floor). The class says, 'ten'. Add another 10, the class says, 'twenty'. Continue adding tens as the class counts by tens with you. Once you get to 100 (or whatever number is your goal), take a 10 away and have the class count backward by tens as you take the tens away. Begin this activity counting by tens on the decuple and progress to counting by tens off the decuple. For example, place 4 ones on an image projector (or on the floor). Add 10, class says, 'fourteen'. Continue to count by tens until the target number is reached. Then remove the tens to count backward. This activity should also be done with the tens screened.

Notes:

- The purpose of this activity is to have the children establish the counting by tens pattern and then to make the link between addition and subtraction. In IA9.3, this is used to solve addition and subtraction tasks.
- Counting by tens could also be illustrated using a hundred chart.

- This activity is effective in small groups or one-to-one. Give each child a few tens. Children take turns putting in or taking out the tens as they count. These can also be screened.
- Do not always stop at 100. Children need practice counting by tens past 100 and counting forward and backward off the decuple beyond 100 (e.g. 104, 114, 124).
- Numbers in the teen range can present difficulties (e.g. 147, 137, 127, ?).

ACTIVITY IA9.3: Ten More or Ten Less

Intended learning: To add 10 to a number or subtract 10 from a number.

Materials: Base-ten materials, a large screen and a whiteboard for recording.

Description: Use base-ten material (bundling sticks, Unifix cubes, base-ten blocks, etc.) to add a 10. Place several tens on an image projector (or on the floor), and screen them. Add one more 10. You might need to leave this 10 unscreened at first. Ask: *How many in all?* Begin with decuples (40, 50, 60) and progress to numbers with tens and ones, such as 48 + 10 and 89 – 10. Variation: use a whiteboard as the screen for the tens and ones. Record the starting number on the board. The addition or subtraction number sentence can also be recorded.

Notes:

- In this activity only one 10 is added or subtracted. In IA9.4, this is extended to adding and subtracting decuples.
- This activity is suitable for whole class, small group or one-to-one.
- Add tens to 3-digit numbers to extend the tens pattern beyond 100.

ACTIVITY IA9.4: Add or Subtract Tens

Intended learning: To add tens to a number and subtract tens from a number.

Materials: Base-ten materials, a large screen and a whiteboard for recording.

Description: Use base-ten material (bundling sticks, Unifix cubes, base-ten blocks, and so on) to add tens. Place several tens on the overhead or carpet and screen them. Add a few more tens. You may need to leave these tens unscreened at first. Ask: *How many in all?* Begin with decuples (40, 50, 60) and progress to numbers with tens and ones, such as 64 + 30 and 59 – 20. Variation: use a whiteboard as the screen for the tens and ones. Record the beginning number on the board. You could also record the addition or subtraction number sentence and the child's strategy.

Notes:

- This activity is suitable for whole class, small group or one-to-one.
- Add tens to numbers in the hundreds to extend the tens pattern past 100.
- Children can chose to jump or split to solve these tasks.

ACTIVITY IA9.5: Playing with Money

Intended learning: To use the setting of money to support learning of 2-digit addition and subtraction.

Materials: One dollar notes (or coins) and ten dollar notes (or play money)

Description: Children in pairs or individuals with a set of $1 notes (or coins) and $10 notes.

- Make these amounts: $24, $56, $99, and so on.
- Make $48. *How many dollars to make $50?* Make $34. *How much will I take away to make $30?* And so on.
- Make $43. Make $30 and $13. *How much is this?* Have children make $50 and $14. *How much is this?* Give similar tasks ($60 and $12, $20 and $16, etc.). Follow up with some mental tasks of this type (without using the money).
- Demonstrate an addition task using money without bridging the decuple (e.g. $34 and $23). Give some of these tasks and follow up with similar mental tasks.
- Demonstrate an addition that bridges the decuple (e.g. $37 and $25). Have children make these amounts. *How much altogether?* See if some children have $50 + $12. Do others have $62? Discuss these results.
- Give other 2-digit additions. After each task, give the children a mental task to see if they can solve the addition without using the money.
- Advertisements can be cut out of newspapers. Have children cut out or bring in items, or create pictures with the cost next to them. The children select two items to buy and take the number of tens and ones indicated in the cost. They then count the total number of tens and total number of ones to find the total cost of the two items.

Notes:

- Ten cent and one cent coins can be used if available in the currency.
- This activity is suitable for whole class, small group or one-to-one.
- Children can add 3-digit numbers by using $100 bills (£100 notes).
- Children can also select more than two items to buy.
- Using $5 bills (£5 notes) as well would encourage adding using five as a reference point.
- Teachers may prefer to introduce this activity via newspaper advertisements and setting up a shop.

ACTIVITY IA9.6: Addition Tasks with Screened Materials

Intended learning: To add tens and ones without regrouping.

Materials: Base-ten materials, a large screen, and board and paper for recording.

Description: Using base-ten material, place a representation of a 2-digit number on the overhead or carpet and screen it. Add some tens. Have children record their answer as you record the number sentence (e.g. 43 + 20 = 63) on the board for all to see. You could also discuss and record children's strategies on a board. Still using the base-ten material, add another two tens and a one to the 63 then screen and write the resulting addition task on the board. Once again, children solve this and write down their answers, then the strategies are discussed. Do several of these addition tasks, adding ones then adding tens. Any strategies and patterns are discussed. Once children learn to add the tens then the ones, give a variety of tasks such as 25 + 14, 67 + 21, 51 + 34, 48 + 22.

Notes

- This activity is suitable for whole class, small group or one-to-one.
- Some children might use a jump strategy to solve these tasks.

ACTIVITY IA9.7: Subtraction Tasks with Screened Materials

Intended learning: To subtract tens and ones without regrouping.

Materials: Base-ten materials, a large screen, and board and paper for recording.

Description: Using base-ten material, place several 2-digit numbers on the overhead or carpet and screen them. Take away a few tens. Have children record their answer as you record the number sentence (e.g. 74 – 20 = 54) on the board for all to see. You could also record children's strategies on the board. Replace the 74 and screen them. Take away 2 tens and a one. Children record their answer as you record the number sentence (74 – 21 = 53). The next problem could be 74 – 22 using screened base-ten materials. Do several problems such as these, taking away an additional one each time. Look for patterns and discuss how tasks were solved. Once children learn how to subtract the tens and then the ones, give varied problems such as 58 – 22, 85 – 33, 96 – 41.

Notes:

- This activity is suitable for whole class, small group or one-to-one.
- Some children might use a jump strategy to solve these tasks.
- Encourage jump strategies, as they can be more easily adapted than split strategies, for subtraction with regrouping.

ACTIVITY IA9.8: Split the Subtrahend (Decuples)

Intended learning: To subtract tens and ones with or without regrouping.

Materials: Base-ten materials, a large screen, and board and paper for recording.

Description: Place several tens (e.g. 8 tens) on an image projector (or on the floor). Be sure to use tens material that can be taken apart (for example, bundling sticks). Ask: *What would happen if you took 20 away?* (60). Then ask: *What if one is taken away?* (59). Record the problem as 80 – 20 – 1 = 59 and as 80 – 21. Continue with other decuples. Gradually increase the number of ones being taken away. When children gain competence introduce screening of the materials.

Notes:

- This activity is suitable for whole class, small group or one-to-one.
- Children should also be able to solve tasks with subtrahends that are multiples of five.
- Some children might use a jump strategy to solve these tasks.
- Encourage jump strategies, as they can be more easily adapted than split strategies, for subtraction with regrouping.
- Progress to tasks such as 63 take 20 and then take another one (63 – 20 – 1 = 42).

ACTIVITY IA9.9: Making Bundles of Ten

Intended learning: To link bundles of tens and ones with 2-digit numerals.

Materials: Popsicle sticks or other tens material, dice or spinners.

Description:

- Groups of up to four children sit in a circle with a bundle of popsicle sticks in the middle. Each rolls a die and picks up that number of sticks from the bundle.
- When they have ten sticks they bundle them together with a rubber band.
- After all the sticks are used each child figures out how many they each have.
- Discuss the game with the whole class and write down the number of groups and number of individual sticks. Link the tens digit in the total with the number of bundles of ten.

Notes:

- Have each child work out how many sticks they have after each throw. Try to get them to solve this without counting the sticks. The other children can check the result.
- Each child could record each new addition on a record sheet where they write in the number on the die and the new total.
- Change the die to one with numerals 7, 8, 9, 10, 11, 12 or other numbers (or use a spinner). More sticks will be required as these numbers get larger.
- Other tens material can be used in place of the sticks.

ACTIVITY IA9.10: Make and Break Numbers

Intended learning: To use **arrow cards** to support identifying and building numerals.

Materials: A set of large arrow cards and sets of arrow cards for individual use.

Description:

- Display a 50 arrow card. Ask the children to say the number. Repeat this for other decuples (e.g. 70). Now use two arrow cards to display 2-digit numbers such as using 50 and 6 to make 56. Have children make these numbers using their own arrow cards.

Notes:

- This activity can provide a basis for knowledge of the tens and ones structure of 2-digit numerals.
- The activity can be extended to include 3-digit and 4-digit numerals.
- Suitable for whole class or groups.
- Arrow cards are also useful for developing conceptual place value knowledge.

(see Figure 9.2).

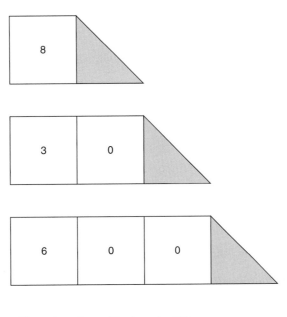

These 3 cards combine to make 638

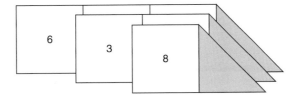

Figure 9.2   Arrow cards

Learning Trajectory

Table 9.1 Learning Trajectory: 2-Digit Addition and Subtraction – Split Strategies

Topics	Page Ref.	Assessment Task Groups	Instructional Activities
Review addition and subtraction in the ranges 1 to 10 and 1 to 20	161		IA9.1
Higher decade addition and subtraction without and with bridging the decuple, using addition and subtraction facts in the range 1 to 10		A9.1	IA9.1
Review counting by tens forwards and backwards on and off the decuple			IA9.2
Adding and subtracting 10 to a number			IA9.3
Adding and subtracting decuples to a number			IA9.4 IA9.5
Higher decade addition and subtraction, bridging the decuple 47 + 5, 62 – 6, etc.	161–163		
Review partitioning and combining 2-digit numbers	163	A9.2	
Partitioning and combining involving non-standard forms		A9.3	IA9.5
Adding two 2-digit numbers without regrouping	163–164	A9.4	IA9.6
Subtraction involving two 2-digit numbers without regrouping	163–164	A9.5	IA9.7
Adding two 2-digit numbers with regrouping	163–164	A9.4	IA9.6
Subtraction involving two 2-digit numbers with regrouping	163–164	A9.5	IA9.7 IA9.8

Topics	Page Ref.	Assessment Task Groups	Instructional Activities
Review jump strategy for addition and subtraction			
Give tasks where children can choose either a jump or a split strategy and discuss children's solutions			
Place value tasks	164–165		IA 9.9
			IA9.10

10
Early Multiplication and Division

Summary

This chapter focuses on the development of early multiplication and division knowledge. This includes the emergent notions of repeated equal groups and sharing, the development of skip counting and the use of arrays in teaching multiplication and division. Also explained are the ideas of numerical composite and abstract composite unit – important milestones in the development of numerical thinking, the idea of commutativity, and the inverse relationship between multiplication and division.

Key topics: 6.6, 7.6, 8.1, 8.6, 9.6   Chapter: 7

Topic Overview

This chapter focuses on the development of children's knowledge of the arithmetic operations of multiplication and division. This begins with very simple notions of equal groups and sharing and learning number word sequences of multiples (for example, 3, 6, 9 …), and extends to developing facile strategies to work out multiplication and division tasks in the range 1 to 100. In the following section, this development is described in detail. Further information on instruction related to multiplication and division is available in Wright et al. (2012) *Developing Number Knowledge: Assessment, Teaching & Intervention with 7–11-year-olds* (see Bibliography).

Repeated Equal Groups and Sharing

In Chapter 4 we saw that children's initial ideas of addition arise from the idea of combining two groups of items. In similar vein, children's initial ideas of multiplication are linked to combining a number of groups, each of which contain an equal number of items, for example, combining six groups each of which contains three items. This situation is referred to as repeated equal groups

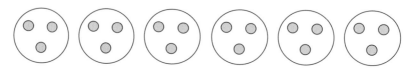

Figure 10.1   Multiplication as repeated equal groups

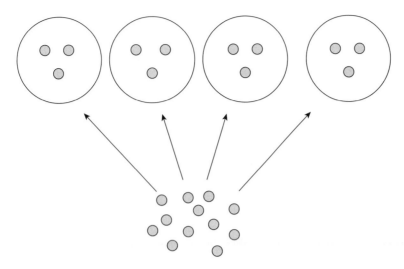

Figure 10.2   Sharing into equal groups

(see Figure 10.1). Finally, children's initial ideas of division are linked to sharing a collection of items into equal groups (see Figure 10.2).

Children should be provided with experiences that involve the activity of making repeated equal groups where the number in each group and the number of groups is specified, for example: *Make six groups of three, five groups of four, eight groups of two*. Children should also be provided with experiences that involve the activity of sharing a given number of items into a specified number of equal groups, for example: *Share eight items into four equal groups, ten items into two equal groups, fifteen items into three equal groups*. Activities can also involve everyday materials and situations in which repeated equal groups or

Photo 10.1   Making equal groups

sharing arise naturally, for example: *How many legs on four chairs? How many fingers on six hands?* For all the above activities, it is important to foster in children the development of the appropriate mathematical language, for example: three groups of four, eighteen shared into six equal groups.

Number Word Sequences of Multiples – Skip Counting

Number word sequences of multiples are sequences such as 'two, four, six, eight, …' – the sequence of multiples of two; and 'five, ten, fifteen, twenty, …' – the sequence of multiples of five. The activity of saying such sequences is typically referred to as counting-by-twos, counting-by-fives, and so on. This is also referred to as skip counting. It is important to keep in mind the distinction between, on the one hand, merely saying the sequence of multiples and,

Photo 10.2 Counting by twos

on the other hand, using the sequence of multiples to count the items in repeated equal groups, for example, six groups of two. Learning the common sequences of multiples is important as a basis for multiplication and division. Typically, children's learning of these sequences proceeds in the following order: by twos, by tens, by fives and by threes. Of course, children begin to learn each new sequence before the previous sequence is known completely. The sequences by other numbers in the range 1 to 10, that is, by fours, sixes, sevens, eights and nines, generally are not learned to the same extent as those stated earlier. Nevertheless, knowledge of these sequences will constitute an important basis for automatizing the basic facts of multiplication. Activities such as number rhymes can be useful for learning the common sequences (by twos, fives, tens and threes).

Counting Repeated Equal Groups

When children are learning the common sequences of multiples (twos, fives, and so on), they should also be given experiences in using these sequences in situations involving materials, that is, situations involving repeated equal groups of items. In these situations, teachers can demonstrate for children, counting by twos, by fives, and so on. For example, counting a collection of 20 red counters by twos involves moving a pair of counters together, in coordination with saying each word in the sequence – two, four, six, eight, and so on. It is tempting to regard activities such as counting by twos, by fives, and so on, as simple and straightforward activities that children can easily learn through imitation of the teacher. However, there is a tendency on the part of the teacher to imagine that the child, as well as imitating the teacher's actions also imitates the teacher's thinking. On the other hand, close observation of children counting by twos and so on can reveal interesting limitations on their thinking. For example, a child who had been shown how to count by twos was asked to count a collection of counters by twos. The collection contained nine counters. The child counted by twos – two, four, six, eight, in coordination with moving a pair of counters for each number word. After saying 'eight' he moved the final counter and said 'ten'. That there was one counter rather than two remaining did not seem to be problematic for the child. To emphasize the point being made: as obvious as it might seem to an adult that, when counting a collection of counters by twos, each number word refers to two counters, this is not necessarily obvious to children! As another example, children might regard the number of items in a collection as being dependent on how it is counted (by ones, by twos, by threes, and so on).

Division as Sharing or Measuring

In an earlier section, division was explained as arising from situations involving sharing into equal groups. In this context there are essentially two different kinds of situations that give rise to division and, as a teacher, it is important to take account of these. Try the following situation for yourself. You will need two sets of 12 counters, for example, blue and red. Use the red counters to solve the following task: arrange 12 counters into 3 equal groups. Use the blue counters to solve the following task: arrange 12 counters into groups of 3. Draw a diagram corresponding to your solution of each of the two tasks. Each of these corresponds to 12 ÷ 3. Alternatively, one could say there are two different ways that the problem 12 ÷ 3 can be demonstrated using a collection of 12 counters and using the number 3. These are called (a) sharing or partitive division and (b) measuring or quotitive division. To interpret 12 ÷ 3 in the sense of sharing is to regard the divisor (3) as indicating the number of equal groups. To interpret 12 ÷ 3 in the sense of measuring is to regard the divisor (3) as indicating the number in each of the equal groups. From the children's perspective, a division situation leads to a division expression 12 ÷ 3, rather than an expression leading to a situation. That is to say, it is usual for teachers to present children with a division situation before presenting the written expression.

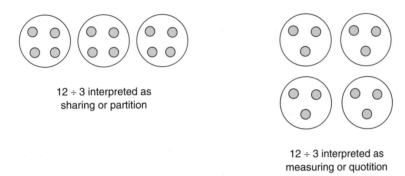

12 ÷ 3 interpreted as
sharing or partition

12 ÷ 3 interpreted as
measuring or quotition

Figure 10.3   Division as sharing or measuring

Figure 10.3 shows examples of division in the sharing and measuring senses. The typical approach in teaching is to begin by working wholly or mainly with one only of the situations, typically the sharing situation. The thinking underlying this is that sharing into a given number of equal groups is typically a very common experience for young children. Ultimately children should be familiar with each of these two division situations. Given a number story relating to either situation, children should be able to generate the corresponding division expression. Try for yourself to write five number stories involving simple division in the sharing sense and similarly write five number stories involving simple division in the measuring sense. For each story, write the appropriate division expression.

Abstract Composite Unit

As children become more facile at working with repeated equal groups and sharing, and thinking in terms of multiples, they are able to think more abstractly about the numbers involved in multiplication and division situations. A major advancement is the ability to regard as a unit a number larger than one when it is appropriate to do so. Thinking of this kind is referred to as **unitizing**. Prior to this advancement, children who can think abstractly about numbers are able to think of numbers as composites but not as units. Steffe and Cobb (1988) referred to these two levels of thinking as a numerical composite and an abstract composite unit. These are explained in Figure 10.4. Developing the idea of an abstract composite unit is fundamental for learning multiplication and division. For example, with the idea of an abstract composite unit, a child who is asked how many threes in 18 can think abstractly in terms of repeated threes. Because the child can regard three as a unit (as well as a composite), they can think in terms of counting the units, that is, how many units of three make 18?

Figure 10.4   Numerical composite and abstract composite unit

Using Arrays

As described above, experience with counters and so on organized into repeated equal groups can provide an important basis for the early development of multiplication and division ideas. As children's knowledge of multiplication and division develops, arrays can be very useful. Arrays in this sense consist of rectangular arrangements of dots in rows and columns. We use the term 'multiplied by' to read a multiplication sentence (equation). Thus 5 × 4 is read as '5 multiplied by 4'. Thus we can regard 5 × 4 as meaning 5 + 5 + 5 + 5, and 4 × 5 as meaning 4 + 4 + 4 + 4 + 4. Related to this, we regard a 5 × 4 array, for example, as consisting of 4 rows of 5 dots (Figure 10.5). Thus, in a 5 × 4 array, the first number (5) indicates the number of dots in each row and the second number (4) indicates the number of rows.

Initially, children can explore the idea that there are the same number of dots in each row (similarly in each column). It is important to move children beyond the activity of counting the

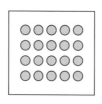

A 5 × 4 array has 5 columns
and 4 rows

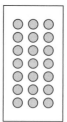

A 3 × 7 array has 3 columns
and 7 rows

Figure 10.5   Using arrays in multiplication

dots by ones. In teaching situations, arrays can be used on an image projector in ways so that some or all of the rows are each screened by a strip. In this situation children are encouraged to count by multiples corresponding to the number in each row. This can be extended by screening the whole array, and encouraging children to visualize the array in order to count the dots in multiples. The array can then be unscreened so that each row is covered by a strip, and children can again count the dots in the array in multiples.

Commutativity and Inverse Operations

As children's knowledge of multiplication and division develops, two important ideas arise – commutativity and inverse. The idea of commutativity was discussed in Chapter 7, in the context of addition. Commutativity also applies to multiplication (but not subtraction and division). In the case of multiplication, commutativity refers to the principle that when any two numbers are multiplied they can be multiplied in either order without affecting the answer, for example, $6 \times 4 = 24$ and $4 \times 6 = 24$. This is sometimes expressed as follows: for any two numbers a and b, $a \times b = b \times a$. Figure 10.6 shows demonstrations of the idea of commutativity using sets and arrays. Arrays are ideal for demonstrating the idea of commutativity. As seen in Figure 10.6, the array for 6×4 can be turned through 90 degrees to show 4×6.

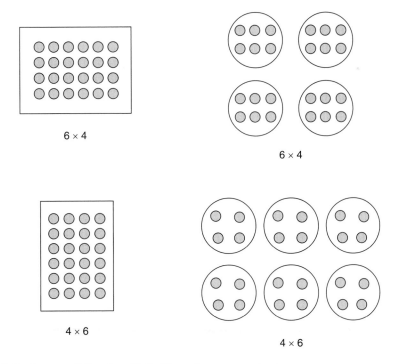

Figure 10.6   Commutativity of multiplication using arrays and sets

Multiplication and division are inverse operations, that is, division is the inverse of multiplication and multiplication is the inverse of division. The preceding statement refers to the principle that if a given number is multiplied by any number and the answer is then divided by the same number, then the answer is equal to the original number. This is demonstrated in Figure 10.7.

$$6 \times 11 = 66 \qquad\qquad 100 \div 4 = 25$$

$$66 \div 11 = 6 \qquad\qquad 25 \times 4 = 100$$

Figure 10.7   Multiplication and division are inverse operations

Children should develop sound knowledge of the principles of commutativity and inverse operations. This includes not only being implicitly aware of these principles but being able to use them flexibly. Examples of using commutativity are: (a) using the known fact of 7 multiplied by 2 makes 14 ($7 \times 2 = 14$), to work out 2 multiplied by 7; and (b) working out 5 multiplied by 9 in order to work out 9 multiplied by 5. Examples of using the inverse operations principle are: (a) using the known fact 5 multiplied by 4 makes 20 ($5 \times 4 = 20$) to work out $20 \div 4$; and (b) using the known fact 6 multiplied by 7 makes 42 ($6 \times 7 = 42$) to try to work out $42 \div 7$.

Extending Multiplication and Division Knowledge

Children's work in multiplication and division extends from the ideas of equal groups and sharing, to the development of abstract composite unit. These ideas are further extended to include the principles of commutativity and inverse operations. During this time most of the work in multiplication and division is in the range 1 to 100. Within this range, children will begin to habituate some of the simplest basic facts of multiplication such as doubles (4×2) and squares (6×6). As well, children can use doubling of known facts to work out other facts, for example, 4 sixes is double 2 sixes, 8 fives is double 4 fives. When children have developed a range of facile multiplication and division strategies in the range 1 to 100, they are ready to work on habituating basic fact knowledge and extending multiplication and division to include 2-digit factors, for example, 30×2, 23×3.

 ASSESSMENT TASK GROUPS

List of Assessment Task Groups

A10.1: Counting by Twos, Fives, Tens and Threes
A10.2: Multiplication – Items and Groups Visible
A10.3: Multiplication – Items Screened and Groups Visible

A10.4: Multiplication – Items and Groups Screened
A10.5: Quotitive Division – Number in Each Group Given
A10.6: Partitive Division – Number of Groups Given
A10.7: Multiplication using Arrays
A10.8: Division using Arrays
A10.9: Multiplication Basic Facts Involving 2, 10 and 5 as Multipliers
A10.10: Relational Thinking: Commutative and Distributive Principles
A10.11: Relational Thinking: Multiplication and Division as Inverses

TASK GROUP A10.1: Counting by Twos, Fives, Tens and Threes

Materials: None.

What to do and say: *Can you count by twos? Go on.* Similarly by fives, tens and threes.

Notes:

- Try to determine in each case (twos, threes, and so on), the limit of the child's fluent skip counting.
- In the case of counting by threes, for example, children might use counting-by-ones to figure out the next multiple of three: 3, 6, 9, 12, … 13, 14, 15. Counting-by-ones in this way involves a double count, that is, the child has to keep track of the number of counts after 12 (three counts).
- The more facile children can also be asked to count by fours and sixes, for example. When counting by fours or sixes, children sometimes use a non-counting addition strategy to determine the next multiple. For example, when counting by sixes, the child uses adding through 10, to determine that 24 is the next count after 18.
- The task of counting by tens also occurs in Task Group A8.1.

TASK GROUP A10.2: Multiplication – Items and Groups Visible

Materials: Cards containing repeated equal groups as follows: 6 groups of 3 dots, 3 groups of 5 dots, 8 groups of 2 dots.

What to do and say: Display the card showing 6 groups of 3. *What do you see? How many groups are there? What do you notice about each group? How many dots are in each group? How many dots altogether?* Similarly with 3 groups of 5, 8 groups of 2, and so on.

Notes:

- Try to gauge the extent to which the child is aware that the groups contain the same number of dots.
- Children might use counting-by-ones, skip counting or more advanced strategies; for example, knowing automatically that 6 threes are 18, or using the known facts of 5 twos and 3 twos to work out 8 twos.
- Children might use counting-by-ones out of convenience. Using counting-by-ones to solve this task does not necessarily indicate that the child cannot use a more advanced strategy when the items are screened, for example.

TASK GROUP A10.3: Multiplication – Items Screened and Groups Visible

Materials: Cards containing repeated equal groups as follows: 5 groups of 2 dots, 7 groups of 5 dots, 5 groups of 4 dots. On each card use small cardboard lids to screen each group separately. For example, the first card has 5 small lids with each lid concealing a circle of 2 dots.

What to do and say: Place out the card with 5 groups of 2, with the lids closed. *How many lids are there? Each of those lids has two dots under it. How many dots altogether?* If the child is not able to solve the task, lift each of the five lids. *How many dots are there in each group? How many dots altogether?* Similarly with 7 groups of 5, 5 groups of 4, and so on.

Notes:

- Try to gauge the extent to which the child correctly construes the task, that is, the extent to which the child understands that there are repeated equal groups.
- Children might solve these tasks by counting-by-ones. For example, the child solves the first task by counting from 1 to 10, making two counts for each lid: 1, 2 ... 3, 4 ... 5, 6 ... 7, 8 ... 9, 10. Alternatively, children might count by twos, making one count for each lid: 2, 4, 6, 8, 10.

Photo 10.3 Repeated equal groups –items screened, groups visible

- Children who use counting-by-ones might use fingers to keep track of the dots in each circle. For example, on the task involving 7 groups of 5 dots, this would involve raising five fingers sequentially, seven times. Alternatively, the child might count on from five, and raise five fingers sequentially, six times.

TASK GROUP A10.4: Multiplication – Items and Groups Screened

Materials: Cards containing repeated equal groups as follows: 3 groups of 4 dots, 4 groups of 5 dots, 5 groups of 3 dots. On each card use small cardboard lids to screen each group separately and a large lid to screen all of the groups. For example, the first card has 3 small lids and one large lid to conceal the 3 small lids.

What to do and say: Place out the card with 3 groups of 4. Have the small lids screening the items in each group and the large lid screening the 3 small lids. *This card has 3 groups of 4. How many dots altogether?* If the child is not able to solve this task, lift the large lid. *How many lids are there? Each of those lids has 4 dots under it. How many dots altogether?* If the child is again not able to solve the task, lift each of the 3 small lids. *How many dots are there in each group? How many dots altogether?* Similarly with 4 groups of 5, 5 groups of 3, and so on.

Notes:

- Try to gauge the extent to which the child correctly construes the task, that is, does the child seem to understand that there are repeated equal groups?
- Using skip counting to solve the task in its initial form (items screened and groups screened) requires a double count, that is, the child needs to keep track of the number of skips: 4 (1), 8 (2), 12 (3) → 12, as well as the number of items.
- Using counting-by-ones to solve the task in its initial form (items screened and groups screened), requires a triple count, that is, the child needs to keep track of the number of items in each group, as well as the number of groups and the number of items altogether.
- As in Task Groups A10.2 and A10.3, children might use counting-by-ones, skip counting or more advanced strategies. It is common for children to use fingers to keep track when using counting-by-ones or skip counting.
- Some children who use counting-by-ones involving a triple count use their fingers to keep track in two different ways. For example, one hand is used to keep track of the items in each group and the other is used to keep track of the number of groups. At the same time, they are mentally keeping track of the number of items altogether.

TASK GROUP A10.5: Quotitive Division – Number in Each Group Given

Materials: Cards containing repeated equal groups as follows: 6 groups of 3 dots, 3 groups of 5 dots, 8 groups of 2 dots.

What to do and say: Flash the card showing 6 groups of 3. The dots on this card are put into groups of 3, and there are 18 dots altogether. *How many groups of 3 are there?* Similarly with 3 groups of 5, 8 groups of 2, and so on.

Notes:

- Try to gauge the extent to which the child correctly construes the task, that is, does the child seem to understand that there are repeated equal groups of 3 (for the first task)?
- Children might use skip counting to solve this task and in doing so, use fingers to keep track of each count.
- Children might count by ones and keep track of each set of three counts. In some cases this might involve using fingers to keep track in two different ways, for example, the fingers of one hand are used to keep track of the ones in each three and the fingers of the other hand are used to keep track of the number of threes.
- Children might skip count to 9 or 12, and then count by ones.

TASK GROUP A10.6: Partitive Division – Number of Groups Given

Materials: Cards containing repeated equal groups as follows: 5 groups of 2 dots, 7 groups of 5 dots, 5 groups of 4 dots. On each card use small cardboard lids to screen each group separately. For example, the first card has 5 small lids with each lid concealing a circle of 2 dots.

What to do and say: Place out the card with 5 groups of 2. *How many lids are there?* Each lid has the same number of dots under it and there are 10 dots altogether. *How many dots under each lid?* Similarly with 7 groups of 5, 5 groups of 4, and so on.

Notes:

- Try to gauge the extent to which the child correctly construes the task, that is, does the child seem to understand that there are repeated equal groups of 2 (for the first task)?
- The notes in Task Groups A10.2 to A10.5 also apply to this Task Group.

TASK GROUP A10.7: Multiplication using Arrays

Materials: A 5 × 6 array (6 rows of 5 dots) and 2 × 7 array. Screen.

What to do and say: Place out the 5 × 6 array and, in doing so, screen all but the first row (5 dots). *What do you see? How many dots in the row?* The array has 6 rows of 5 dots. *How many dots altogether?* Place out the 2 × 7 array and, in doing so, screen all but the first row (2 dots). *What do you see? How many dots in the row?* The array has 7 rows of 2 dots. *How many dots altogether?*

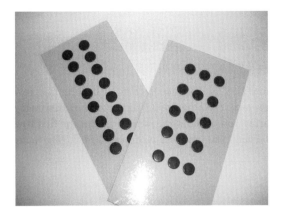

Photo 10.4 Using arrays

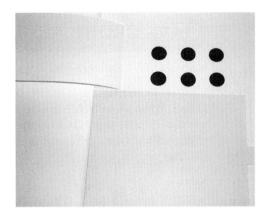

Photo 10.5 Using a partially screened array for multiplication (1)

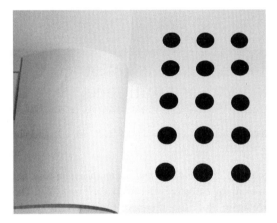

Photo 10.6 Using a partially screened array for multiplication (2)

Notes:

- Children who can solve tasks involving repeated equal groups might not be able to solve tasks involving arrays.
- Try to gauge the child's sense of an array. This includes familiarity with the notions of rows and columns, and knowing that each row is equal in number and similarly for each column. This can be done via a preliminary task in which an array is displayed and open questions, for example, *What do you see?* can be posed.
- Try to determine if the child uses counting-by-ones, skip counting or more advanced strategies.
- The notes in Task Group A10.3 about strategies involving skip counting and counting-by-ones apply here as well.

TASK GROUP A10.8: Division using arrays

Materials: A 3 × 5 array (5 rows of 3 dots) and 2 × 8 array. Screen.

What to do and say: Place out the 3 × 5 array and, in doing so, screen all but the first row (3 dots). *What do you see? How many dots in the row? The array has 15 dots altogether. How many rows does the array have?* Place out the 2 × 8 array and, in doing so, screen all but the first row (2 dots). *What do you see? How many dots in the row? The array has 16 dots altogether. How many rows does the array have?*

Notes:

- The notes in Task Group A10.3 about strategies involving skip counting and counting-by-ones apply here as well, as do the notes in Task Group A10.5.
- Try to determine if the child uses counting-by-ones, skip counting or more advanced strategies.

TASK GROUP A10.9: Multiplication Basic Facts Involving 2, 10 and 5 as Multipliers

Materials: Expression cards of the form 1 × 2, 2 × 2, 3 × 2, … 10 × 2, and similarly for 10 and 5 as multipliers

What to do and say: *I am going to show you a card with a multiplication basic fact. Tell me the answer as quickly as you can.* First, present the cards in order from 1 × 2 to 10 × 2. Then mix up the cards and present the cards in turn again. Put aside the cards for which the child is incorrect or does not answer in two seconds. Similarly for 10 and 5 as multipliers.

Notes:

- The purpose of this task is to determine which of these easiest basic facts the child has habituated.
- If the child is unsuccessful on the first run when the cards are in order, do not present the second run (cards not in order).
- Children who answer within about two seconds will either know the fact or use a relatively sophisticated strategy, that is more advanced than counting-by-ones or skip counting.
- For children who are successful with 2, 5 and 10, other multipliers can be used: 3, 4 and 9; and finally 6, 7 and 8.
- An alternative is to use cards with the constant factor on the left hand side, that is, 2 × 1, 2 × 2, 2 × 3 to 2 × 10. These two approaches accord with the two different common forms of tables of basic facts, that is, constant factor on the left and constant factor on the right.

TASK GROUP A10.10: Relational Thinking: Commutative and Distributive Principles

Materials: Cards on which tasks are written: 3 × 7, 7 × 3; 4 × 8, 4 × 9; 5 × 8, 5 × 5, 5 × 13.

What to do and say: Commutativity. Display the following: 3 × 7 (read as 7 threes). *Can you work this out?* If the child is correct, display the following immediately beneath the previous card: 7 × 3 (read as 3 sevens). *Can you use this (3 × 7) to work out this (7 × 3)?*

Distributive principle – extending a known fact. Display the following: 4 × 8 (read as 8 fours). *Can you work this out?* If the child is correct, display the following immediately beneath the previous card: 4 × 9 (read as 9 fours). *Can you use this (4 × 8) to work out this (4 × 9)?*

Distributive principle. Display the following: 5 × 8 (read as 8 fives). *Can you work this out?* If the

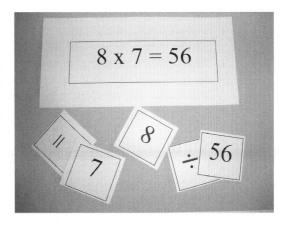

Photo 10.7 Relational thinking

child is correct, display the following immediately beneath the previous card: 5 × 5 (read as 5 fives). *Can you work this out?* If the child is correct, display the following immediately below the previous two cards: 5 × 13. *Can you use this (5 × 8) and this (5 × 5) to work out this (5 × 13)?*

Notes:

- Knowledge of these kinds of relationships is important for the development of mental computation.
- The notion of commutativity (see first task) can also be tested in the context of an array being turned through 90 degrees. For example, using a 4 × 7 array (*How many dots?*). Turn the array so it becomes a 7 × 4 array (*How many dots now?*).
- Additional examples for extending a known fact (second task): use 6 × 10 = 60 to work out 6 × 9; use 8 × 4 = 32 to work out 8 × 8; use 3 × 7 = 21 to work out 6 × 7.

TASK GROUP A10.11: Relational Thinking: Multiplication and Division as Inverses

Materials: Cards on which tasks are written: 5 × 9, 45 ÷ 9, 8 × 4, 32 ÷ 4.

What to do and say: Display the following: 5 × 9 (read as 9 fives). *Can you work this out?* If the child is correct, display the following immediately beneath the previous card: 45 ÷ 9 (read as 45 divided by 9). *Can you use this (5 × 9) to work out this (45 ÷ 9)?* Similarly, display 8 × 4 and so on.

Notes:

- Multiplication and division are said to be inverse operations because if a number (e.g. 5) is multiplied by another number (e.g. 4) and the result (20) is divided by the same number (4), we obtain the number we started with (5). Similarly, if 20 is divided by 4 and the result (5) is multiplied by 4 we obtain the number we started with (20).
- Knowing that multiplication and division are inverse operations is important for the development of mental computation.
- Some children are able to solve this task because they are familiar with the format (written form) of a multiplication equation and its corresponding division equation. Thus, when a child solves this task it can be interesting to ask in an open-ended way about their solution.

 INSTRUCTIONAL ACTIVITIES

List of Instructional Activities

IA10.1: Count Around – Multiples
IA10.2: Trios for Multiples
IA10.3: Quick Draw Multiples
IA10.4: Rolling Groups
IA10.5: Lemonade Stand
IA10.6: Array Flip
IA10.7: Dueling Arrays
IA10.8: Mini Multo
IA10.9: Four's a Winner
IA10.10: I Have/Who Has
IA10.11: Multiplication Match-up
IA10.12: Introducing Division
IA10.13: Division Array Cards

ACTIVITY IA10.1: Count Around – Multiples

Intended learning: To develop facility with number word sequences in multiples.

Materials: None.

Description: Children form a circle and count in turn. The progression of counting sequences in this activity supports children in moving from counting-by-ones to counting using a sequence of multiples. The first rounds involve a verbal count by ones with emphasis being placed on the multiples of a selected number, initially focusing on the first ten multiples. For example, for multiples of three, the count would be *1, 2, 3, 4, 5, 6, 7, 8, 9 …* with the children who have a count that is a multiple of three calling it out loudly while raising their arms in the air. In subsequent rounds, the counts for the numbers not in the multiple sequence are de-emphasized. This might include going from a normal vocal count to a whisper count to an action, such as a clap or snap, to represent the count. This brings the multiple sequence to more prominence. Finally, Count Around can be played with only the multiples being said in sequence.

Notes:

- Knowledge of number word sequences in multiples is separate from knowledge of the group structure. That is, children who can recite skip counting sequences might not understand that when counting in multiples, what they are counting is an abstract composite unit.
- Sequences for multiples should also include starting not only at the beginning of the sequence, but also at different places within the sequence.
- Sequences for multiples should also include counting backwards by multiples. For example, starting at 30 and counting backwards by threes.

ACTIVITY IA10.2: Trios for Multiples

Intended learning: To identify sequences of numerals representing three consecutive multiples.

Materials: Numeral card deck containing four each of the first ten multiples of a given number (for example, for multiples of three, the deck would contain four each of the numbers 3, 6, 9, 12, 15, 18, 21, 24, 27, 30).

Description: Two or three players are each dealt five cards from a deck of numeral cards containing multiples of a given number. The remaining cards are placed face down, forming a draw pile, and the top card is turned over and placed beside the stack, forming a discard pile. The goal is to collect a series, or trio, of three consecutive multiples (for threes, an example is 9, 12, 15). At their turn, a player may take either the top card from the draw pile or the top card from the discard pile. If the player's hand contains a trio the cards are displayed on the table and saved by that player. Whether or not a trio is formed, the player's turn ends by selecting a card from their hand and placing it in the discard pile. If the draw pile is depleted, the discard pile is shuffled to form a new draw pile. The game ends when one player is out of cards.

Notes:

- The number of cards held in each player's hand can be increased to add to the potential trios that can be formed.
- To increase the level of difficulty, combine the decks for several sets of multiples. Children then must decide what sequence they are working on for a given number and which other numbers fit into that sequence.

ACTIVITY IA10.3: Quick Draw Multiples

Intended learning: To generate sequences of multiples with numerals, both forwards and backwards.

Materials: Numeral card deck containing four each of the first ten multiples of a given number (e.g. for multiples of three, the deck would contain four each of the numbers 3, 6, 9, 12, 15, 18, 21, 24, 27, 30).

Description: Two players are each dealt 15 cards from a deck of numeral cards containing multiples of a given number. These cards are placed in a stack face down in front of the player. The remaining ten cards are divided into two stacks of five and placed face down between the players with space enough between the stacks to turn up and display cards to start the play action. The larger stack in front of the player is the draw pile for that player. Each player draws three cards from their own draw pile. Next, both players simultaneously turn over a card from the middle stacks. A play is made from a player's hand by placing the next multiple, either forwards or backwards, on top of one of the turned up cards. Both players play at the same time and may make a series of plays, so long as the plays are made one card at a time. For example, in a game using multiples of five, if a 25 is turned up a player may play either a 20 or a 30. An example of a sequence of cards is 30, 35, 40, 35, 30, 25, 20 (remember the next card can be the multiple of five before or after the previous card). As cards are played during the game, the player replenishes their hand from their draw pile. A player cannot have more than three cards at any one time. When neither player can play a card, new starter cards are turned up. If the starter cards are all used, the cards in the center are shuffled and placed face down for new starter cards. The first player to play all cards from their draw pile is the winner.

Note:

- Children should have prior experience reciting multiple sequences, forwards and backwards, starting at different places within the sequence.

ACTIVITY IA10.4: Rolling Groups

Intended learning: To develop strategies for multiplication using a repeated unit. To develop facility with counting in multiples.

Materials: One die with the numbers 2, 3, 3, 4, 4, 5 (to generate the number in each group), one deca-die with numbers 0–9 (to generate the number of groups), nine strips of each of the following: 2 items, 3 items, 4 items, 5 items (see Figure 10.8).

Description: Children roll one die to generate the number of groups and another die to generate the number in each group. Using the numbers generated by rolling the dice, the child places on the table the number of strips of the specified size. Children count to get the total number. Children may work individually, in pairs or in small groups.

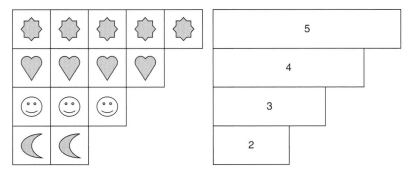

Figure 10.8 Strips for Rolling Groups

Notes:

- Encourage the children to count in multiples.
- Children might demonstrate differing abilities in counting to find the total, for example: (a) using a multiple count (skip counting), such as **3**, **6**, **9**, **12**; (b) using a stress count, such as 1, 2, **3**, 4, 5, **6**, 7, 8, **9**; (c) using a combination of stress and multiple counts, such as **3**, **6**, **9**, 10, 11, **12**, 13, 14, **15**.
- Each strip provides the child with a reference for both the group and the number of items in each group (i.e. the strip is a container that holds the given number of items).
- Observe how the children arrange the strips. Do they arrange them in a row or column structure or do they place them in a line?
- Asking children how they got their total or asking them if they could arrange the strips another way can provide insight into the child's knowledge and skills.
- As needed, change the numbers on the die representing the number in each group to give children practice with the multiple sequences they do not already know.
- To move children away from using visible items to count, replace the strips having individual items with strips that only contain a numeral to represent the quantity in each strip.
- To modify this task so that it is based on an area model (Figure 10.9), children could color rows or columns on grid paper.
- To modify this task so that it is based on a linear model (Figure 10.10), children could show hops on a number line.
- Children could record the resulting equation on a piece of paper.
- Products could be verified using a calculator.
- Other dice and sets of strips could be created for work on other multiples.

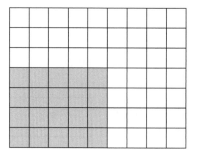

Figure 10.9   Using an area model to illustrate four groups of 5

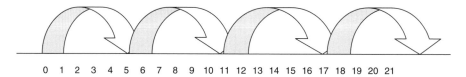

0 1 2 3 4 5 6 7 8 9 10 11 12 13 14 15 16 17 18 19 20 21

Figure 10.10   Using a linear model to illustrate four groups of 5

ACTIVITY IA10.5: Lemonade Stand

Intended learning: To develop strategies for multiplication. To form equal groups of a specified size and determine the total with individual items concealed.

Materials: Ten-sided die with numerals 1 to 10, regular die with dots 1 to 6, 10 opaque cups, lids for the cups or cardboard covers, 60 small cubes, Lemonade Stand record sheet.

Description: Pairs of children take turns preparing cups with ice-cubes for lemonade orders. Player A rolls both dice. The numeral die indicates how many cups and the dot die indicates how many ice-cubes are to be placed in each cup. This player sets out the appropriate number of cups, puts the indicated number of cubes into each cup, and places lids on the cups. The player must then work out how many ice-cubes were used for the entire order. The number of cups, number of ice-cubes per cup, and the total number of ice-cubes are recorded on the Lemonade Stand record sheet. Player B then rolls the dice and completes the task as above. The winner of the round is the player who used the most ice-cubes. More rounds are completed in the same way.

Notes:

- The lids are used intentionally to conceal the individual items within the groups, while the cup is available as a marker to indicate the group.
- Encourage the children to count in multiples. Children might demonstrate differing abilities in counting to find the total, for example: (a) using a multiple count (skip counting), such

as **3**, **6**, **9**, **12**; (b) using a stress count, such as 1, 2, **3**, 4, 5, **6**, 7, 8, **9**; (c) using a combination of stress and multiple counts, such as **3**, **6**, **9**, 10, 11, **12**, 13, 14, **15**.

- The dice can be customized to set the number of groups and the number within each group for different ability levels.

LEMONADE STAND					
ROUND 1					
	PLAYER 1			PLAYER 2	
Number of Cups	Number of Ice-cubes	Total Number of Ice-cubes	Number of Cups	Number of Ice-cubes	TOTAL Number of Ice-cubes
ROUND 2					

Figure 10.11   Lemonade Stand record sheet

ACTIVITY IA10.6: Array Flip

Intended learning: To develop strategies for multiplication and division. To use array structures to support the use of repeated groups.

Materials: Numeral and array cards for the first ten multiples of a given number, partially covered array cards for the first ten multiples of a given number.

array cards face down   numeral cards face down

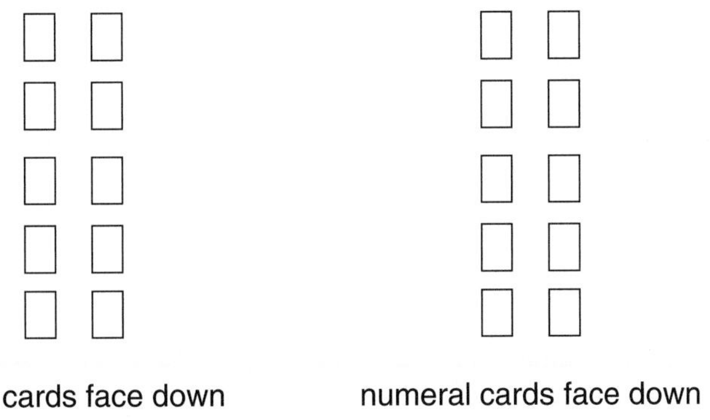

Figure 10.12   Layout of array and numeral cards

Description: Pairs of children place array cards face down in a 2 × 5 arrangement (see Figure 10.12). The numeral cards are also placed face down in a 2 × 5 arrangement. Children take turns turning over one array card and one numeral card trying to match the array to its product (see Figure 10.13). The game continues until all cards have been matched.

Notes:

- Children will need experiences forming equal groups and forming arrays, before undertaking this activity.
- Arrays with covers that leave one row and one column visible and that can be lifted, could be supportive (see Figure 10.14).
- Cards showing the groups as collections can be substituted for the array cards.
- Cards with multiplication expressions can be substituted for the numeral cards, for example, 4 × 5 instead of 20.
- Pay close attention to the strategies children use to determine the matching product or array; for example: (a) Are they counting each group by ones? (b) Are they using skip counting, or a combination of counting-by-ones and skip counting? (c) Do they use their fingers to keep track of the items in each group, the number of groups, or both? (d) Do they use multiplication facts? If so, for which products?
- The activity could be changed to a Fish format by making four sets of the numeral and array cards. Having five cards in their hand, children ask for the product or describe the array needed to make a match. For example, the child asks, 'Do you have four rows of five'?

ACTIVITY IA10.7: Dueling Arrays

Intended learning: To develop strategies for multiplication and division. To determine the number of rows or the total for a partially covered array structure with all but one row hidden.

Materials: Dueling array cards.

Description: The class forms a double circle with one child standing behind a child who is sitting. The teacher shows a dueling array card to a pair of children (see Figure 10.15). The first of the two children who answers correctly holds the standing position. The turn moves to the next pair of children.

Notes:

- Prior to using this activity, children should be able to find the total for array structures with all dots visible.
- Children should have at least partial knowledge of the accompanying skip counting sequences prior to using this activity.
- Children of similar abilities can be paired for this activity.
- Differentiate for pairs by selecting cards of appropriate difficulty.
- Give children time to work out the answer, carefully watching for the child's strategy.
- For some children it might be necessary to make complete dot arrays with removable covers.

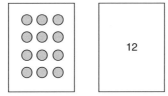

Figure 10.13   Array and numeral cards

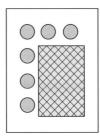

Figure 10.14   Partially screened array card

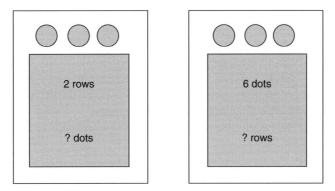

Figure 10.15   Examples of dueling array cards

ACTIVITY IA10.8: Mini Multo

Intended learning: To develop automaticity with multiplication facts.

Materials: Mini Multo game board.

Description: Players begin by filling in a table on the Mini Multo game board with nine different multiples, chosen from the first ten multiples, of a selected number for the round (see Figure 10.16). These can be placed in any arrangement. The teacher, acting as the caller, shuffles the deck of numeral factor cards, 1 to 10, and places the stack face down. The teacher selects the top card and announces the factor to the players. The players then independently determine the product of the called factor and the selected number for the round. If the product appears in the filled-in table, that box is crossed out. The winner is the first player(s) who has three boxes in a row marked off vertically, horizontally or diagonally. The products can be verified against the factor cards that were called.

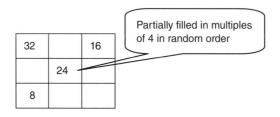

Figure 10.16   Mini Multo game board

Notes:

- Children should have previously developed strategies for finding products that are to be used in this activity.
- Introduction of this activity might include explaining how the play will take place, but with little help given as to what numbers the children should place on their game board.
- Mini Multo can be differentiated to meet the needs of individual children. Within the same round, all children could be using multiples of the same number or children could select, or be assigned, different numbers to generate sets of multiples. The results can still be verified for any set of multiples based on the factor cards that are called during the game.
- This activity is appropriate for whole class or small groups.
- A child could take the role of the caller and could use a calculator to verify the products for the called numbers.
- This activity can be extended by using the sum of two dice to determine the called factor instead of the cards. This allows for the possibility of using a multiple more than one time on the board, as some multiples would be more likely than others. Although this will probably not be immediately apparent to the children, over time strategies for filling in the table of multiples will emerge. A larger table of multiples might also be used in this case. A record-keeping system should be used to keep track of what factors were called.

ACTIVITY IA10.9: Four's a Winner

Intended learning: To use multiplication and division in determining products and factors.

Materials: Four's a Winner game board (see Figure 10.17), game markers in two colors, two see-through markers for the factor strips.

Description: Pairs of children take turns forming factor pairs and covering the product on the game board with a game marker. To begin the game, place factor markers on the ones in each factor strip. Player A moves a factor marker anywhere on either of the factor strips and places one of their colored markers on the product of the two indicated factors. Player B now moves one of the factor markers on either of the factor strips and covers the resulting product with a colored marker. (Note: for each turn, a player may move only one of the factor markers.) Players continue alternating turns. The winner is the first player to cover four spaces in a row, horizontally, vertically or diagonally.

Notes:

- Children should have facility with strategies for multiplication and division and some level of automaticity before playing this game.
- Relational knowledge for multiplication and division is important in this activity, as children might select two numbers to multiply or might have selected a number they would like to capture and must determine what factors could be used.
- In addition to the practice with multiplication and division, this activity is rich with underlying strategies for play. Over time children will develop strategies for blocking and for factor selection that limits their opponent's options.

64	20	9	16	48	4	54	14	25
49	32	36	10	32	81	42	35	12
21	63	7	15	63	20	45	24	16
14	72	18	8	35	28	12	40	8
2	56	12	27	4	18	8	24	36
15	6	72	30	16	9	42	6	40
30	18	36	48	27	56	24	3	54
12	28	21	6	24	18	10	5	45

FACTOR

1	2	3	4	5	6	7	8	9

×

1	2	3	4	5	6	7	8	9

FACTOR

Figure 10.17 Four's a Winner game board

ACTIVITY IA10.10: I Have/Who Has

Intended learning: To use multiplication and division in determining products and factors.

Materials: I Have/Who Has cards for twos, threes, fours and fives.

Description: I Have/Who Has cards are distributed to the children (one per child). The teacher begins the round by posing the first task (*Who has …*). All children work out the answer and check to see if the answer is on their card. The child who holds the card with the correct answer responds by reading their card (*I have … who has …*), posing a new task for the group. Play continues in this way until the teacher has the correct answer.

Notes:

- Children can be instructed to work out each item individually, record the answer on paper or whiteboard, and display to the teacher. This holds all children accountable for all task items and allows the teacher to assess an individual child's work.
- The teacher might need to assist some children to read the cards, as the written language for these concepts might prove difficult. The emphasis for this activity is on verbally based tasks.
- Certain cards can be assigned to specific children to match capabilities and allow for success.
- I Have/Who Has can be played by the whole class or in small groups. When used in small groups, each child will be responsible for more than one card.
- Sets of I Have/Who Has cards can be created to work on a variety of topics and for a variety of levels.

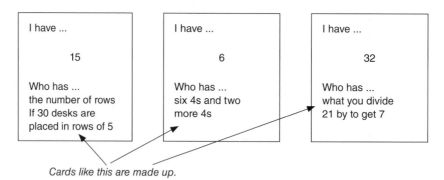

Cards like this are made up.

Figure 10.18   Cards for I Have/Who Has

ACTIVITY IA10.11: Multiplication Match-up

Intended learning: To support children to learn the multiplication facts and link these with equal groups or arrays.

Materials: Multiplication, numeral and group cards (see diagram), player sheet if needed.

Description: Children are arranged into groups of two to four players. Three types of cards are piled up between the players: multiplication task (red), product (green) and equal groups (yellow) (other colors will suffice). Each player in turn selects a card and places it on their sheet. The aim is to complete as many rows as possible before the cards are used up.

Notes:

- The cards can be placed on a table or on the floor rather than using a prepared sheet.
- Array cards can be used instead of the yellow equal group cards.
- As an alternative, children could work on one sheet between two and take turns to choose a card and place it on the sheet. This becomes a cooperative rather than a competitive task.

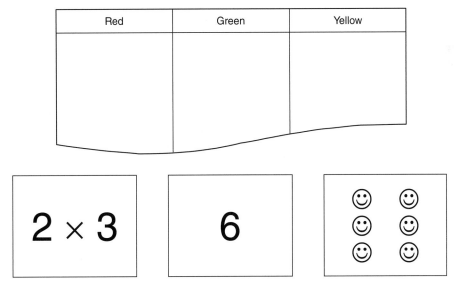

Figure 10.19   Multiplication Match-up sheet and cards

ACTIVITY IA10.12: Introducing Division

Intended learning: To introduce quotitive (sharing) and partitive division.

Materials: Counters, lids (or cups etc.).

Description:
Partitive (sharing) division

- Sharing between two: Teacher sets up 12 counters and 3 plates. *We want to put the same number of counters on each plate. How many counters will there be on each plate?* Give other tasks sharing an even number of items between two people. See if children can find the answer to these sharing divisions without using the counters. Have children check to see if their answer is correct.

- Sharing between two, four and five: Use activities similar to those above, sharing among three, four and five people. Introduce a range of sharing activities such as having 12 children divide equally into 2 groups, 3 groups, 4 groups.
- Give children individually or in pairs 20 counters and 5 containers (plates, cups, squares of paper, etc.) and repeat tasks like those above. *Share (or divide) 15 counters into 3 equal groups.*

Quotitive (grouping) division

- *There are 12 counters and there are 3 on each plate. How many plates are there?* Have the class think about this task and ask for someone to explain their solution using plates and counters. Give other tasks of this type.
- Give individuals or pairs a pile of counters (say 20) and give them tasks similar to those used in sharing between two (above). Discuss the solutions. Encourage children to try to solve the tasks in their head and then check the result with the counters and lids.

Notes:

- Simple sharing tasks can be given to young children.
- As children develop multiplication concepts, teachers should encourage their use in solving division tasks.

ACTIVITY IA10.13: Division Array Cards

Intended learning: To develop strategies to solve quotitive division tasks.

Materials: Array cards.

Description: Children in pairs take turns to select a card and work out how many rows. The answer can be checked on the reverse side of the card. A record sheet for each player to record the task and their answer can be prepared.

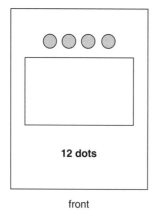

12 dots

front

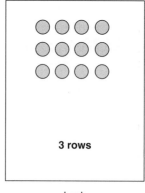

3 rows

back

Figure 10.20   Array cards

Notes:

- An alternative is for students to do this activity individually.
- This is a self-checking activity which frees the teacher to observe children more closely or assist specific children.

Learning Trajectory

Table 10.1 Learning Trajectory: Early Multiplication and Division

Topics	Page Ref.	Assessment Task Groups	Instructional Activities
Counting by 2s, 5s, 10s and 3s	179–180	A10.1	IA10.1 IA10.2 IA10.3
Multiplication – items and groups visible		A10.2	IA10.4
Multiplication – items screened and groups visible		A10.3	IA10.4 Turn the individual cards over so the items can't be seen 1A10.5
Multiplication – items and groups screened		A10.4	1A10.5
Quotitive division – number in each group given	180–181	A10.5	IA10.12
Partitive division – number of groups given	180–181	A10.6	IA10.12
Multiplication using arrays	182–183	A10.7	1A10.6 1A10.7
Division using arrays	182–183	A10.8	IA10.13
Multiplication basic facts involving 2, 10 and 5 as multipliers		A10.9	1A10.8 1A10.9 1A10.10 IA10.11
Relational thinking (a) commutative and distributive principles (b) multiplication and division as inverses	182–183	A10.10 A10.11	1A10.10

Glossary

Addend. A number to be added. In 7 + 4 = 11, 7 and 4 are addends, and 11 is the sum.

Additive task. A generic label for tasks involving what adults would regard as addition. The label 'additive task' is used to emphasize that children will construe such tasks idiosyncratically, that is, differently from each other and from the way adults will construe them.

Arithmetic rack. See Appendix 1.

Array. See Appendix 1.

Arrow cards. See Appendix 1.

Automaticity. A capacity to determine quickly the value of calculations (e.g. 7 + 9, 4 × 8), typically referring to the basic facts. Also referred to as **automatization**. Related terms are 'automatized knowledge' and 'habituated knowledge', that is, knowledge that is immediately available.

Automatization. See **Automaticity**.

Automatized knowledge. See **Automaticity**.

Backward number word sequence (BNWS). A regular sequence of number words backward, typically but not necessarily by ones, for example, the BNWS from 10 to 1, the BNWS from 82 to 75, the BNWS by tens from 83.

Base-ten dot materials. See Appendix 1.

Bundling sticks. See Appendix 1.

Combining. An arithmetical strategy involving combining (i.e. in a sense adding) two numbers whose sum is in the range 1 to 10, without counting, for example 4 and 3, 7 and 2.

Commutative. Addition is said to be a commutative operation because, for any two numbers, the order of adding does not change the result, for example, 7 + 4 = 4 + 7. Multiplication is also a commutative operation whereas subtraction and division are operations that are not commutative.

Complexifying. We use this term to refer to making the current mathematics more complex. For example, progressing from (a) adding to finding a missing addend, (b) adding a 10 to adding a 10 and 2 ones, and (c) doubling a number to doubling a number and adding one. Thus complexifying is a dimension (theme) of progressive mathematization.

Counting-back-from. A strategy used by children to solve removed items tasks, for example 11 remove 3 – 'eleven, ten, nine … eight'. Also referred to as counting-off-from or counting-down-from.

Counting-back-to. Regarded as the most advanced of the counting-by-ones strategies. Typically used to solve missing subtrahend tasks, for example, have 11, remove some, and there are eight left – 'eleven, ten, nine … three'. Also referred to as counting-down-to.

Counting-by-ones. Initial or advanced arithmetical strategies which involve counting-by-ones only. Examples of initial counting-by-ones strategies are perceptual and figurative counting, which involve counting-from-one. Examples of advanced counting-by-ones strategies are counting-up-from, counting-up-to, counting-back-from and counting-back-to.

Counting-on. An advanced counting-by-ones strategy used to solve additive tasks or missing addend tasks involving two hidden collections. Counting-on can be differentiated into counting-up-from for additive tasks and counting-up-to for missing addend tasks. Counting-on is also referred to as counting-up.

Counting-up-from. An advanced counting-by-ones strategy used to solve additive tasks involving two hidden collections, for example, 7 and 5, is solved by counting up 5 from 7.

Counting-up-to. An advanced counting-by-ones strategy used to solve missing addend tasks, for example, 7 and how many make 12, is solved by counting from 7 up to 12, and keeping track of 5 counts.

Count number. When an additive or subtractive task is solved in the usual way using counting-on or counting-back the count number is the number of counts the student makes. Count numbers are usually in the range 2 to 5.

Decrementing by tens. See **Incrementing and decrementing by tens**.

Decuple. A multiple of ten (e.g. 10, 20, 30, 180, 240). Distinguished from decade which means a sequence of ten numbers, for example, from 27 to 36 or a period of ten years.

Difference. See **Minuend**.

Discrete-based reasoning. When solving a task involving counting-on or counting-back, where the student's reasoning seems to focus on the items in turn. See also **Interval-based reasoning**.

Digit. The digits are the ten basic symbols in the modern numeration system, that is 0, 1, … 9.

Digit cards. See Appendix 1.

Early number. A generic label for the number work in the first three years of school and learned by children around 4 to 8 years of age. Also known as 'early arithmetic'.

Emergent. The term 'emergent' is used in cases where the child is not able to count perceptually. Thus the child is unable to count a collection of say, 12 or 15 counters. The child might not know the number word sequence or might not correctly coordinate each number word with an item to be counted.

Empty number line (ENL). See Appendix 1.

Facile. Used in the sense of having good facility, that is, fluent or dexterous, for example, a facile counting-on strategy, or facile with the backward number word sequence.

Figurative. Figurative thought involves re-presentation of a sensory-motor experience, that is a mental replay of a prior experience involving seeing, hearing, touching, and so on. Figurative counting may be: figural, in which visualized items constitute the material which is counted; motor, in which movements constitute the material which is counted; or verbal, in which number words constitute the material which is counted.

Five-wise pattern. A spatial pattern for a number in the range 1 to 10 made on a ten-frame (two rows and five columns). The five-wise patterns are made by progressively filling the rows. For example, a five-wise pattern for 8 has a row of five and a row of three, a five-wise pattern for 4 has a row of four dots.

Flashing. A technique which involves briefly displaying (typically for half a second) some aspect of an instructional setting, for example, a ten-frame with 8 red and 2 green counters is flashed.

Formal algorithm. A standard written procedure for calculating with multi-digit numbers that relies on the conventions of formal place value; for example, the column-based procedures for adding, subtracting, and so on, contrasted with an informal strategy, for example, solving 58 + 25 by adding 58 and 20, and then 78 and 5.

Formal arithmetic. Arithmetic at the adult level involving formal notation rather than involving informal notation such as an empty number line or a setting such as base-ten materials.

Forward number word sequence (FNWS). A regular sequence of number words forward, typically but not necessarily by ones, for example the FNWS from 1 to 20, the FNWS from 81 to 93, the FNWS by tens from 24.

Habituated knowledge. See **Automaticity**.

Incrementing and decrementing by tens. Refers to the ability to say immediately the number that is ten more (incrementing) or ten less (decrementing) than a given number.

Instructional setting. See **Setting**.

Interval-based reasoning. When solving a task involving counting-on or counting-back, where the student's reasoning seems to focus on the interval from one number to the next. See also **Discrete-based reasoning**.

Irregular spatial configuration. A configuration of dots that does not take the form of a pattern such as the patterns on dice or dominos.

Jump strategy. A category of mental strategies for 2-digit addition and subtraction. Strategies in this category involve starting from one number and incrementing or decrementing that number by tens or ones.

Knowledge. A collective term for all of what the child knows about early number. The term 'knowledge' is sometimes juxtaposed with 'strategies' and in that case refers to knowledge not easily characterized as a strategy (for example, knowing the names of numerals).

Mathematics Recovery (MR). A program originally developed in schools in New South Wales which has been implemented widely in schools in a range of countries. The program focuses on intensive teaching for low-attaining children and an extensive program of specialist teacher development.

Micro-adjusting. Making small moment-by-moment adjustments in interactive teaching which are informed by one's observation of student responses.

Minuend. In subtraction of standard form, for example $12 - 3 = 9$, 12 is the minuend, 3 is the subtrahend and 9 is the difference. Thus the difference is the answer obtained in subtraction, the subtrahend is the number subtracted and the minuend is the number from which the subtrahend is subtracted.

Missing addend task. An arithmetical task where one addend and the sum are given, for example $9 + \square = 13$.

Missing subtrahend task. A subtractive task where the minuend and the difference are given, for example, $11 - \square = 8$.

Non-canonical. The number 64 can be expressed in the form of $50 + 14$. This form is referred to as a non-canonical (non-standard) form of 64. Knowledge of non-canonical forms is useful in addition, subtraction, and so on.

Non-count-by-ones. A class of strategies which involve aspects other than counting-by-ones and which are used to solve additive and subtractive tasks. Part of the strategy may involve counting-by-ones but the solution also involves a more advanced procedure. For example, $6 + 8$ is solved by saying 'six and six is twelve – thirteen, fourteen'. Also referred to as grouping strategies.

Notating. Writing which relates to numbers and numerical reasoning. Thus purposeful writing in an arithmetical situation, for example, notating a jump strategy on an empty number line.

Number. A number is the idea or concept associated with, for example, how many items in a collection. We distinguish between the number 24, that is, the concept, the spoken or heard number word 'twenty-four', the numeral '24', and the read or written number word 'twenty-four'. These distinctions are important in understanding children's early numerical strategies.

Number word. Number words are names or words for numbers. In most cases in early number, the term 'number word' refers to the spoken and heard names for numbers rather than the written and read names.

Numeral. Numerals are symbols for numbers, for example, '5' and '27'.

Numeral cards. See Appendix 1.

Numeral identification. Stating the name of a displayed numeral. The term is used similarly to the term 'letter identification' in early literacy. When assessing numeral identification, numerals are not displayed in numerical sequence.

Numeral recognition. Selecting a nominated numeral from a randomly arranged group of numerals.

Numeral roll. See Appendix 1.

Numeral roll and multi-lid screen. See Appendix 1.

Numeral roll and window. See Appendix 1.

Numeral sequence. A regularly ordered sequence of numerals, typically but not necessarily a forward sequence by ones, for example the numerals as they appear on a numeral track.

Numeral track. See Appendix 1.

Numerosity. The numerosity of a collection is the number of items in the collection.

Ordering numerals. See **Sequencing numerals**.

Pair-wise pattern. A spatial pattern for a number in the range 1 to 10 made on a ten-frame (two rows and five columns). The pair-wise patterns are made by progressively filling the columns. For example, a pair-wise pattern for 8 has four pairs, a pair-wise pattern for 5 has two pairs and one single dot.

Partitioning. An arithmetical strategy involving partitioning a number into two parts without counting, for example, when solving 8 + 5, 5 is partitioned into 2 and 3.

Perceptual. Involving direct sensory input – usually seeing but may also refer to hearing or feeling. Thus perceptual counting involves counting items seen, heard or felt.

Progressive mathematization. This term is used to describe progression of children's learning and thinking in terms of advancement in mathematical sophistication.

Quinary. This term refers to the use of five as a base in some sense, and typically in conjunction with, rather than instead of, ten as a base. The arithmetic rack may be regarded as a quinary-based instructional device.

Regrouping task. In the case of addition of two 2-digit numbers, a task where the sum of the numbers in the ones column exceeds 9, for example, in 37 + 48, 7 + 8 exceeds 9. In the case of subtraction involving two 2-digit numbers, a task where, in the ones column, the subtrahend exceeds the minuend, for example in 85 – 48, 8 exceeds 5. Similarly applied to addition and subtraction with numbers with three or more digits. The term non-regrouping is used in the case of an addition task where the sum of the numbers in the ones column does not exceed 9 and in the case of a subtraction task where, in the ones column, the minuend exceeds the subtrahend.

Regular spatial configuration. A configuration of dots that takes the form of a standard pattern such as the patterns on dice or dominos.

Removed items task. A subtractive task where the minuend and the subtrahend are given, for example, 11 – 3 = □.

Screening. A technique used in the presentation of instructional tasks which involves placing a small screen over all or part of an instructional setting (for example, screening a collection of six counters).

Sequencing numerals. Putting in order, a set of numerals that constitute a standard sequence, for example, the numerals from 1 to 10 or from 46 to 55. When the set of numerals does not constitute a standard sequence the term ordering numerals is used, for example: 9, 12, 18, 21.

Setting. A setting is a situation used by the teacher when posing arithmetical tasks. Settings can be: (a) materials (e.g. numeral track, ten-frame, counters); (b) informal written; (c) formal written; or (d) verbal. The term setting refers not only to the material, writing or verbal statements but also encompasses the ways in which these (materials, writing or verbal statements) are used in instruction and feature in students' reasoning. Thus the term setting encompasses the often implicit features of instruction that arise during the pedagogical use of the setting.

Split strategy. A category of mental strategies for 2-digit addition and subtraction. Strategies in this category involve splitting the numbers into tens and ones and working separately with the tens and ones.

Strategy. A generic label for a method by which a child solves a task. A strategy consists of two or more constituent procedures. A procedure is the simplest form of a strategy, that is, a strategy that cannot be described in terms of two or more constituent procedures. For example, on an additive task involving two screened collections a child might use the procedure of counting the first collection from one and then use the procedure of continuing to count by ones, in order to count the second collection.

Subitizing. The immediate correct assignation of a number word to a small collection of perceptual items.

Subtractive task. A generic label for tasks involving what adults would regard as subtraction. The label 'subtractive task' is used to emphasize that children will construe such tasks idiosyncratically, that is, differently from each other and from the way adults will construe them.

Subtrahend. See **Minuend**.

Sum. See **Addend**.

Symbolizing. Used in a very broad sense – developing or using symbols in the context of numerical reasoning.

Task. A generic label for problems or questions presented to a child.

Temporal sequence. A sequence of events that occur sequentially in time, for example, sequences of sounds or movements.

Ten-frame. See Appendix 1.

Ten-frames – 10-dot cards. See Appendix 1.

Ten-frames – combinations. See Appendix 1.

Ten-frames – five-wise. See Appendix 1.

Ten-frames – pair-wise. See Appendix 1.

Ten-frames – partitions. See Appendix 1.

Unitizing. A conceptual procedure that involves regarding a number larger than one as a unit, for example, 3 is regarded as a unit of 3 rather than 3 ones, and 10 is regarded as a unit of 10. Unitizing enables students to focus on the unitary rather than the composite aspect of the number.

Appendix
Instructional Settings

Arithmetic rack. An instructional device consisting of two rows of ten beads which can be moved like beads on an abacus. In each row the beads appear in two groups of five, demarcated by color. The rack is used to support students' additive reasoning in the range 1 to 20. See Figure 7.1 and Photos 7.2 and 7.3.

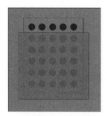

Array. A rectangular grid of dots used as a setting for multiplication, for example, a 6 × 4 array has six rows and four columns. See Figure 10.5 and Photo 10.4.

Arrow cards. A set of 36 cards with a card for each of the following numerals: 1, 2, …9; 10, 20, … 90; 100, 200, … 900; and 1000, 2000 … 9000. The cards are used to build multi-digit numerals, and each card has an arrow on the right hand side to support students' orienting and locating the cards. See Figure 9.2.

Base-ten dot materials. Materials consisting of strips with 1 to 9 dots, strips with 10 dots and squares with 100 dots. Dots are grey or black in order to demarcate a 5 in the 6- to 9-dot strips, two 5s in the 10-dot strip and two 50s in the 100-dot square. See Figure 8.2 and Photo 8.2.

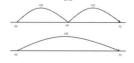

Bundling sticks. Wooden sticks used to show tens and ones. Rubber bands are used to make bundles of 10 and groups of 10 tens.

Digit cards. A set of cards used to build numerals. Each card displays a digit (i.e. 0, 1, 2 … 9). A set includes several cards for each digit, in order to account for numerals with repeating digits (e.g. 464, 3333).

Empty number line (ENL). A setting consisting of a simple arc or line which is used by students and teachers to record and explain mental strategies for adding, subtracting, multiplying and dividing. See Figures 1.2 to 1.6.

Numeral cards. A set of cards with each card displaying a numeral. See Photos 3.3 and 3.4.

Numeral roll. An instructional setting consisting of a long strip of paper containing a relatively long sequence of numerals, increasing from left to right, for example, from 1 to 120 or 80 to 220. See Photos 3.1, 3.2 and 3.8.

Numeral roll and window. A numeral roll threaded through a slotted card so that one numeral only is displayed.

Numeral roll and multi-lid screen. A numeral roll and a screen with 10 or more lids enabling screening and unscreening of individual numerals.

Numeral track. An instructional setting consisting of a strip of cardboard containing a sequence of numerals and for each numeral, a hinged lid which can be used to screen or display the numeral. See Figure 3.1 and Photos 3.5 and 3.6.

Ten-frame. An instructional setting consisting of a card with a 2 × 5 rectangular array used to support students' additive reasoning in the range 1 to 10. See Figure 5.5 and Photos 5.4 to 5.7.

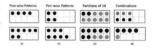

Ten-frames – 10-dot cards. Ten-frames with 10 dots of one color.

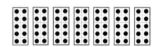

Ten-frames – combinations. A set of ten-frames with the different combinations of (a) 0 to 5 dots in the upper row and (b) 0 to 5 dots in the lower row, typically with the rows in differing colors. A total of 36 cards.

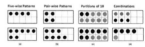

Ten-frames – five-wise. A set of 11 ten-frames showing the five-wise patterns for 0, 1, … 10. See Figure 5.7 and Photos 5.6 and 5.7.

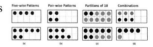

Ten-frames – pair-wise. A set of 11 ten-frames showing the pair-wise patterns for 0, 1, … 10. See Figure 5.6 and Photos 5.4 and 5.5.

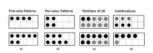

Ten-frames – partitions. A set of 11 ten-frames showing the partitions of 10 demarcated by color (i.e. 10 and 0, 9 and 1, 8 and 2, … 0 and 10). Typically, a five-wise set and a pair-wise set.

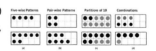

Bibliography

Anghileri, J. (2000) *Teaching Number Sense*. London: Continuum.

Anghileri, J. (ed.) (2001) *Principles and Practices of Arithmetic Teaching*. Buckingham: Open University Press.

Aubrey, C. 1993 'An investigation of the mathematical knowledge and competencies which young children bring into school', *British Educational Research Journal*, 19(1): 27–41.

Baroody, A. (1985) 'Mastery of basic number combinations: internalization of relationships or facts?', *Journal for Research in Mathematics Education*, 16(2): 83–98.

Baroody, A. (2006) 'Why children have difficulties mastering the basic number combinations and how to help them', *Teaching Children Mathematics*, 13(1): 22–31.

Beishuizen, M. (1993) 'Mental strategies and materials or models for addition and subtraction up to 100 in Dutch second grades', *Journal for Research in Mathematics Education*, 34: 394–433.

Beishuizen, M. (1999) 'The empty number line as a new model', in I. Thompson (ed.), *Issues in Teaching Numeracy in Primary Schools*. Buckingham: Open University Press, pp. 157–168.

Beishuizen, M. (2001) 'Different approaches to mastering mental calculation strategies', in J. Anghileri (ed.), *Principles and Practices in Arithmetic Teaching: Innovative Approaches for the Primary Classroom*. Buckingham: Open University Press, pp. 119–130.

Beishuizen, M. and Anghileri, J. (1998) 'Which mental strategies in the early number curriculum? A comparison of British ideas and Dutch Views', *British Education Research Journal*, 34: 519–538.

Bobis, J. (1996) 'Visualisation and the development of number sense with kindergarten children', in J. Mulligan and M. Mitchelmore (eds), *Children's Number Learning: A Research Monograph of MERGA/AAMT*. Adelaide: Australian Association of Mathematics Teachers, pp. 17–34.

Bobis, J., Clarke, B., Clarke, D., Thomas, G., Wright, R., Young-Loveridge, J. and Gould, P. (2005) 'Supporting teachers in the development of young children's mathematical thinking: three large-scale cases', *Mathematics Education Research Journal*, 16(3): 27–57.

Carpenter, T.P., Fennema, E., Franke, M.L., Levi, L. and Empson, S.B. (1999) *Children's Mathematics: Cognitively Guided Instruction*. Portsmouth, NH: Heinemann.

Carruthers, E. and Worthington, M. (2006) *Children's Mathematics: Making Marks, Making Meaning*. London: Sage.

Cayton, G. A. and Brizuela, B. M. (2007) 'First graders' strategies for numerical notation, number reading and the number concept', in J.H. Woo, H.C. Lew, K.S. Park and D.Y. Seo (eds), *Proceedings of the 31st Conference of the International Group for the Psychology of Mathematics Education* (Vol. 2). Seoul: PME, pp. 81–88.

Clarke, B., McDonough, A. and Sullivan, P. (2002) 'Measuring and describing learning: the early numeracy research project', in A. Cockburn and E. Nardi (eds), *Proceedings of the 26th Annual Conference of the International Group for the Psychology of Mathematics Education* (Vol. 1). Norwich, UK: PME, pp. 181–185.

Clarke, D., Sullivan, P., Cheeseman, J. and Clarke, B. (2000) 'The early numeracy research project: developing a framework for describing early numeracy learning', *Mathematics Education Beyond 2000. Proceedings of the Twenty-third Annual Conference of the Mathematics Education Research*

Group of Australasia. Freemantle, WA, 5–9 July 2000. Perth WA: Mathematics Education Research Group of Australasia, 180–187.

Clements, D. and Sarama, J. (eds) (2004) *Engaging Young Children in Mathematics*. Mahwah, NJ: Lawrence Erlbaum.

Clements, D. and Sarama, J. (2009) *Learning and Teaching Early Math – The Learning Trajectories Approach*. New York: Routledge.

Clements, D.H. and Sarama, J. (2011) 'Early childhood mathematics intervention', *Science* 333(6045): 968–970.

Cobb, P. (1991) 'Reconstructing elementary school mathematics', *Focus on Learning Problems in Mathematics*, 13(3): 3–33.

Cobb, P. and Bauersfeld, H. (eds) (1995) *The Emergence of Mathematical Meaning: Interaction in Classroom Cultures*. Hillsdale, NJ: Lawrence Erlbaum.

Cobb, P. Gravemeijer, K., Yackel, E., McClain, K. and Whitenack, J. (1997) 'Mathematizing and symbolizing: the emergence of chains of signification in one first-grade classroom', in D. Kirshner and J.A. Whitson (eds), *Situated Cognition Theory: Social, Semiotic, and Neurological Perspectives*. Mahwah, NJ: Lawrence Erlbaum, pp. 151–233.

Cobb, P., McClain, K., Whitenack, J. and Estes, B. (1995) 'Supporting young children's development of mathematical power', in A. Richards (ed.), *Proceedings of the Fifteenth Biennial Conference of the Australian Association of Mathematics Teachers*. Darwin: Australian Association of Mathematics Teachers, pp. 1–11.

Cobb, P. and Wheatley, G. (1988) 'Children's initial understandings of ten', *Focus on Learning Problems in Mathematics*, 10(3): 1–36.

Cobb, P., Wood, T. and Yackel, E. (1991) 'A constructivist approach to second grade mathematics', in E. von Glasersfeld (ed.), *Radical Constructivism in Mathematics Education*. Dordrecht: Kluwer, pp. 157–176.

Cobb, P., Yackel, E. and McClain, K. (eds) (2000) *Symbolizing and Communicating in Mathematics Classrooms: Perspectives on Discourse, Tools, and Instructional Design*. Mahwah, NJ: Lawrence Erlbaum.

Copley, J. (ed.) (1999) *Mathematics in the Early Years*. Reston, VA: National Council of Teachers of Mathematics.

Denvir, B. and Brown, M. (1986) 'Understanding of number concepts in low attaining 7–9 year olds: Part 1. Development of descriptive framework and diagnostic instrument', *Educational Studies in Mathematics*, 17: 15–36.

Dowker, A.D. (2004) *Children with Difficulties in Mathematics: What Works?* London: DfES.

Dowker, A.D. (2005) *Individual Differences in Arithmetic: Implications for Psychology, Neuroscience and Education*. Hove: Psychology Press.

Ellemor-Collins, D. and Wright, R.J. (2007) 'Assessing student knowledge of the sequential structure of numbers as a significant aspect of multi-digit addition and subtraction', *Educational and Child Psychology*, 24(2): 54–63.

Ellemor-Collins, D. and Wright, R.J. (2008) 'How are your students thinking about arithmetic? Videotaped interview-based assessment', *Teaching Children Mathematics*, September: 106–111.

Ellemor-Collins, D. and Wright, R.J. (2009) 'Structuring numbers 1 to 20: developing facile addition and subtraction', *Mathematics Education Research Journal*, 21(2): 50–75.

Ellemor-Collins, D. and Wright, R.J. (2011a) 'Developing conceptual place value: instructional design for intensive intervention', *Australian Journal of Learning Difficulties*, 16(1): 41–63.

Ellemor-Collins, D. and Wright, R.J. (2011b) 'Unpacking *mathematisation*: an experimental framework for arithmetic instruction', in B. Ubuz (ed.), *Proceedings of the 35th Conference of the*

International Group for the Psychology of Mathematics Education (Vol. 2). Ankara, Turkey: PME, pp. 313–320.

Flexer, R. (1986) 'The power of five: the step before the power of ten', *Arithmetic Teacher*, 31: 5–9.

Fosnot, C.T. and Dolk, M. (2001a) *Young Mathematics at Work: Constructing Multiplication and Division*. Portsmouth, NH: Heinemann.

Fosnot, C. and Dolk, M. (2001b) *Young Mathematicians at Work: Constructing Number Sense, Addition and Subtraction*. Portsmouth, NH: Heinemann.

Fountas, I.C. and Pinnell, G.S. (1996) *Guided Reading: Good First Teaching for All Children*. Portsmouth, NH: Heinemann.

Fuson, K. (1988) *Children's Counting and Concepts of Number*. New York: Springer-Verlag.

Fuson, K.C., Richards, J. and Briars, D. (1982) 'The acquisition and elaboration of the number word sequence', in C.J. Brainerd (ed.), *Progress in Cognitive Development: Vol. 1 Children's Logical and Mathematical Cognition*. New York: Springer-Verlag, pp. 33–92.

Fuson, K.C., Wearne, D., Hiebert, J., Human, P., Olivier, A., Carpenter, T. and Fenema, E. (1997) 'Children's conceptual structure for multidigit numbers and methods of multidigit addition and subtraction', *Journal for Research in Mathematics Education*, 38: 130–163.

Geary, D.C., Hoard, M.K., Nugent, L. and Bailey, D.H. (2013) 'Adolescents' functional numeracy is predicted by their school entry number system knowledge', *PLoS ONE*, 8(1): e54651. doi:10.1371/journal.pone.0054651.

Gelman, R. and Gallistel, C. (1978) *The Child's Understanding of Number*. Cambridge, MA and London: Harvard University Press.

Ginsburg, H.P. (1997) *Entering the Child's Mind: The Clinical Interview in Psychological Research and Practice*. New York: Cambridge University Press.

Ginsburg, H., Jacobs, S. and Lopez, L.S. (1998) *The Teacher's Guide to Flexible Interviewing in the Classroom: Learning What Children Know About Math*. Boston, MA: Allyn and Bacon.

Gould, P. (2012) 'What number knowledge do children have when starting kindergarten in NSW?' *Australian Journal of Early Childhood*, 37 (3): 105–110.

Gravemeijer, K.P.E. (1991) 'An instruction-theoretical reflection on the use of manipulatives', in L. Streefland (ed.), *Realistic Mathematics Education in Primary School*. Utrecht: Freudenthal Institute, pp. 57–76.

Gravemeijer, K.P.E. (1994) *Developing Realistic Mathematics Education*. Utrecht: CD-B Press.

Gravemeijer, K.P.E. (1997) 'Mediating between concrete and abstract', in T. Nunes and P. Bryant (eds), *Learning and Teaching Mathematics: An International Perspective*. East Sussex: Psychology Press, pp. 315–343.

Gravemeijer, K.P.E., Cobb, P., Bowers, J. and Whitenack, J. (2000) 'Symbolizing, modeling, and instructional design', in P. Cobb, E. Yackel and K. McClain (eds) *Symbolizing and Communicating in Mathematics Classrooms: Perspectives on Discourse, Tools, and Instructional Design*. Mahwah, NJ: Lawrence Erlbaum, pp. 335–373.

Gray, E.M. (1991) 'An analysis of diverging approaches to simple arithmetic: preference and its consequences', *Educational Studies in Mathematics*, 33: 551–74.

Gray, E. and Tall, D. (1994) 'Duality, ambiguity, and flexibility: a "proceptual" view of simple arithmetic', *Journal for Research in Mathematics Education*, 25(2), 116–140.

Hatano, G. (1982) 'Learning to add and subtract: a Japanese perspective', in T.P. Carpenter, J.M. Moser and T.A. Romberg (eds), *Addition and Subtraction: A Cognitive Perspective*. Hillsdale, NJ: Lawrence Erlbaum Associates, pp. 211–222.

Heirdsfield, A. (2001) 'Integration, compensation and memory in mental addition and subtraction', in M. Van den Heuvel-Panhuizen (ed.), *Proceedings of the 25th Conference of the*

International Group for the Psychology of Mathematics Education (Vol. 3). Utrecht, Netherlands: PME, pp. 129–136.

Hewitt, D. and Brown, E. (1998) 'On teaching early number through language', in A. Olivier and K. Newstead (eds), *Proceedings of the 22nd Conference of the International Group for the Psychology of Mathematics Education* (Vol. 3). Stellenbosch, South Africa: PME, pp. 41–48.

Hiebert, J., Carpenter, T.P., Fenema, E., Fuson, K.C., Wearne, D., Murray, H., Oliver, A. and Human, P. (1997) *Making Sense: Teaching and Learning Mathematics with Understanding*. Portsmouth, NH: Heinemann.

Hughes, M. (1986) *Children and Number: Difficulties in Learning Mathematics*. New York: Basil Blackwell Inc.

Jacobs, V.R., Ambrose, R., Clement, L. and Brown, D. (2006) 'Using teacher-produced videotapes of student interviews as discussion catalysts', *Teaching Children Mathematics*, 12(6): 276–281.

Kamii, C. (1985) *Young Children Reinvent Arithmetic*. New York: Teachers College Press.

Kamii, C. (1986) 'Place value: an explanation of its difficulty and educational implications for the primary grades', *Journal of Research in Early Childhood Education*, 1: 75–86.

Kamii, C. and Dominick, A. (1998) 'The harmful effects of algorithms in grades 1–4', in L.J. Marrow (ed.), *The Teaching and Learning of Algorithms in School Mathematics: 1998 Yearbook*. Reston, VA: National Council of Teachers of Mathematics, pp. 130–140.

Kaufman, E.I., Lord, M.W., Reese, T.W. and Volkmann, J. (1949) 'The discrimination of visual number', *The American Journal of Psychology*, 62(4): 498–525.

Klein, A.S., Beishuizen, M. and Treffers, A. (1998) 'The empty number line in Dutch second grades: realistic versus gradual program design', *Journal for Research in Mathematics Education*, 29(4): 443–464.

Lambdin, D.V. (2003) 'Benefits of teaching through problem-solving', in F.K. Lester and R. Charles (eds), *Teaching Mathematics Through Problem-solving: Pre-kindergarten – Grade 6*. Reston, VA: NCTM, pp. 3–13.

Maclellan, E. (2010) 'Counting: what it is and why it matters', in I. Thompson (ed.), *Teaching and Learning Early Number* (2nd edn). Buckingham: Open University Press, pp. 72–81.

McClain, K. and Cobb, P. (1999) 'Supporting children's ways of reasoning about patterns and partitions', in J.V. Copley (ed.), *Mathematics in the Early Years*. Reston, VA: National Council of Teachers of Mathematics, pp. 113–18.

McClain, K. and Cobb, P. (2001) 'An analysis of development of sociomathematical norms in one first-grade classroom', *Journal for Research in Mathematics Education*, 32: 236–266.

Menne, J. (2001) 'Jumping ahead: an innovative teaching programme', in J. Anghileri (ed.), *Principles and Practices in Arithmetic Teaching: Innovative Approaches for the Primary Classroom*. Buckingham: Open University Press, pp. 95–106.

Mix, K., Huttenlocher, J. and Levine, S. (2002) *Quantitative Development in Infancy and Early Childhood*. Oxford: Oxford University Press.

Mulligan, J.T. (1998) 'A research-based framework for assessing early multiplication and division', in C. Kanes, M. Goos and E. Warren (eds), *Proceedings of the 21st Annual Conference of the Mathematics Education Research Group of Australasia* (Vol. 2). Brisbane: Griffith University, pp. 404–411.

Mulligan, J.T. and Mitchelmore, M.C. (1997) 'Young children's intuitive models of multiplication and division', *Journal for Research in Mathematics Education*, 28: 309–330.

Mulligan, J. and Mitchelmore, M. (2009) 'Awareness of pattern and structure in early mathematical development', *Mathematics Education Research Journal*, 21(2): 33–49.

Munn, P. (1997) 'Writing and number', in I. Thompson (ed.), *Teaching and Learning Early Number*. Buckingham: Open University Press, pp. 19–33.

Munn, P. (2010) 'Children's beliefs about counting', in I. Thompson (ed.), *Teaching and Learning Early Number* (2nd edn). Buckingham: Open University Press, pp. 9–19.

Olive, J. (2001) 'Children's number sequences: an explanation of Steffe's constructs and an extrapolation to rational numbers of arithmetic', *The Mathematics Educator*, 11(1): 4–9.

Papic, M., Mulligan, J. and Mitchelmore, M.C. (2011) 'Assessing the development of preschoolers' mathematical patterning', *Journal for Research in Mathematics Education*, 42(3), 237–268.

Pepper, K. and Hunting, R. (1998) 'Preschoolers' counting and sharing', *Journal for Research in Mathematics Education*, 29: 164–183.

Piaget, J. (1941) *The Child's Conception of Number*. New York: Norton.

Pirie, S.E.B. and Kieren, T.E. (1994) 'Growth in mathematical understanding: how can we characterise it and how can we represent it?', *Educational Studies in Mathematics*, 26: 165–190.

Rousham, L. (2003) 'The empty number line: a model in search of a learning trajectory?', in I. Thompson (ed.), *Enhancing Primary Mathematics Teaching*. Buckingham: Open University Press, pp. 29–39.

Sarama, J. and Clements, D.H. (2009) *Early Childhood Mathematics Education Research: Learning Trajectories for Young Children*. New York: Routledge.

Shulman, L.S. (1986) 'Those who understand: knowledge growth in teaching', *Educational Researcher*, 15(2): 4–14.

Simon, M. (1995) 'Reconstructing mathematics pedagogy from a constructivist perspective', *Journal for Research in Mathematics Education*, 26(2): 114–145.

Steffe, L.P. (1988) 'Children's construction of number sequences and multiplying schemes', in J. Hiebert and M. Behr (eds), *Number Concepts and Operations in the Middle Grades*. Hillsdale, NJ: Erlbaum, pp. 119–141.

Steffe, L.P. (1992a) 'Learning stages in the construction of the number sequence', in J. Bideaud, C. Meljac and J. Fischer (eds), *Pathways to Number: Children's Developing Numerical Abilities*. Hillsdale, NJ: Lawrence Erlbaum, pp. 83–88.

Steffe, L.P. (1992b) 'Schemes of action and operation involving composite units', *Learning and Individual Differences*, 4(3): 259–309.

Steffe, L.P. (2004) 'On the construction of learning trajectories of children: the case of commensurate fractions', *Mathematical Thinking and Learning*, 6(2): 129–162.

Steffe, L.P. and Cobb, P. (with E. von Glasersfeld) (1988) *Construction of Arithmetic Meanings and Strategies*. New York: Springer-Verlag.

Steffe, L.P., von Glasersfeld, E., Richards, J. and Cobb, P. (1983) *Children's Counting Types: Philosophy, Theory, and Application*. New York: Praeger.

Stephan, M., Bowers, J., Cobb, P. and Gravemeijer, K. (2003) *Supporting Students' Development of Measuring Conceptions: Analyzing Students' Learning in Social Context, JRME Monograph #12* (Vol. 12). Reston, VA: National Council of Teachers of Mathematics.

Streefland, L. (ed.) (1991) *Realistic Mathematics Education in Primary School*. Utrecht: CD-B Press.

Sullivan, P., Clarke, D.M., Cheeseman, J. and Mulligan, J. (2001) 'Moving beyond physical models in learning multiplicative reasoning', in M. Van den Heuvel-Panhuizen (ed.), *Proceedings of the 25th Annual Conference of the International Group for the Psychology of Mathematics Education* (Vol. 4). Utrecht: PME, pp. 233–240.

Tabor, P. (2008) 'An investigation of instruction in two-digit addition and subtraction using a classroom teaching experiment methodology, design research, and multilevel modeling'. Unpublished PhD thesis, Southern Cross University, Lismore, New South Wales.

Thomas, J. and Harkness, S. (2011) 'Implications for intervention: categorising the quantitative mental imagery of children', *Mathematics Education Research Journal*, 25: 231–256.

Thomas, J. and Tabor, P. (2011) 'Developing quantitative mental imagery', *Teaching Children Mathematics*, 19: 175–183.

Thomas, J., Tabor, P. and Wright, R. (2011) 'First graders' number knowledge', *Teaching Children Mathematics*, 17: 298–308.

Thompson, I. (1994) 'Young children's idiosyncratic written algorithms for addition', *Education Studies in Mathematics*, 36: 333–345.

Thompson, I. (1997a) 'Mental and written algorithms: can the gap be bridged?', in I. Thompson (ed.), *Teaching and Learning Early Number*. Buckingham: Open University Press, pp. 97–109.

Thompson, I. (ed.) (1997b) *Teaching and Learning Early Number*. Buckingham: Open University Press.

Thompson, I. (ed.) (1999a) *Issues in Teaching Numeracy in Primary Schools*. Buckingham: Open University Press.

Thompson, I. (1999b) 'Written methods of calculation', in I. Thompson (ed.), *Issues in Teaching Numeracy in Primary Schools*. Buckingham: Open University Press, pp. 167–183.

Thompson, I. (ed.) (2003a) *Enhancing Primary Mathematics Teaching*. Buckingham: Open University Press.

Thompson, I. (2003b) 'Place value: the English disease?', in I. Thompson (ed.), *Enhancing Primary Mathematics Teaching*. Buckingham: Open University Press, pp. 181–190.

Thompson, I. and Bramald, R. (2002) *An Investigation of the Relationship Between Young Children's Understanding of the Concept of Place Value and Their Competence at Mental Addition (Report for the Nuffield Foundation)*. Newcastle upon Tyne: University of Newcastle upon Tyne.

Thompson, I. and Smith, F. (1999) *Mental Calculation Strategies for the Addition and Subtraction of 2-digit Numbers (Report for the Nuffield Foundation)*. Newcastle upon Tyne: University of Newcastle upon Tyne.

Threlfall, J. (2002) 'Flexible mental calculation', *Educational Studies in Mathematics*, 50(1): 29–47.

Threlfall, J. (2010) 'Development in oral counting, enumeration and counting for cardinality', in I. Thompson (ed.), *Teaching and Learning Early Number* (2nd edn). Buckingham: Open University Press, pp. 61–71.

Tolchinsky, L. (2003) *The Cradle of Culture and What Children Know about Writing and Numbers before Being Taught*. Mahwah, NJ: Lawrence Erlbaum.

Treffers, A. (2001) 'Grade 1 (and 2) – Calculation up to 20', in M. van den Heuvel-Panhuizen (ed.), *Children Learn Mathematics*. Utrecht: Freudenthal Institute, Utrecht University/SLO, pp. 43–60.

Treffers, A. and Beishuizen, M. (1999) 'Realistic mathematics education in the Netherlands', in I. Thompson (ed.), *Issues in Teaching Numeracy in Primary Schools*. Buckingham: Open University Press, pp. 27–38.

Treffers, A. and Buys, K. (2001) 'Grade 2 and 3 – calculation up to 100', in M. van den Heuvel-Panhuizen (ed.), *Children Learn Mathematics*. Utrecht: Freudenthal Institute, Utrecht University/SLO, pp. 61–88.

Van den Heuvel-Panhuizen, M. (1996) *Assessment and Realistic Mathematics Education*. Utrecht: Freudenthal Institute, Utrecht University.

Van den Heuvel-Panhuizen, M. (ed.) (2001) *Children Learn Mathematics: A Learning–teaching Trajectory with Intermediate Attainment Targets*. Utrecht: Freudenthal Institute, Utrecht University.

Van de Walle, J.A. (2004) *Elementary and Middle School Mathematics: Teaching Developmentally* (5th edn). Boston, MA: Pearson.

Von Glasersfeld, E. (1995) *Radical Constructivism: A Way of Knowing and Learning*. London: Falmer.

Von Glasersfeld, E. (1982) 'Subitizing: the role of figural patterns in the development of numerical concepts', *Archives de Psychologie*, 50: 191–318.

Von Glasersfeld, E. (1987) 'Learning as a constructive activity', in C. Janvier (ed.), *Problems of Representation in the Teaching and Learning of Mathematics*. Hillsdale, NJ: Lawrence Erlbaum Associates, pp. 3–17.

Vygotsky, L.S. (1963) *Mind in Society: The Development of Higher Psychological Processes*. Cambridge, MA: Harvard University Press (trans. M. Lopez-Morillas, original work published 1934).

Wheatley, G. and Reynolds, A. (1999) *Coming to Know Number*. Tallahassee, FL: Mathematics Learning.

Wigley, A. (1997) 'Approaching number through language', in I. Thompson (ed.), *Teaching and Learning Early Number*. Buckingham: Open University Press, pp. 113–122.

Willey, R., Holliday, A. and Martland, J.R. (2007) 'Achieving new heights in Cumbria: raising standards in early numeracy through Mathematics Recovery', *Educational and Child Psychology*, 24(2): 108–118.

Worthington, M. and Carruthers, E. (2003) *Children's Mathematics: Making Marks, Making Meaning*. London: Sage.

Wright, R.J. (1989) 'Numerical development in the kindergarten year: a teaching experiment'. Doctoral dissertation, University of Georgia [DAI, 50A, 1588; DA8919319].

Wright, R.J. (1991a) 'An application of the epistemology of radical constructivism to the study of learning', *Australian Educational Researcher*, 18(1): 75–95.

Wright, R.J. (1991b) 'The role of counting in children's numerical development', *Australian Journal of Early Childhood*, 16(2): 43–48.

Wright, R.J. (1991c) 'What number knowledge is possessed by children entering the kindergarten year of school?', *Mathematics Education Research Journal*, 3(1): 1–16.

Wright, R.J. (1992) 'Number topics in early childhood mathematics curricula: historical background, dilemmas, and possible solutions', *Australian Journal of Education*, 36: 125–142.

Wright, R.J. (1994a) 'Mathematics in the lower primary years: a research-based perspective on curricula and teaching practice', *Mathematics Education Research Journal*, 6(1): 23–36.

Wright, R.J. (1994b) 'A study of the numerical development of 5-year-olds and 6-year-olds', *Educational Studies in Mathematics*, 36: 35–44.

Wright, R.J. (1996) 'Problem-centred mathematics in the first year of school', in J. Mulligan and M. Mitchelmore (eds), *Research in Early Number Learning: An Australian Perspective*. Adelaide: AAMT, pp. 35–54.

Wright, R.J. (1998) 'Children's beginning knowledge of numerals and its relationship to their knowledge of number words: an exploratory, observational study', in A. Olivier and K. Newstead (eds), *Proceedings of the 22nd Conference of the International Group for the Psychology of Mathematics Education* (Vol. 4). Stellenbosch, South Africa: PME, pp. 201–208.

Wright, R.J. (2000) 'Professional development in recovery education', in L.P. Steffe and P.W. Thompson (eds), *Radical Constructivism in Action: Building on the Pioneering Work of Ernst von Glasersfeld*. London: Falmer, pp. 134–151.

Wright, R.J. (2001) 'The arithmetical strategies of four 3rd-graders', in J. Bobis, B. Perry and M. Mitchelmore (eds), *Proceedings of the 25th Annual Conference of the Mathematics Education Research Group of Australasia* (Vol. 4). Sydney: MERGA, pp. 547–554.

Wright, R.J. (2003) 'Mathematics Recovery: a program of intervention in early number learning', *Australian Journal of Learning Disabilities*, 8(4): 6–11.

Wright, R.J. (2008a) 'Interview-based assessment of early number knowledge', in I. Thompson (ed.), *Teaching and Learning Early Number* (2nd edn). Buckingham: Open University Press, pp. 193–204.

Wright, R.J. (2008b) 'Mathematics Recovery: an early number program focusing on intensive intervention', in A. Dowker (ed.), *Mathematics Difficulties: Psychology and Intervention*. San Diego, CA: Elsevier, pp. 203–223.

Wright, R.J. (2013) 'Assessing early numeracy: significance, trends, nomenclature, context, key topics, learning framework and assessment tasks', *South African Journal of Childhood Education*, 2: 21–40.

Wright, R.J., Ellemor-Collins, D. and Tabor, P. (2012) *Developing Number Knowledge: Assessment, Teaching & Intervention with 7–11-year-olds*. London: Sage.

Wright, R.J., Martland, J. and Stafford, A. (2006a) *Early Numeracy: Assessment for Teaching & Intervention* (2nd edn). London: Sage.

Wright, R.J., Martland, J., Stafford, A. and Stanger, G. (2006b) *Teaching Number: Advancing Children's Skills & Strategies* (2nd edn). London: Sage.

Yackel, E. (2001) 'Perspectives on arithmetic from classroom-based research in the United States of America', in J. Anghileri (ed.), *Principles and Practices in Arithmetic Teaching: Innovative Approaches for the Primary Classroom*. Buckingham: Open University Press, pp. 15–31.

Young-Loveridge, J. (1989) 'The development of children's number concepts: the first year of school', *New Zealand Journal of Educational Studies*, 34(1): 47–64.

Young-Loveridge, J. (1991) *The Development of Children's Number Concepts from Ages Five to Nine* (Vols 1 and 3). Hamilton: University of Waikato.

Young-Loveridge, J. (2002) 'Early childhood numeracy: building an understanding of part-whole relationships', *Australian Journal of Early Childhood*, 27(4), 36–42.

Index

2-digit addition and subtraction: jump strategies 135–160
  assessment task groups 142–148
  adding and subtracting involving a decuple and a number from 1 to 9 139
  adding and subtracting involving a non-decuple and a number from 1 to 9 139
  identifying jump strategies 158
  instructional activities 149–158
  learning addition and subtraction through a decuple 138–139
  recording on an empty number line 156–157
  with support of a hundred chart 155
2-digit addition and subtraction: split strategies 137–138, 161–177
  assessment tasks groups 165–167
  instructional activities 169–175
  some children's preferences for split strategies versus jump 137–138
2-digit addition and subtraction without and with regrouping 146–148
2-digit addition and subtraction using transforming, compensating and other strategies 148–159
2-digit numbers
  addition with and without regrouping 168
  combining and partitioning involving non-canonical (non-standard) forms 167–168
  difficulty with names 36
  learning to increment and decrement 139
  learning to increment and decrement on the decuple 139
  learning to increment and decrement off the decuple 140
  partitioning and combining involving 167
  subtraction with and without regrouping 169
  using the setting of money 172
2-digit numerals
  See number words and numerals
3-digit addition, subtraction and place value
  developing strategies 165
  incrementing and decrementing by tens 165
  incrementing and decrementing by hundreds 165
  number words and numerals to 1000 164–165

3-digit numbers
  hundreds, tens and ones structure 28
  extending to thousands, millions and decimals 28
3-digit numerals 35

abstract composite unit *see* multiplication and division
addend *see* glossary
addition
  adding tens to a 2-digit number 146, 149–150, 171
  adding tens and ones without regrouping 172–173
  adding through five 75
  beginning through counting by jumping to 10 141
  by compensation 141
  by jumping to 10 141
  by transforming 141
  from a decuple 142–143
    higher decade addition and subtraction 161–162
    beyond the decade – addition 162
    beyond the decade – subtraction 162
    within the decade – addition 162
    within the decade – subtraction 162
    sequences in 162–163
  in the range 1 to 4 from a given number 104–105
  in the range 1 to 20 124–126
  making combinations to 20 126–127
  using doubles, fives and tens 121–122, 131
  tasks involving five and ten 129–130
  to a decuple 143–144
  using ten-plus combinations 127–128
  with spatial patterns in the range 1 to 10, assessment task 79–80
  with 11,
  see also counting, advanced
additive tasks
  see also Glossary
  two screened collections 97
arithmetic rack
  see also Appendix 1
  see also numbers 1 to 20
  adding two numbers with the sum in the range 1 to 20 113–115

arithmetic rack *cont.*
  making numbers 112
  progressing to mental strategies 117
  reading numbers112
  subtraction in the range 1 to 20 116
  subtraction on the 111
arrays, use of
  see also Appendix 1
  see multiplication and division
arrow cards 174–175
  see also Appendix 1
arrow notation 163
assessment,
  observational 25
  tasks 4
  videotaped interviews. 25
  written 25
assessment Task Groups
  formal 24
  list of 36
  rational 24
  ways to use 25
assessment tasks,
  advanced counting, addition and subtraction
    96–100
  as instructional activities 26
  as a source of teachers' learning 26
  in early counting and addition 76–80
automaticity 20
  see also Glossary
automatized knowledge 75

Backward Number Word Sequences (BNWSs) 9
  see Appendix 1
  see also Glossary
  assessment task 38–39
  by 10s on and off the decuple 149, 170–171
  facility with 34
  instructional activities 45
base ten materials
  see also Appendix 1
  focus on the use of 161
  base ten blocks 163
  bundling sticks 163
bead bar *see* Bead string
bead board 131–132
bead string 102–103
  with ten catcher 149–150
block scheduling *see* organizing instruction
branching 164
bundling sticks
  see Appendix 1
bunny ears 81–82

Classroom Instructional Framework for Early
    Number (CIFEN) 2, 10–11
Collaborative Learning Model *see* organizing
    instruction
combining and partitioning numbers 3, 23
  see also Glossary
  approaches to teaching 71
  doubles to 10 71
  doubles to 20 71
  five and ten structure as reference points 3
  five pluses 71
  instructional activities 80–91
  involving 2-digit numbers 165,
      167–168, 176
  involving non-canonical forms 165,
      167–168
  partitioning numbers 2 to 5 71
  partitioning numbers 6 to 10 71
  small numbers 71
  using doubles 3
  using spatial patterns 73
  without using counting-by-ones 71–72, 74–75
commutativity 118, 132, 178, 183–184, 191
  see also Glossary
comparative addition and subtraction, *see*
    subtraction
compensating, *see* strategies
  solving comparison tasks 109
complexifying
  see progressive mathematization
  see also Glossary
conceptual place value *see* place value
conventions for reading and writing
    numbers 4
counting,
  advanced assessment task groups
      96–100
  back from a given number 105–106
  coordinating words and items 56
  development of 3
  emergent 3, 53, 56–57
  figurative 3, 53, 55–57
  importance of 53
  instructional activities 100–109
  in the range 2 to 5 only 95
  levels of sophistication in 53
  perceptual 3, 53–57
  primitive strategies 94
counting –back-from, *see* strategies
  see also Glossary
counting-back-to, *see* strategies
  see also glossary
  counting backwards in the range 1–100 101

counting-back-to, *see* strategies *cont.*
  counting backwards from a given number
    101–102
  counting backwards to solve missing subtrahend
    tasks 107–108
counting-by-ones, *see* strategies
  advanced, *see* strategies
counting-forward-from-one-three-times, *see*
  Strategies
counting forward in the range 1–100 101
counting-from-one, *see* strategies
counting-on, *see* strategies
  instructional activities 49–50, 101–109
counting-on-from, *see* strategies
  counting on from a given number
    100–102
  counting on to solve missing subtrahend tasks
    107–108
counting-on-to, *see* strategies
counting-up-from, *see* strategies
  see also Glossary
counting-up-to, *see* strategies
  see also Glossary
  to solve missing addend tasks 106–107

decrementing by tens *see* Glossary
decuples *see* Glossary
  assessment tasks involving 142–144, 146,
    165–169
  confusion with 38
  difficulty crossing 43
  incrementing and decrementing by tens
    165–166, 170
  incrementing and decrementing off the 137,
    165–166
  incrementing and decrementing versus
    counting-by-ones 140
  instructional activities involving 152, 159–160,
    170–176
  omitting 37–38
  pronunciation of 37
  reading numerals as 39
  saying next lowest 38
  subtracting through 137–138
  sequencing 40
designing Instruction 10
difference between 107–109
  see also minuend
digit cards *see* Appendix 1
digits 33
  instructional activity 46
discrete-based reasoning 96
  see also Glossary

distancing the setting *see* progressive
  mathematization
domino patterns, *see* Strategies
  naming and visualizing assessment task 77
doubles
  1 to 5 71
  6 to 10 72
  addition using 118, 121
  arithmetic rack 112
  automate knowledge of 118
  describing 114
  domino flashes and 87–88
  domino snap 88
  emerging knowledge of 71
  finger patterns and 74
  flashed 86, 124
  flexible working with 117, 134
  near 116
  realising the structure of 114
  spatial arrangement 131
  subtraction using 118, 122–123
  to 20 72
double ten frame 111–112
drop-down notation 164
dropping back to one 34

early counting 51–70
  additive tasks involving two screened collections
    57, 60, 70
  comparing small collections 57
  establishing a collection of specified numerosity
    54, 57, 70
  establishing the numerosity of a collection 54,
    57–58, 66–68, 70
  establishing the numerosity of two collections
    54, 57–58, 70
  increase and decrease in the range 1 to 6
    57–58, 70
  instructional activities 61, 70
  learning trajectory 70
early multiplication and division, *see*
  multiplication and division
early number knowledge 2, 34
early number learning 33–36
emergent *see* Glossary
empty number line (ENL) 15–16, 136, 140, 163
  see also Appendix 1
  as a notating device versus ENL as a means of
    solving a task 136–137
  recording 2-digit addition and using a jump
    strategy 153–155
extending the range of numbers *see* progressive
  mathematization

facile 17, 82
    see also Glossary
figurative see Glossary
finger patterns
    adding two numbers in the range 1 to 5 75
    and advanced count-by-ones strategies 95–96
    as spatial configurations 71
    assessment tasks 76
    combining and partitioning 73
    combinations of 74
    contrasting three solution strategies 96
    correcting 73
    current view of 73
    encouraging 74
    extending the range to 6 to 10 74
    for multiplication and division 178,181, 184
    making 72
    numbers in the range 1 to 5 73
    numbers in the range 6 to 10 73
    numbers in the range 6 to 10 using 5 as a
        reference 74
    to support and augment arithmetical thinking 73
    why and when 73
    with addition and subtraction 163–165, 168
five-frame 72, 84–85
five as a reference point 74–75
five and ten as reference points 74, 131–132
    see also strategies
five-wise patterns on a ten frame 17, 75, 78, 86, 91
    see also Glossary
    naming and visualizing assessment task
        78–79, 119
five-wise patterns on two ten-frames 119
flashing see Glossary
formal algorithms 31
    see also Glossary
    for adding and subtracting see learning to add
        and subtract with two 2-digit numbers
forward number word sequences (FNWSs)
    see also Glossary
    warm up activity 13
    assessment task 37
    by 10s on and off the decuple 142, 149, 170–171
    extending knowledge of 20, 50
    facility with 34
    instructional activities 42, 50, 149
    relating numeral identification to FNWS 48
five and ten structure of numbers 71
flashing 9, 14

Glossary 206–213
guiding principles for classroom teaching (GPCT)
    5–8, 10, 12

habituated knowledge 75
    see also Glossary
horizontal number sentences 163–164
higher decade addition and subtraction follow the
        pattern 170

identifying numerals
    instructional activity 48
    in the range 1 to 100 101
incrementing and decrementing 2-digit numbers
    see also Glossary
    flexibly by tens and ones 140, 145
    off the decuple 140
    on the decuple 139
    versus counting-by-ones 140
incrementing and decrementing by 10s on and off
        the decuple 144
incrementing and decrementing by several
        10s 140
incrementing and decrementing by 100s,
incrementing flexibly by 10s and ones see
        Incrementing and decrementing 2-digit
        numbers
informal strategies versus formal algorithms see
        learning to add and subtract with two 2-digit
        numbers
instruction
    assessment, the crucial basis for 2
    classroom organization 2
    designing 1–2
    intensive 1
    organizing 1
    teaching and learning cycle 2
    website 4
instructional activities 2, 4, 26, 41
instructional setting see Glossary
instructional sequences 2
interval-based reasoning see Glossary
irregular spatial configuration see Glossary
inverse operations 183–184, 192

jump strategies see Glossary
    see also Strategies
    advantages of 136
    jump versus split 137
    other means of notating 136
    the role of the ENL 137

knowledge see Glossary

locating numbers in the range 1 to 100 102–103
    assessment task 41
    instructional activity 43

learning pairs and discussion model *see* organizing instruction
learning to add and subtract with two 2-digit numbers
  formal algorithms for adding and subtracting 31
  informal strategies versus formal algorithms 31
learning trajectory
  2-digit addition and subtraction using jump strategies 156, 159–160
  2-digit addition and subtraction using split strategies 176
  advanced counting, addition and subtraction 109–110
  definition of 2
  early counting and addition 70
  early multiplication and division 205
  instructional activities relevant to 10
  number words and numerals 51–52
  progression of learning topics 10
  specific topics 10
  structuring numbers 1 to 10 91
  structuring numbers 1 to 20 133–134

Mathematics Recovery program *see* Glossary
micro-adjusting *see* Glossary
minuend 94, 107
  see also Glossary
missing addend tasks 15, 97–98
missing subtrahend tasks 99
money, using the setting of 172
multiplication and division,
  abstract composite unit 181–182
  assessment task groups 184–192
  basic facts 190
  commutative principle *see* multiplication and division relational thinking
  commutativity 183
  counting repeated equal groups 180
  determining products and factors 200–202
  developing automaticity 199–200
  distributive principle *see* Multiplication and Division relational thinking
  division as sharing or measuring 180–181
  early 178–179, 181–183
  equal groups 178, 196–197
  extending knowledge 184
  instructional activities 192–204
  inverse operations 183–184
  number word sequences of multiples 178, 192–194
  numerical composite 182
  partitive division 188, 203–204
  quotitive division 187, 203–205

multiplication and division *cont.*
  relational thinking 191
    commutative principle 191
    distributive principle 191
    multiplication and division as inverses 191
  repeated equal groups 178–182, 185–189, 194–196
  sharing 178–179
  skip counting 179–180
  unitizing 182
  use of arrays 182–183, 188–190, 197–199, 202–203

near doubles 116
  flexible working with 117, 134
near ten-plus cards 17
non-canonical (non-standard) forms *see* 3-digit addition, subtraction and place value
  see also Glossary
non-count-by-ones *see also* Glossary
  5 and 10 as a reference point 131
  adding to 10 56
  adding through 10 56
  bridging to 10 56
  child example 56
  doubles *see* doubles
  facile 135
  flexible strategies for addition and subtraction 135
  See also jump strategies
notating *see* progressive mathematization
  see also Glossary
number *see* Glossary
numbers 33
  non-canonical forms *see* 2-digit numbers
numbers 1 to 20,
  making and reading on the arithmetic rack 111–112, 133
number knowledge 5, 7–10, 12–13, 20
number line *see* empty number line
number words *see also* Glossary
  are names 33
  Asian languages 36
  basis of early arithmetical strategy 74
  developing facility with 33–34
  encountering 34
  emerging familiarity with 34
  learning about 33
  referred to as numerals 33
  spoken or heard 33
  teen numbers 35
number word after 34, 36–37, 51–52
  assessment tasks 37

number word after *cont.*
  instructional activities 43–45
  teen/decade confusion 35
number words and numerals 3
number words and numerals to 1000 *see* 3-digit
   addition, subtraction and place value
number word before
  assessment task 36
  confusion with number word after 39
  dropping back strategy 39
  in range 1 to 20 52
  using FNWS to locate NWB 39
number word sequences 34
numeral cards
  see Appendix 1
numerals 33
  see also Glossary
numeral identification
  see also Glossary
  assessment task 39–40
  instructional activities 45, 48, 52
numeral sequence *see* Glossary
numeral recognition
  see also Glossary
  assessment tasks 36, 39
  instructional activities 45, 52
numeral roll 37, 42, 50
  see also Appendix 1
  and window *see also* Appendix 1
numeral track *see also* Appendix 1
  activities 43–45
numerals
  12/21 confusion 39, 41
  confusion with letters 35
  developing facility with 34
  from 1 to 10 35
  from 11 to 20 35
  from 20 to 99 35
  identifying 34, 39, 41, 48
  instructional activity 45
  learning about 34
  naming 34
  non-sequential 46
  ordering 36, 40–41
  reading 47
  reversal 39
  sequences 36, 40–41
  teen difficulty 35
  using arrow cards to support and build 174
  using bundles of tens and ones 174
  write 34
numeration system 33
numerosity *see* Glossary

ordering numerals 36, 52
  assessment task 40–41
  errors when 41
  instructional activities 45, 47–48
organizing instruction
  block scheduling 22
  collaborative learning model 18, 20
  learning pairs and discussion model 19
  rotational groups model 20–22

pair-wise patterns on a ten frame 75,
   77–79, 91
  see also Glossary
  naming and visualizing assessment task
   77–78
  pair-wise patterns 1–10 118–119
  pair-wise patterns 11 to 20 120
partitions of 5 and 10
  see also Glossary
  assessment task 79
perceptual *see* Glossary
partitioning and combining involving 2-digit
   numbers 167
place value,
  additive sense of 30
  alternative view 29
  conceptual 29
  difficulties 28–29, 35
  in the range 1 to 100 30–31
  new approach 28
  teaching through addition and subtraction
   29–30
  traditional view 29
perceptual counting *see* counting
perceptual replacements 96
problem-centred lessons 12
progressive mathematization *see* Glossary
  complexifying 9
  distancing the setting 9
  extending the range of numbers 9

quinary pattern *see* five-wise patterns
  see also Glossary

regrouping task *see* Glossary
regular spatial configuration *see* Glossary
removed items task 93, 96, 98–99
  see also Glossary
  use of counting back to solve 99
repeated equal groups *see* multiplication and
   division
rotational groups model *see* organizing
   instruction

screened collections
  developing verification 94
  imagining 94
  versus word problems 94
screening 51
  see also Glossary
sequencing numerals *see* Glossary
  assessment task 40
  instructional activities 42–43, 47
  non-sequential 46
setting *see* Glossary
sharing, *see* multiplication and division
skip counting, *see also* multiplication and division
  developing limit of fluency 185
  development of 178
  keeping track in 187
  need for double counting 18
  problem with reciting 193
  speed of response 190
spatial patterns,
  ascribing number to regular patterns 82–83
  combinations to five 84–85,89–90
  domino patterns 87–88
  five and ten frame flashes 85–86
  instructional activities 81–91
  partitions of 5 and 10 89–90
  subitizing 72,83–84
  see also five-wise patterns
  see also pair-wise patterns
split strategy *see* Glossary *see also* strategies
  assessment task groups 165–169
  alternative means of notating 137
  choosing split or jump 177
  developing facility with 163–164
  development of 61, 163
  ease of 163
  focus on 161
  notating 163–164
  prior knowledge for 163
  some children's initial preference for split
    strategies 137–138
  splitting 164
  using drop-down notation 164
  value of base-ten blocks and bundling sticks 163
strategies *see* Glossary
  adding through five 75
  compensating 142, 148
  counting-by-ones56, 135–136, 140, 143
    advanced 92–99, 111
    advanced in the range 20 – 100 95
    in multiplication 185–187, 189–190, 193, 198
    advanced strategies, task type and solutions 93
  counting-from-one 92, 110

strategies *see* Glossary *cont.*
  counting-back-from 74, 92–93, 99, 111
  counting-back-to 74, 92–93, 99–100, 111
  counting-forward-from-one-three-times for
    addition 94
  counting-forward-from-one-three-times for
    subtraction 94
  counting-on 74, 80, 92–93, 96–98, 108–109,
    111, 140
  counting-on-from 74
  counting-on-to 74
  counting-up-from 92–93, 95, 97
  counting-up-to 92–93, 98–100, 106
  developing strategies for addition, subtraction,
    missing addends and missing subtrahends
    tasks 158–159
  five as a reference point 74–75
  fostering the development of a range of
    strategies 140, 163
  fostering the development of jump strategies
    136–138
  grouping strategies 135
  informal 31
  jump 31–32, 135–160
  means of notating for 163
  non-count-by-ones 75, 92, 110, 135
  non-counting strategies 111
  prior knowledge for 163
  split 31–32, 135, 137, 140–141, 147–148
    assessment task groups 165–166
  splitting 164
  split-jump for addition 140, 147
  split-jump for subtraction 141
  ten as a reference point 74
  transforming 141–142, 148
  using drop-down notation 164
  value of base-ten blocks and bundling sticks 163
split-jump strategy *see* strategies
structuring numbers
  in the range 1 to 10 71–91
  assessment tasks 75–80
  instructional activities 80–90
  learning trajectory 91
structuring numbers,
  in the range 1 to 20 111–134
  assessment task groups 118–123
  instructional activities 123–132
subitizing *see* Glossary *see* also spatial patterns,
subtraction
  as adding up 117
  as finding the difference 116
  as partitioning 117
  as take away 116

subtraction *cont.*
  bare numbers 100
  by adding up 117, 141, 148
  by compensation 141
  by jumping to 10 141
  by transforming 141
  comparative subtraction 97, 99–100, 110
  counting back 99, 101, 103, 107–108
  from a 2-digit number 142, 146, 160
  from a decuple 142–143
  in the range 1 to 4 by counting back from a
        given number 103–104
  on the arithmetic rack 116–117
  higher decade 161–163, 165–166,
        170, 176
  progressing to mental strategies 117
  to a decuple 143–144
  subtracting tens from a 2 digit number 146
  tens and ones without regrouping 172–173
  using doubles, fives and tens 122–123
  with minuend in the range 11–20
  with minuend less than, or equal to,
        10 116
  with regrouping 137, 142, 147–148, 153, 160,
        165, 168–169, 173–174, 176
  without regrouping 147, 150, 152, 160,
        169–170, 173–174, 176
  with spatial patterns in the range 1 to 10,
  see also Counting, advanced
subtractive task *see* Glossary
subtrahend *see* minuend
sum *see* addend
symbolizing *see* Glossary

task *see* Glossary
teaching and learning cycle 10, 12–13
teaching number,
  emerging approaches 26–28
  traditional approaches 26–28
temporal patterns
  see also Glossary
  counting and copying 57, 60
  developing conceptually based 69
temporal sequences
  counting and copying 57, 61, 70
  more difficult than counting collections 61
ten as a reference point 74
ten-dot cards *see* Appendix 1
ten-frame combinations *see* Appendix 1
ten-frames 133
  see also Appendix 1
  five wise *see* Appendix 1
  pair wise *see* Appendix 1
  partition
  ten-plus cards 17
teen numbers 29, 35, 48
ten-wise patterns
  for 15 to 20 121
  naming and visualizing 120–121
transforming, *see* strategies

unitizing 182
  see also Glossary

verbally base strategies 6,

zone of proximal development 3